FIGHTING BLIND

FIGHTING BLIND

A GREEN BERET'S STORY
OF EXTRAORDINARY COURAGE

Major Ivan Castro

and

Jim DeFelice

ST. MARTIN'S PRESS 📖 NEW YORK

www.stmartins.com

Design by Meryl Sussman Levavi

Library of Congress Cataloging-in-Publication Data

Names: Castro, Ivâan, 1967– author. | DeFelice, Jim, 1956– author.
Title: Fighting blind : a Green Beret's story of extraordinary courage /
    Ivan Castro and Jim DeFelice.
Description: First edition. | New York : St. Martin's Press, 2016. | Includes
    bibliographical references.
Identifiers: LCCN 2016014596| ISBN 9781250076540 (hardcover) |
    ISBN 9781466887985 (e-book)
Subjects: LCSH: Castro, Ivâan, 1967– | Iraq War, 2003–2011—Personal narratives,
    American. | United States. Army. Special Forces—Officers—Biography. |
    Soldiers—United States—Biography. | Male long-distance runners—Biography. |
    Blind athletes—United States—Biography. | Blind—United States—Biography.
Classification: LCC DS79.766.C38 A3 2016 | DDC 362.4/1092 [B] —dc23
LC record available at https://lccn.loc.gov/2016014596

Our books may be purchased in bulk for promotional, educational, or business use. Please contact your local bookseller or the Macmillan Corporate and Premium Sales Department at 1-800-221-7945, extension 5442, or by e-mail at MacmillanSpecial Markets@macmillan.com.

First Edition: November 2016

10 9 8 7 6 5 4 3 2 1

Dedicated to my kids and family.

In memory of Ralph Porras and Justin Dreese, the men who died alongside me in Iraq.

With thanks to all who served, and to their families.

Contents

FIGHTING BLIND

Prologue

On September 2, 2006, I woke up in hell, a dry, hot place of unrelenting torment and constant danger, otherwise known as Yusufiyah, Iraq. I got up without breakfast, threw some gear in my pack, and set out to do two things: relieve my men so they could eat, and find us a better place to do our jobs. We were snipers—I was the head of a sniper-scout team protecting a task force searching the tangled grounds of an al Qaeda training camp, a factory of death that had already cost us a pair of lives. We were part of the 82nd Airborne, tasked to work with some special operation units and other operators in a sweep in one of the most dangerous areas of Iraq. Just southwest of Baghdad, the region was a cauldron of hate, a place where Sunni and Shia fighters regularly faced off. The day before, we had seized a half-built power plant that al Qaeda terrorists had been using to assemble bombs and teach recruits how to use rifles and mortars. That night the commander ordered my unit to take up a position on a building a special op unit had abandoned because enemy mortars had zeroed in on it.

I thought it was a stupid order, but I couldn't argue with him over the radio, and in any event I had to find a better vantage point to mount our overwatch before asking permission to go there. That was my intention as I climbed the makeshift ladder to the roof that morning.

As a soldier, you're trained to see the world in a special way; it's a dangerous place, you look for all possibilities of danger. As a sniper, you sharpen those skills to the max. You survey a field and you don't just see brush; you see anomalies in that brush, and realize you're about to be attacked.

That morning as I scanned the countryside beyond the roof, I saw things as a soldier and a sniper, as an officer in charge of an elite team of fighters, and as a human being. I saw a beautiful sun rising over a desert, a shallow canal filled with murk and rushes, a cluster of hovels that under other circumstances might have seemed bucolic. I saw shades of yellow and brown, light blue streaked with white, drab gray, deep black. I saw red bloodstains turned black; I saw rusted wrecks of a once-promising enterprise. I saw waves of heat filtering upward in the distance. It was a beautiful morning in an ugly place.

I got to work. From my vantage on the top of the roof I eyed a half-constructed building tall enough to command the countryside. It would also offer some shade, an important consideration in the Iraqi summer.

I dropped to my knee to make my call to the battalion commander. At that moment, something exploded to my right.

It was a mortar round. It had fallen next to the building, hitting the ground a few yards to my right.

"Get off the roof!" I yelled to the men nearby. "Get off!"

The words were still in my mouth as the next round landed square on the roof.

■ ■ ■

The explosion changed my life irrevocably. It left me blind, and close to death.

Quite literally, September 2, 2006, was the darkest day of my life. That mortar shell continues to haunt me.

And yet . . .

While the mortar shell sent me on a journey filled with unfathomable lows, there have also been incredible highs. It has been a journey of and through darkness. But it has also been a journey of light. I've done things I never would have been able to do before that explosion.

Why? I never really asked myself that question, or examined what I did, until another journey just recently, one to the literal ends of the earth. It was there, under a sky of unrelenting light, that I reached a place where I could begin to understand not just what happened to me or why I've pushed beyond it, but what it might mean to others. It was a journey to the South Pole, figuratively and literally. It was a trip I'd never have attempted if I could see.

The journey left me with a need to reach out to others, as others have reached out to me, to share what I have been through, and what I still hope to achieve. But how do I talk to them about being blind? How do I talk to you?

Every reference you have, every allusion and metaphor, involves the negation of sight: seeing things that are around you taken away. But imagining that they are not there does not describe blindness.

Imagining a lack of color, or a world where it is always night, doesn't really correlate to being completely blind. Pondering a world where darkness has no dimension and no end is a shabby substitute for living blind. Wandering endlessly through a dream where you can never wake, moving in a world where the exterior mimics and sometimes mocks the interior regions conjured by your mind . . . words can barely hint at the real experience.

Contemplating never-ending isolation is a pale facsimile of the actual experience of blindness. Becoming helpless when you have always been the man others counted on—that seems more a prank than the actual experience.

There are no metaphors or similes that adequately describe the world, and thus there are no metaphors or similes that can plumb the depths of being blind. The most pernicious turn out to be the ones that call it absence and loss, even though in many ways they are the most accurate of all.

Blindness is loss and absence and isolation and helplessness, for me at least, who lived so long in the sighted world. But to think of blindness as any of those words is like thinking of the ocean as a single drop of water. These are all negatives, without possibilities, and being blind is not a continual state of depression, or even of loss.

How do I talk to you about war?

Bare descriptions run cold. Pure emotions sound hollow. Arrangements of words on a page, even of pictures on a screen— these are as bad as metaphors of blindness. Real knowledge of danger and death, of violence and faith, cannot be found in books or lectures. War, like blindness, is a world of its own. Its dimensions are smaller and more brutal than those of the universe, but it, too, allows for no simple metaphors. War is its own paradox: its end is no end, its seed both death and life. The soldier who survives it joins a brotherhood whose members are together, yet alone. They fold themselves in the past even as they try to move ahead.

Or so it has been for me.

How can I talk to you about strength and will, despair and surrender? Of triumph? Of small victories that lead not to greatness but to something just as worthy, just as human? How do you talk about perseverance despite odds?

Those, at least, are emotions all humans feel, or at least strive to understand. They are the common ground that binds us together, no matter what war we've been in, no matter what struggles we have had, blind or sighted, rich or poor. To overcome despair, even one solitary time, is something every human aspires to. To be brave, even under the most mundane circumstance, is something we might all achieve. No matter how trivial a challenge, overcoming it makes everyone of us an achiever. Beating setbacks, overcoming obstacles—each achievement tells us we are worth something in the universe, reminds us that we exist not just as worms, but as humans.

These are things that touch every soul. And so I will start

there, even if at times I question the meaning of those things—
of courage, of strength, and even achievement itself.

And I will start with the cold, the numbing cold that left
my toes bruised and fingers unusable, cold without parallel on
the earth, the cold of the South Pole. I'll give you excerpts from
my diary, and then the memories the cold provoked. For it was in
that cold, and in the struggle to survive it, that I began to understand both blindness and war, and I came to appreciate how we
move beyond them.

ONE

EARLY DAYS

We set out today. The teams lined up shoulder to shoulder for the camera. There was a blast of a horn, and we were off.

Three teams, all with wounded war veterans, are racing against each other to reach the South Pole.

Whether we win or not—and we will win—I'll be the first blind American and the first wounded American serviceman to make it. The first Puerto Rican as well. At least as far as I know.

We ski with a small sled of equipment tied to our waists. Because I can't see, I'm guided by another team member, gently tugged by a line tied to his sled. The terrain is anything but smooth—wind-swept snow and ice form an endless sea of sastrugi, shallow ridges formed on the ice by wind and erosion. They're like waves of ice and frozen snow, hard as a rock. Skiing over them is a challenge; at times it's more like stomping. The sastrugi are a hazard for everyone, but especially me. Being blind, I have no idea of their size or shape. I slip and slide at every push. Soon after we started this morning, I tripped and fell face-first into the snow; some of the other members of the team had to pull me out.

Everyone knows the South Pole is cold, but you need to have the sweat on your fingers freeze in your mittens before you can really understand cold. And only when that happens at the warmest time of day do you understand the South Pole.

There are twelve veterans in the race, along with guides and Prince Harry of Great Britain. We're divided into three teams: American, British, Commonwealth. We plan to ski from 9 A.M. to 5 P.M. every day for the next two weeks until we reach the Pole. That's some two hundred miles across the high plain of Antarctica to the exact bottom of the earth. The race is sponsored by Walking With the Wounded, a British charity with the backing of Prince Harry. The group does extreme things to raise money and tell the world that being wounded doesn't mean giving up.

The race to the South Pole is the organization's most ambitious event yet. It's garnered major media: a BBC special is planned; there's talk of a TV special in the States. My focus, though, is winning the thing. Blind or not, I'm coming in first.

1

A Simple Man

I was born in Hoboken, New Jersey, and lived the first few years of my life in the New York City area, but if you ask me, I'll tell you I'm Puerto Rican. Puerto Rico is where I mostly grew up. It's where the best memories of my childhood are. I have a lot of family there, and friends, and while it's changed in the thirty years since I last called it home, it's a place that remains close to my heart.

Both my mom, Juana Gloria Dones, and my dad, Jose Castro, were from the Commonwealth. Their parents were poor farmers; in fact, they worked plots right next to each other in Trujillo Alto, a landlocked, bucolic town in the northeast. Both raised cattle and sometimes horses; they grew bananas, plantains, oranges, grapefruit, yucca, pumpkins—if you could put the seed in the ground and get it to sprout, one of my grandparents would try it. My dad's father made rum from sugarcane and even set up a little grocery store to sell his wares—it amounted to three tree stumps and a plank of wood, according to family legend. Today, we'd call this creative boutique family farming; back then it was subsistence living.

Farming wasn't in my father's blood, and like a lot of Puerto Ricans in the 1950s and early 1960s, he left to find work in the New York area. He got a job in Union City, a gritty New Jersey town directly across from New York City's Hell's Kitchen, the colorful name for what at the time was little more than a ghetto of recent immigrants. He sent for my mom; they soon moved to West New York—another nearby New Jersey town—and spent over a decade and a half in the metropolitan area. I was born in Hoboken on August 11, 1967, a latecomer to the family—my sister, Olga, and brother, Joe, are thirteen and fourteen years older than me, respectively.

Before you ask—no, Ivan is not a typical Spanish or Puerto Rican name, although I've been surprised to find many other Hispanic *Ivans* as I've gone through life. As far as I know, there was no special reason for it; my parents just liked the sound.

My sister and I were close, despite the age difference; she would babysit me when she came home from school, taking over for one of my aunts. According to family lore, I was a fussy eater when I was small. My sister loves to tell a story about how this drove my mother to distraction until one day, possibly at wit's end, she grabbed a Halloween mask and put it on to encourage me to eat.

I'm not exactly sure how this worked—she seems to have slid food in my mouth every time I laughed—but apparently it became a nightly ritual for quite awhile. She would mug, I would laugh, and in the food went.

My father, God bless his soul, was a good man in many ways: kind and generous toward me, fun to be with. He worked hard. But he had a drinking problem, and too often when he drank he would gamble—not the best combination. My dad always thought it would make him rich, but then, so do most gamblers.

He also tended to be jealous of any attention my mother got. Since she was a beautiful woman, she got a lot. This was all a very bad combination, unfortunate for them, I'm sure.

One day when I was five, my father showed up at home drunk; he ended up passing out on one of the beds. This apparently was the end for my mother. She took me in hand and we went to her sister's house in the Bronx.

We never went back. My parents' marriage was effectively over. They remained relatively cordial, even after they divorced a short time later. My brother and sister, who were still going to school, stayed with my father until they got jobs; many years later, my father ended up living on property my mom owned next to her house in Puerto Rico. But there was never any illusion or talk of them getting back together romantically.

My mother had been a hard worker before the separation; now she worked even harder. She had a job in a textile factory—the garment industry was having its last hurrah in New York—then eventually saved enough money to purchase a bodega, a small neighborhood grocery store very common in urban America at the time.

The part of the Bronx where I grew up was like Puerto Rico north. I'd get out of school and walk home to the sound of conga music. Spanish was common here, and it had a Caribbean accent. It was a first language for many of my peers. We lived across the street from a Catholic church, which for many families was as much a community hub as a place of worship.

But New York was also a dangerous place in the late sixties and early seventies. Sometime around 1975, with crime increasing throughout the city, a shooting very close to my mother's store shook her badly.

"That's it," she announced when she came home. "We are selling and moving."

We left the Bronx and went to Jersey City, across the Hudson, where my mom bought another bodega and candy store. She soon met and fell in love with a man from the Dominican Republic, Osbado Alvarez. Somewhere around there, she saved enough money to buy an apartment building, then another; investing with an uncle, Mom ended up with four or five buildings in the area of Wayne Street, near a pencil factory.

I remember playing with my cousins in the sticky asphalt-covered street, building ramps from grayed plywood so we could fly over the street curbs with our bikes. I remember the Italian deli with the freshly cured salami hanging in the window, maroon-red speckled with brown and crisscrossed by white twine. I remember my gray blazer and tie for Catholic school, the nuns in their habits with starched curves and bleached white collars. I remember the red handles of the shovels in the window of the hardware store, and curiously bright colors of the wheelbarrows that lined the way inside. I remember the flowers I would sometimes buy with a few pennies for my mother on the way home—white daisies, yellow mums.

In summer we would open up the hydrants and let the water flow out—silvery water with drops that glittered against the flaked-red fire hydrants. The Twin Towers rose across the skyline, twin peaks of lofty ambition waiting in the future. Disco music shuffled from white plastic transistor radios and bulky black-and-silver boom boxes. Whatever cares my mother might have had—and I know there were many, between business and her marriage—they didn't intrude into my world or those of the other kids. We played and ran and rode our bikes. If all I remember today is laughter, that is the way memory often works: polishing out the blemishes from predominantly happy times.

Around 1977, Mom found out that her parents were ill. Caring for your parents is very important in Latino culture and especially on the island, so she and I moved back to Puerto Rico.

You can imagine the culture shock. From English to Spanish. From very urban to very rural. We hadn't been rich in the United States, but we were solidly middle class/blue collar. Puerto Rico, even near the capital of San Juan where we lived, was solidly poor. There were pans under the beds and an outhouse in the back. Mosquitos were kept at bay with nets. We were considered lucky because our kitchen was inside. We didn't have hot water, but there was a wood-fired stove.

TV? Yes, but only a single channel.

I don't remember how well I did in school the first year we moved. Probably not too well—everything was in Spanish, and mine was far from polished. It wasn't until I started attending the Antilles Military Academy the next year that I felt comfortable. It was more than just the fact that most of the kids at the private school spoke English; there was something about the rigor of the classes that attracted me. Structure and discipline were what I needed as a young teenager, and the military drills and lessons that came when I reached high school age funneled my energy.

The academy was expensive; even with her sacrifices, my mother was only able to send me because my father took his Social Security money and gave it to her for the tuition. She worked several jobs, and so did I. I'd come home and go right out selling fruit and vegetables at a busy intersection; when the other kids saw me, they made fun. I guess they didn't understand the benefits of work, let alone the necessities of bringing in an income when you aren't born rich.

For me, those were important lessons, ones I learned entirely by doing—almost by osmosis, absorbing them from Mother and the rest of my family. Working hard, striving to make things better: These became second nature, habits that I never questioned.

I wasn't the greatest student. Drilling, shooting, physical fitness (PT)—those classes I was great at. English, so-so. History, math—there were more interesting things to do than hit the books.

Our track team was studded with kids on scholarship, but I still managed to make the team, running in cross-country and the longer racing events. My memory is hazy, but I remember being somewhere in the middle, not too fast but above the worst. I was five feet eight and probably a little pudgy; not exactly the best build for a distance runner. I don't remember competing in many races, and I know I didn't come in first in any of them.

With one exception.

Even when you weren't scheduled to compete, you were expected to attend the meets. I was standing around at one of those events during my senior year when one of our coaches mentioned to another that we didn't have anyone for the racewalking competition.

"Hey, Castro," said the coach, glancing toward me. "Ever speed walked?"

"No."

"Want to try?"

"Sure!" I said. "What do I have to do?"

He took me aside and quickly showed me how to move my hips and arms. The instruction maybe lasted sixty seconds, but it was good enough to propel me to first place, and by quite a margin. Beginner's luck? Maybe. But I still took home the ribbon.

Racewalking—also known as speed walking, which is what we called it at my school—is not exactly a glamor event. It sounds a bit soft—*walk*, not run?—and looks a bit ridiculous. All of which would explain why all my friends thought it hilarious that I was now a "champion" racewalker.

The coach told me I had potential. I'm not sure I believed him, until I used it to get into college a short time later.

Very lackadaisical about my college plans, I didn't bother researching, let alone applying to colleges until well into the spring. At that point—maybe panicking—I frantically looked around for a school that would take me. I applied to the University of Puerto Rico's main campus in San Juan—after the deadline— only be told, duh, too late. And, duh, your grades are not good enough to make an exception.

As a consolation prize, the university agreed to accept me to their branch in Humacao. The college was more rural, its standards easygoing.

It was also far away. So I wondered—maybe I was a good enough speed walker to get into San Juan?

Worth a try, no?

I went over one day to see how I might go about getting in. Wandering into the gym, I eventually found the track coach talking with some of his team members and other coaches. I introduced myself, and he led me over to his office, a sweaty little closet at the far end of the locker room.

"I'm hoping to be on the track team as a speed walker," I told him. "I have come in first and my coach at Antilles says I have talent."

He looked over at his assistant. "Do we have a speed walker?"

Apparently not, judging from the man's expression.

"OK," he told me. "Try out."

"When?"

"Now."

I was in street clothes: tight jeans and leather moccasins, no socks. It was ninety-five degrees out and if the humidity wasn't near 100 percent, this wasn't Puerto Rico.

"Go test him," the coach told his assistant.

The poor man grunted unenthusiastically, then led me outside, where he took out a watch and told me to go for it.

I started lapping the track. I glanced at him as I came around the first time; he was drenched in sweat.

I did a few more laps before he stopped me.

"But I'm not done," I said.

"We'll use your average so far," he said. "You're consistent and besides, it's too hot out here."

Whatever the average was, it was enough to get me a full scholarship to the San Juan campus.

Racewalking is not just walking fast; it requires a certain kind of technique. For me, swinging the hips was critical, and easy—I liked to dance, and even better, I liked to do anything that would get the girls watching, and there were few better ways than swinging your hips back and forth in those days. A friend and I used to practice all over campus, collecting catcalls from the girls. Call it reverse sexual harassment; we ate it up.

Scholarship or no, I was a lousy student. Maybe the scholarship had something to do with it—in some ways I didn't feel as if I had to work very hard for it. My studies were rarely my main focus. I was still working when I could, both at home and at a retail store in a local mall, but I was also spending a lot of time on the beach. In fact, when I describe my life back then, I'm more often to call myself a beach bum than a college student. I started blowing off classes soon after I arrived, with predictable results.

There was one area of study that I cared about: military science. I enrolled in the Reserve Officers' Training Corps or ROTC program at the school, with the vague idea of becoming an officer in the U.S. Army when I graduated. The way it worked at the time, you made a commitment in your third year; at that point, you would receive a stipend and join the army in return. You weren't guaranteed to become an officer; among other things, you had to keep your grades up and prove you had the proper character. But it was a good route. I joined the National Guard, which in theory might have also helped me advance, but theory met reality on the sandy beaches of San Juan, and guess which won?

If I'd been more serious about my studies, I could have stayed in the program, graduated from college, and become a second lieutenant at age twenty-one. Maybe I'd be a general now.

Things didn't go that way. I was less and less motivated to go to any class that didn't have the letters ROTC attached to it. My grades went south. I didn't have the mix of credits I would have needed to get that officer contract, and I wasn't all that committed to getting them, either. I was still living at home, and days when I wasn't at school or work were mostly spent swimming and lazing on the sand. At night, a friend and I would race our cars down the treacherous mountain roads at night to get to Old San Juan, where we'd party and club until all hours. Coming home we'd snap off the car lights and drive outrageously fast on the narrow lanes, sometimes hitting eighty mph on roads that you'd have to be out of your mind to do twenty on.

In the end, though, I wasn't made to be a party animal. The military was calling.

2

All Out

The first time I jumped from a plane, I was hooked. And even though I was part of the U.S. Army's storied paratrooper training program, I wasn't even in the service. I qualified for airborne before I even enlisted.

I was chosen for the U.S. Army program during the summer of 1987, while still in college. Even though I was only ROTC, I was mixed in with regular soldiers. It was my first real introduction not only to jumping, but to being on my own in the States.

I loved it.

I went with four other ROTC cadets, none of whom could speak English as well as I could. That made me the de facto leader of the group—and the person the others relied on for notes and explanations.

Unfortunately, that also made me the center of attention for the instructors, who probably thought we were goofing around. I must have done a million push-ups in that class.

They say you always remember your first jump from a plane, but mine's mostly a blur. I see myself in the aircraft—I don't even remember the type, though I would guess a C-130—as it lumbers to altitude. I look in the face of the guy next to me and wonder, do I look as scared as he does?

From there, everything moves extremely fast—a good thing, because any pause would give me a chance to back out. I go out, the wind smacks me, my whole body is yanked suddenly—and then I have the most peaceful feeling in the world, floating to the ground.

Bliss lasted for half a second. Then I got to work, checking my risers (the lines to the parachute), my altitude, my body posture. A few dozen checks and I got ready to land.

Jumping is the easy part. Landing is hard. I tried to relax my legs as I hit and rolled, absorbing the shock like the instructors had told me.

Then I wanted to do it again. *Airborne all the way!* College never stood much of a chance after that summer. I returned home pumped on the military, and bored as ever of books.

Somewhere between my love for the army and my ambivalence about school, I came to a point where I had to decide my future. I was wandering around in a way, not getting anywhere fast, likely to flunk out of college, and unsure of what I wanted to do. I was still living with my mom, though by this time I had built a little apartment on the second floor of the family house. One night I was having dinner with her, and for some reason that I can't recall, I started telling her that I was terribly unhappy.

My mother was a no-nonsense person, and understood me better than I understood myself.

"You love the military," she told me after my brief woe-is-me speech. "It's what excites you the most."

"Yes, but—"

"No but. It's simple."

It was. The next day I went to the recruiter with a friend who had also been thinking of enlisting. I told him I wanted to be a Ranger. (Besides being highly qualified for light infantry, Rangers are trained to jump out of planes.) For some reason he couldn't guarantee a spot; instead he offered me a slot in a mechanized unit. I didn't want that—I wanted to be infantry, light on my feet.

And I wanted to jump out of airplanes.

"What about the 82nd Airborne?" I asked, naming the army's elite paratrooper unit.

"No slots. But we do have the 101st. They're air assault, not airborne, but they do have units that are airborne qualified."

Long story short, both my friend and I ended up with an assignment to the 101st Airborne Division. The 101st is a storied division; those are the guys who told the Germans "Nuts!" when ordered to surrender during the Battle of the Bulge in World War II. At the time, and for most of the 101st's history, the division was airborne—the main fighting units dropped into battle from airplanes. The modern 101st travels by air as well, but rather than parachuting from airplanes, as a general rule their chariots of choice are helicopters.

It's not as much fun as jumping out of airplanes, but the army didn't ask for my opinion. As a lowly private—I did make PFC—I wasn't asked for much of anything. Rather I was told: Do this, do that, and put some hustle into your step.

I was assigned to the 187th Regiment, known as the Rakkasans—a nickname that was earned from the Japanese in World War II, who called us (roughly speaking) "falling umbrella men." No one envied my assignment—the 187th was known as a tough brigade, one where you couldn't duck work or get out of training.

Exactly what I needed.

I realized the day I arrived at their camp in Fort Campbell, Kentucky, that things were going to be a little different than they had been in ROTC. Rather than being driven out to the field where my company was exercising, we marched double-time. I soon found that the unit marched *everywhere*; trucks were for the other guys.

I was placed in second squad, second platoon, Bravo Company—twos were wild for me. The team leader was a tall Puerto Rican sergeant named Jimenez who took me under his wing the first day by pointing me toward a Black Hawk helicopter and telling me to get aboard. We pushed out into the dark, a dozen helicopters all told, and hit our objective like a well-oiled machine.

Except for me. I didn't know how to unlatch my safety harness.

Imagine the scene: It's late at night, an entire chalk, or formation, of helicopters sets down. The company hits the ground running. More helicopters are coming in. Then everything grinds to a halt—the helicopters can't take off, the others can't come in, all because one very wet-behind-the-ears Private First Class, Ivan all-I-want-to-do-is-jump-out-of-aircraft Castro, who is so green that he doesn't even know how to unlatch a seatbelt.

The crew chief, seeing that I was messing up his flight, came over, unbuckled the belt, then pushed me out of the aircraft.

That solved one problem, but left me with another: Where the hell was I supposed to go?

My squad had moved to its assignment, which was to secure the landing zone and provide security for the succeeding waves. They ought to have been nearby, but I couldn't spot them.

The night filled with dust and grit and shouts as the next wave of helicopters came in. Lost, I did the only thing I could think of—I started running.

"Sergeant Jimenez!" I shouted as I ran. "Sergeant Jimenez!"

I'd like to say I found him in short order, but the truth is I didn't find him for quite a while. It may not even have been until the ground portion of the exercise was concluded—my memory is mercifully short on the specifics. In any event, he eventually greeted me with a very sensible question:

Where the hell were you?

My answer was suitably unintelligible. I grabbed on to him—figuratively—and basically didn't let go until we were back at camp. Either the sergeant was unnaturally forgiving or he remembered his own first few days in the army; in any event, he became an excellent mentor and friend, helping me not only in training but also to find a place to rent off base.

I needed a place to stay off base because, in the two weeks between enlisting and reporting for duty, I'd gotten married.

Irma and I were a mistake. It's a cliché, yes, but we were way too young to know what we were doing. I had barely settled on

the military. And then we compounded our confusion by having a child.

That was one good thing that came out of the marriage—my son Ivan Eduardo, who was born a few years later, in 1993. Ivan Eduardo was *not* a mistake. And if I can't take as much credit as I'd like for raising him—that was mostly Irma, who was an excellent mom—I still think of him proudly as one of the best things that ever happened to me. He was certainly the best thing to come out of that marriage.

Not to say that there weren't some happy moments, or even that things might not have turned out differently if Irma and I had been older when we hitched. But we weren't. The marriage's ultimate failure was as much my fault as anyone's, if you're assigning blame.

But at that point, we were still in the honeymoon phase. I was looking forward to getting settled in the States, and playing house with my wife.

Uncle Sam had other ideas.

I joined the army in the summer of 1990—right around the time when Saddam Hussein was mobilizing his troops to take over Kuwait. I'd been with my unit only a few days when word came for us to prepare to deploy—we were going to Saudi Arabia.

I had no idea where that was. Frankly, I had barely been at Fort Campbell long enough to know where the front gate was. I hadn't even bought furniture for the apartment when the deployment orders were cut. Irma flew in from Puerto Rico, we bought some furnishings from Sears on credit, got her a car, and said good-bye. I was headed to war.

■ ■ ■

I wasn't ready for war. I doubt anyone can really be ready, certainly not the first time. If you think too much, fear becomes your obsession. But if you don't think enough, you court trouble. Adrenaline is similarly double-edged—you need the energy, but it can easily push you into mistakes.

Looking back, my introduction to combat was pretty benign, very strange—and in some ways absolutely typical, at least for that war. Most of what I experienced was confusion, which is something all soldiers can probably cite as one of their main battlefield experiences.

Iraq invaded Kuwait at the beginning of August 1990; the country was quickly overrun. President George Bush—I'm talking here about George H. W. Bush—proclaimed that the invasion would not stand, and began putting a coalition together to fight Iraq and its dictator, Saddam Hussein. The big fear at the time was that Saddam would invade Saudi Arabia next, and American troops were dispatched within a week to protect the kingdom, beginning a huge buildup.

We were part of that.

Fort Campbell is pretty warm in the summer; Saudi Arabia was an oven. I got off the civilian airliner and instantly pounded a liter of water. Double-decker buses were waiting a short distance away, already baked by the Saudi heat. The bus ride to our tent city was interminable, even more so because all the water we drank when we landed soon had to be expelled. Guys ended up emptying their bladders into bottles, then draining them out the windows.

There's a metaphor about war in there somewhere.

It's hard to imagine now, but at the time the Iraqi army was supposedly the fourth largest in the world. Allegedly hardened by years of war with Iran, it was said to be a top fighting force, well-equipped with modern weapons.

Weapons that included biological and chemical agents. Given the fact that the Iraqi army had used chemicals against the Kurds some years before to crush a rebellion, it was believed that they would be used now against us.

There was massive hype about that, and we spent considerable time training with MOPP suits. The acronym stands for "Mission Oriented Protective Posture"; anyway you define it, the spacesuit-like gear is a massively oppressive pain in the posterior. We had four different levels of protection, which meant four levels of discomfort. MOPP level 1 meant you had just your suit on, no gloves, et cetera. Level 4 was fully dressed, with mask, gloves, top and bottom-sealed, complete with laced-up rubber boots, leaving nothing exposed. Running around in MOPP 4 was about as much fun as it sounds.

My company was "volunteered" to stand guard near the border, and my squad was tasked with watching large ammo dumps—semitrailers stuffed with ammo of every conceivable description and caliber, which were prepositioned for the eventual assault into Iraq and Kuwait. You'd have ten or twenty trucks lined up, waiting. Overhead, jets would boom as they broke the sound barrier—a noise that could sound disconcertingly like an explosion until you got used to it.

The tension was exacerbated by the lack of information. That was possibly the most valuable lesson I learned during Desert Shield. Being left in the dark metaphorically wears on a soldier. Information may not physically improve his condition, but it does make it easier to cope.

I also learned something valuable about being a private and the lowest man on the ladder of rank: You're a few ranks down from cannon fodder.

I was never actually sent out into a minefield to check for mines with my feet, but I do remember one incident at night where we'd been told to get our MOPP gear on. When the all-clear was sounded, everyone looked at me.

"Give me your weapon, soldier," said one of my superiors.

"What?" I said.

"Hand it over."

I complied.

"Break the seal on your mask," he told me.

I glanced around. Clearly I was the guinea pig, or maybe more accurately the canary in the coal mine. I hoped they'd remember the first aid lessons if things didn't go well.

There was no need to worry, then or later. But the joys of being the low man in the unit continued. I'll never forget the smell of the fifty-five-gallon drums of waste fresh from the latrines as I burned them.

Things ratcheted up with the start of the air war in January. We returned to our main base, Camp Eagle, to refit, then took a position close to the border. There was a French unit to our left equipped with massive rocket launchers, the sort that obliterate thousand-square-meter grids in a single salvo. To our right and rear were American units equipped with equally awesome weapons, from artillery to Apache gunships. Our hardware, by contrast, was pretty simple: M16s, squad-level machine guns, a few antitank missiles. But if there was a gap in firepower, our esprit de corps made up for it.

Toward the end of February, army planners spotted dug-in enemy positions over the Saudi border and assigned my unit to take them out. The Iraqis were isolated from the rest of their army and had been softened up by artillery and air strikes. They looked like easy targets.

As our squad's lowest-of-low privates, I had no specialty to speak of. But I was entrusted with an M249, a SAW, or squad-automatic weapon, your basic mobile machine gun, which can play an important role spitting lead in a firefight. I suspect I got the job as much for my ability to haul around a lot of weight as any marksmanship ability; the gun and its ammo was considerably heavier than the standard issue M16s most of the rest of the squad were assigned. I carried six hundred rounds of ammo on my waist, which is a lot of bullets and a lot of weight. (Somewhere in the area of forty pounds, give or take.) Meanwhile, I had an AT4 strapped to my back—roughly another fourteen pounds, not counting the ammo. (The AT4 is an antitank weapon, essentially a modern version of a bazooka. Unlike that World War II classic, the tube on the AT4 is "disposable"; you get one shot.)

The day of our attack, I ran with the rest of my squad to our Black Hawk. There were Apache gunships nearby; the heavy *thump* of their blades reverberated as they took off, heading out first to scout our objective. I found my place inside our helicopter and did what a lot of guys do the first time they're heading to combat: I prayed.

I prayed most of the way, fifteen or twenty minutes of Our Fathers and Hail Marys, basic prayers all good Catholics learn in grammar school, if not before. I was still mouthing my prayers when someone said we were about to land.

The helicopters went in fast and furious, circling around the target as the Apaches darted in and out. The officers and noncoms shouted directions and gave pointers; I lost the details in the blare of the rotors. I did what any soldier does in that situation—I watched the guy next to me, and did what he did.

We'd been tasked to hit an Iraqi army unit some miles behind the line. "Hit" may be an overstatement when describing what actually happened, though; what we really did was mop up the remains of a unit pummeled by a parade of jet fighters, Apaches, and artillery. We expected a fight; what we got were white flags waving from the entrances to the bunkers.

The Iraqi army unit was composed mostly of green recruits who were even lower on the military totem pole than I was. They had no intention of being cannon fodder, and realized that the sensible thing to do was surrender. The appearance of the helicopters was, to them, a blessing, since it signaled the end of the bombing. Literally hundreds of troops streamed from the underground strongholds as we landed.

We herded them into groups away from the bunkers, making sure they had no weapons. They were smiling, happy to give up—we found out that they hadn't been fed or given water for days. Preparing to take them back across the line to Saudi Arabia where they could be processed and interred as prisoners of war was a massive job, and frankly, one that took us by surprise. By evening a succession of Chinook helicopters had barely made a dent in the sea of POWs.

The next thing I knew, I was ordered into a Black Hawk.

Command had decided to pull us back—the prisoners who hadn't been evacuated were to be left in the desert.

If it sounds a little crazy to you, well, don't ask me—I was just a private, doing what I was told. I have no idea what the reasoning was.

The truth is, I felt like I was really *badass* when we got back. The way I saw it, we had just whipped a frontline unit of one of the largest armies in the world. The fact that things had gone off without a hostile shot being fired, let alone without casualties, meant that we were truly the best warriors around.

That feeling evaporated a short time after we landed, when our commander told us we were going back in a few hours.

I wasn't quite as nervous when we crossed the border again the next morning, but I wasn't cocky either. The Iraqis were still eager to give up. The situation was crazy—I remember seeing an OH-58 pilot leaning out of his helicopter with his pistol, herding a small group of prisoners to a place where another helicopter could pick them up.

Eventually, my unit was told to search the bunkers for weapons—and oh, by the way, be on your guard for booby traps. Fortunately, there were none of the latter, but there were plenty of the former. The most plentiful were Russian-made AK-47s, PKMs (a squad-level machine gun), and RPGs or rocket-propelled grenade launchers. What surprised me, though, were American munitions—I saw 60 mm and 81 mm mortar rounds, which I imagine had been sold or given to Iraq during the Iran-Iraq war.

Back safely across the border, we relaxed for a day or so, then began training for another mission, which was planned to take place after the ground invasion began. This one was aimed at capturing a bridge behind the lines. The idea was to seize the bridge and hold it, cutting off the Iraqis as they tried to retreat. In outline, the plan was simple: We'd land on the northern side of the bridgehead, kill any enemy nearby, then race across to the other side and seize the strongpoints at the north.

That outline leaves out the fact that the troops on the other side of the bridge would be firing at us the whole time. And while we would be in the open, they would be behind fortifications and in bunkers.

I was assigned to fire an AT4 at a bunker on the north, then help lead the charge. I had nightmares the day before we were scheduled to go up. Grenades exploded in my face. Gunfire from the bunker took me down. I ran on my own, naked, bullets whizzing around—any horror you can imagine, I dreamed it.

Fortunately, the raid never came off. Within hours of the step-off, the war became a rout. I'm not sure if the Iraqis had already retreated past the bridge, or if the army we were supposed to cut off had simply disintegrated and surrendered. In any event, we were reassigned to take a different position in the desert, dig in, and wait. This time, at least, simple meant easy.

President Bush called a cease-fire shortly after we took that position, ending the ground war exactly one hundred hours after it had started. American troops mopped up and came back to Saudi territory. The 101st, one of the first divisions into the war zone, was ordered to come home.

But not *all* of the 101st. My company was still out in the desert, watching the sand dunes shift, a week or so later when we heard from CNN that the division was being feted with a ticker-tape parade in New York City.

"You gotta be kidding," was about the typical response—assuming you throw a few curse words in there. We must have been out in the desert for a good two weeks before someone figured out that the few camels we saw in the distance weren't an imminent threat.

■ ■ ■

Looking back, I couldn't have asked for an easier introduction to battle. I had been in combat, but never fired my weapon. I'd faced danger, but in a very controlled way—many of the exercises and training missions I'd go on in the coming years were far more dangerous.

None of that kept me from having nightmares when I got back. I dreamed about the mission we didn't go on, saw myself getting shot, swam in sweat-wrapped dreams of fear. It was a month before the nightmares stopped.

And yet, I loved the army. I started thinking about making a career out of it, rather than seeing it as a stopgap because I didn't know how else to straighten myself out. I wanted adventure. I wanted to push myself up the ranks. I wanted to stay in infantry, because that's where the action was. And I wanted to jump out of airplanes, because that's where the fun was. So I ratcheted up my courage and went over to a Pathfinder unit headquartered near my unit at Fort Campbell, and asked if they had room for me.

Things have changed a little since they were established in World War II, but the Pathfinder motto—"first in, last out"—still holds. Pathfinders jump into enemy territory ahead of an airborne attack, preparing to guide aircraft to the assault area. They direct landing operations, arrange resupply, and oversee drop zones. Organized to improve the accuracy of parachute operations in a time of limited technology, today they employ state-of-the-art communications and location gear, working with both airborne and air-assault units.

I still remember how nervous I was walking into the Pathfinders' building to ask for a job. The first sergeant, a Vietnam vet, looked at me skeptically.

"You have to pass a PT test before we consider you," he said gruffly.

I made arrangements and came back a few days later, acing the test. From there it was easy.

The unit was filled with studs, and I learned a lot from them. They sent me to air assault school and then to an NCO leadership class, which qualified me for promotion to E5, sergeant.

I spent two years there; they were some of the happiest years of my early career. But all good things must come to an end, and they did the day I was notified to stand by for a transfer to Germany. The transfer meant that I would be given a new assignment.

The way things shaped up, it looked like I'd end up in a mechanized unit once I reported to Germany. No way did I want to spend my time in a moving coffin. I started desperately looking around for a unit there on jump status. I found Long Range Surveillance, and was lucky enough to get a transfer to a unit after one of the NCOs pulled strings on my behalf.

LRS—we pronounce it "lurse"—acts as the tip of the spear for army units. Often operating behind enemy lines, LRS soldiers scout ahead of the main body, providing intelligence to command and conducting missions to disrupt enemy attacks and defenses. They work in small teams, each man depending on the other, something I came to value highly.

My years as a Pathfinder and LRS really helped me grow as a soldier. I went to a number of "schools"—advanced courses that train you in certain specific areas—that gave my career as a soldier a firm grounding. In Army Pathfinder School for example, I learned how to guide airplanes to target areas and how to prepare drop zones; in Jumpmaster School, I learned how to supervise a parachute jump; in Survival School, I learned how to live in the wilderness with only the barest of tools. As a boy in Puerto Rico studying things like math and science, I'd been a so-so student. Now I became an achiever, striving to be one of the top students in every class I attended. Achieving became important to me in a way that it hadn't before. There had always been a competitive side to me, something that pushed me to be the best at things—you can't compete in sports without that. Now that competitive streak joined itself to a purpose: I wanted to be a good soldier.

No, not a *good* soldier—a *great* soldier. And I realized that to achieve that, I had to study and work harder at it than I ever had before.

That doesn't mean I didn't have fun in Germany. Hell no. I had a blast.

There was a bit of a culture shock, especially at first. A day or two after I first arrived, some new acquaintances asked if

I wanted to go out for ice cream. We drove to a lake, and began walking down the path. It took a few moments, but then with a start I realized we were strolling past a nude beach. I was so young and inexperienced all I felt was embarrassment.

The others laughed at me. We did get the ice cream, though.

I learned to speak German and learned to love the food. I also learned to love the fact that there was no drinking age; I was legal here, unlike in many parts of the States. And I also found that Germans love salsa music—it seemed to be playing everywhere I went, far more than at home in Puerto Rico.

My wife and son lived with me for a little more than a year in Germany, before Irma and I decided the marriage wasn't working. She moved back to the States where she had family and we tried a trial separation, hoping maybe things would change. Ultimately they didn't, and our divorce was finalized in 1996.

There were many reasons: the usual stress factors that all service families go through—frequent separations, stressful jobs, and all the rest. Beyond that, we'd gotten married very young, and inevitably grew apart. My real regrets are for my son: I wish I could have been a better, more present father. I'm not saying I didn't try as hard as I knew then. I *am* saying that I wish I knew better then.

I was very focused on my career and on being a good provider. As important as those things are, it's also important to be there for the first walk across the kitchen floor and endless games of catch in the backyard. Fortunately, Ivan Eduardo's mom was there for him through that, and did a good job raising him, mostly on her own.

My career, though, went very well. I made E5—sergeant—soon after I got to Germany.

Soldiers from E5 to E7—in the army, sergeants, staff sergeants, and sergeants first class—can be thought of as the middle managers of platoons and companies. They lead the enlisted men in the field, carrying out the orders and missions set by the officers. They ensure that things get done back at camp or base.

Senior NCOs with an E8 or E9 rank, regardless of their job,

are experienced leaders. Generally they've been in the army for fifteen years or more, and are usually "subject matter experts" in their particular fields. They also know how the army bureaucracy works, and occasionally doesn't; if you really need something done, they are the men and women to see.

3

Rangers Lead the Way

Civilians tend to see soldiers as, well, soldiers—everyone the same. But, in fact, there are many different specialties and subspecialties which work together to accomplish different missions. Mine was infantryman—a fighter trained to travel and fight light, with a rifle or machine gun, working with other soldiers. Infantryman is probably what comes to mind first when most people think of the army, and that's what I was.

As a combat solider looking to make myself better, I began thinking of going to Ranger school and earning the right to call myself a Ranger. It was and still is the mark of an accomplished light infantryman, one of the best trained and toughest soldiers on the planet.

Army Rangers sometimes trace their history to the French and Indian War, where Robert Rodgers led a group of specially trained men who fought behind enemy lines, attacking supply lines and weakly defended posts. Rodgers's company was composed of British colonists in New Hampshire; they proved so effective that additional units were raised. Rangers in various forms were active on both sides of the Revolution, and the general concept of using lightly armed, highly trained warriors in what became known as irregular warfare remained an important part of military thinking throughout the twentieth century.

Today's U.S. Army Ranger units can be traced to World War II, where they were started under the command of then-Colonel William Darby and participated in a number of important battles, both as a full, coherent unit and, from about the time of D-Day, as individual soldiers assigned to regular army companies.

That dual nature still exists today. To be a Ranger, you have to go through the Ranger course; you can then join the Ranger Regiment, which is composed of Ranger-qualified soldiers and conducts special operations missions, or join a regular infantry unit as one of the senior combat soldiers. Wherever they are, men entitled to wear the Ranger tab are expected to show outstanding courage and prowess in combat.

(A bit more Army nomenclature: The Ranger "tab" is an emblem with the word "Ranger" on it; it signifies that the wearer has completed the Ranger course. A Ranger "scroll" is the emblem signifying that the wearer is a member of the Ranger Regiment. The terms are often confused, even in the army. There is also an ongoing controversy in some quarters about whether you are a "true" Ranger if you are assigned outside the regiment. I'm not wading into that one.)

There were a limited number of slots or openings for Ranger school; my company was granted two. A competition quickly developed to snag one.

On paper, everyone was equally qualified—they'd done well in their evaluations, they were airborne qualified, had gone to various schools, and so on. So the competition came down to a series of PT or physical training demonstrations—like how many push-ups you could do. My goal was to blow everyone else out of the water—and exceed the Ranger school standard at the same time. Pull-ups, push-ups—those were no problem. The tough thing was running five miles in forty minutes or less: I still remember that run.

I was proud as hell when I learned that I had won one of those slots. I'm still proud of it. It meant I'd matured physically as well as mentally, putting that competitive spirit to actual work. No more beach bum; I was going to be the best in my profession.

But if I had any illusions that I'd already "made it," my first days at Ranger school in Fort Benning, Georgia, kicked them in the gut. The humidity was so thick you could cut it with a knife. The heat was terrible. But the weather was nothing compared to the humans in charge.

The Ranger instructors didn't particularly care what we'd done in our army careers up to that point; we had to prove ourselves to them. Proving that you could blow away the minimum Ranger PT standards was no big deal; then why the hell else were you here? Jump into the water with your uniform and gear, swim fifty meters—can't do it? You're gone.

We lost a lot of guys those first few days.

We learned to patrol by doing it without sleep. We toughened ourselves up on an obstacle course called the "Darby Queen" (named after the Rangers' founder, William Darby) and ate meals with only a BFS—a big fucking spoon, if you're into acronyms.

Soldiers were disqualified at every turn. Guys who couldn't hack it were encouraged to drop out—a "real" Ranger would *never* quit, encouraged to do so or otherwise.

That was what the instructors were really going for: guys who would stick it out no matter what. It's a cliché to say that being a special operations soldier is more mental than physical, but it's a cliché for a reason: It's true.

After making it through Camp Darby, we headed to Fort Bliss and a two-week "desert phase," where we learned the basics of fighting in the sandbox. What I remember most is being tired all the time. We had to dodge grenades and rifle fire as well as the weather, but always the worst thing was the fatigue. I didn't just fall asleep on my feet; I literally fell asleep while walking.

One night I ran straight into some concertina wire that I hadn't seen. It took five guys to untangle me; I was cut in a dozen places, including my face.

Quit? You must be joking. Just scratches.

Another night I was part of a patrol wedge, walking at the two o'clock position. I momentarily lost track of where I was, then spotted the wedge leader ahead. I kept walking until I realized he wasn't moving. A few more steps, and I saw he was a bush—the leader was somewhere well off to my left.

Of course, I had a large number of guys behind me, and more behind them. Getting everyone stopped and reoriented, then finding the lead patrol—it was a learning experience.

Our brown T-shirts turned orange with sweat, and there were still weeks to go. We jumped into mountains in Georgia and conducted a combat mission. We worked in the swamps of Florida, slogging through the muck to ambush the enemy. Then came the final test, acting as a platoon sergeant for a lieutenant also taking the course. After all that work, all that suffering . . . I failed.

Technically, it was the lieutenant who flunked. But that only meant that I didn't do a good enough job supporting him, and therefore I failed, too.

I can't tell you how desolate that felt. There were still several days to go—I couldn't just quit, but I knew that nothing I did on the exercises could change my status. I was a goner.

Somehow, some way, the class managed to move through the exercises quickly enough so that I got another chance.

Sleeping while you're on patrol is a real no-no, not just for the sleeper but even more so for his commander. I was acting as platoon sergeant, setting up an ambush on this final exercise. While we were waiting for the "enemy" to appear, my men began nodding off. I ran up and down the line trying to keep them awake, but they were so tired and we had to wait so long that inevitably one or two drifted off.

Naturally, an instructor saw it. This might have meant a washout . . . except that, a little later in that same exercise, I caught someone else on the exercise sleeping.

I was so pissed—these guys were costing me my Ranger tab—that I marched over and kicked him, not softly, then proceeded to dress him down, not politely, for falling asleep.

"Ranger," he growled.

Damn. I realized I'd just kicked one of the instructors.
Oh, well.

I apologized profusely; he growled something and moved on. Somehow the earlier episode had passed by unnoticed, or at least unremarked.

I was paired with another lieutenant, and this time I did a good enough job that we accomplished our mission, a night ambush where we took POWs.

I'd made it. I was a Ranger.

■ ■ ■

Rangers will tell you that the hardest thing about becoming a Ranger isn't the school, or even the missions Rangers are given. Both are difficult, and certainly Rangers pride themselves on taking on the hardest jobs possible. But there are more difficult things than attacking well-protected refineries in Iraq or jumping behind enemy lines to rescue downed airmen. When you are a Ranger you have to live by the highest standards. That's every day, in every way.

"Rangers lead the way" is an unofficial motto that turned the tide on the beaches at D-Day, and there's not a Ranger alive who doesn't know that story and doesn't promise himself that, when faced with those overwhelming and bloody odds, he, too, will jump up and run forward, snatching victory from defeat. School is easy—it's only sixty-five days. Being a Ranger is a lifetime commitment. Other soldiers recognize the Ranger tab on the left shoulder of your uniform, and they expect you to prove yourself. Certainly in combat they'll be counting on you. And you have to set a standard in peace as well—no fluffing off at PT, no cutting out early when work is to be done.

■ ■ ■

I graduated Ranger school in the summer of 1994. After visiting my wife and son and spending a little time in Puerto Rico, I returned to the LRS unit, where I was promoted to staff sergeant. It wasn't long before I was sent back to war—to keep the peace.

Following the death of "President for Life" Josip Broz Tito in 1980, Yugoslavia had been breaking up into different parts, separated primarily by ethnicities. Violence accompanied the dissolution.

In 1992, war broke out between different ethnic factions in the republic of Bosnia and Herzegovina, with Christian Serbs and Croats on one side and Bosnian Muslims on the other. The Serbs were aided and encouraged by the head of the Yugoslav Federation, Slobodan Milošević, a Serb who claimed that the republic had illegitimately split away from Yugoslavia and sought to reunite it with the remaining parts of Yugoslavia that he controlled.

Milošević's personal agenda of power coincided with the goal of creating a large Serbian-dominated state, and his ambitions helped fuel a series of conflicts, including war in Croatia and Kosovo as well as Bosnia. Civilians were targeted for extermination; ultimately, Milošević was charged with war crimes for encouraging the atrocities.

At the very end of 1995, following the signing of the Dayton Peace Accords, NATO intervened. The alliance sent peacekeepers to the Bosnian conflict, charging them with separating the combatants and protecting civilians. My unit was one of the first in.

We drove from Germany to Hungary, stopping at a military base there to brief the mission before proceeding. We hastily set up camp near the runway, in sight of some old Soviet-era MiG jets that looked as if they hadn't flown since Stalin's time. It was winter and we were in the mountains, without buildings or even tents; every morning the frost on my face reminded me how much I hated the cold.

We crossed over the border at Brčko, a small city that had been hit hard in the conflict. The devastation was horrific. We passed buildings riddled with bullets, glass gone from windows, stones pockmarked and peppered with holes. All were deserted; the few civilians who hadn't fled huddled in hiding spots, afraid even of us.

Every one of those holes is a gunshot, I thought. *A lot of those bullets went into people. The blood washed away. Do the ghosts remain?*

For the first time I saw how truly terrible people can be to one another. Most of the victims in this conflict were civilians. The war I had seen in Desert Storm was different than this, far different: army versus army. This felt far more devastating, more evil.

As we drove on to our objective, I realized the bare terrain around us had been forest not long ago. Desperate to keep warm during the winter, the locals had hacked down the trees to survive.

The landscape changed but the overall situation was much the same in Tuzla, a city hard hit during the conflict; even today an attack there by Serbs that killed some seventy-one people and injured two hundred more is remembered as a key event in the war. The inhabitants were very wary and likely feared us as much as they had the Serbs.

We passed on to an old base outside the city, where we set up camp. We were among the first NATO troops in the area, and our supplies had not yet caught up with us. There were roughly two hundred men in our unit; we got two tents to shelter them in. Someone ended up scrounging another, but it was a tight fit until the base was built up. Most of us slept under the stars—a reality nowhere as romantic as that may sound in the cold hills of Bosnia.

What do peacekeepers do?

Damned if I knew then, and I'm not entirely sure I know now. We didn't seem to have much of a mission once we got to Tuzla. After a day or two, one of our officers volunteered us to guard radio relay stations on hilltops surrounding the area. We split up my platoon and took over the posts, convoying out as we watched for ambushes from Serb guerrillas, who were still active in the area.

The biggest danger, though, wasn't guerrillas or even Milošević's forces, which were always rumored to be ready to attack. Land mines were everywhere. Venturing into a field, even to take a leak, was potentially a life-ending event. But the hills and mountains were beautiful—green curves decked with white and brown patches, gradually becoming greener as the weather warmed. Orange-red-tiled roofs clustered along the valleys, and in the distance white-sided buildings looked like lines marking a path through the woods.

Eventually we were given another mission, securing suspected arms caches hidden by the guerrillas. Planning the operations carefully—ambush was always a possibility, as there was no way to completely vet our intel—we ran them typically at night, watching the location for several hours before moving in. These sorts of operations are always routine until they're not; you have to guard against complacency as you set up your security and go in. Fortunately, there were never any incidents, and while we recovered vast amounts of arms, we were never so much as challenged.

■ ■ ■

Ranger school had cemented my career ambitions; having obtained the Ranger tab, I now knew what the next step would be: a spot in Ranger Regiment.

This wasn't necessarily an easy goal to reach. Most noncoms of E6 rank in the regiment have worked their way up through the unit's own ranks. There's no hard-and-fast rule that to reach the coveted position of squad leader and then platoon sergeant you must have put your time in below; still, that's the way most do it. Being Ranger-qualified is a requirement but not a guarantee that you'll be accepted.

I put in for the regiment before leaving the States, but days went by without the orders coming through. Then I got busy in Bosnia. Right about the time I feared I'd been completely forgotten, I finally got word to report to the Ranger Orientation Program at Fort Benning—a prerequisite to getting a permanent post with the 3rd Ranger Battalion, one of the regiment's units based at Fort Benning, Georgia. The program lasted about a week—truthfully I was so happy to be there and so determined to kick butt that everything was a blur. If we had to march, I ran. Gung ho doesn't begin to describe my attitude. Joining the battalion was going to be the pinnacle of my career.

I was lying on a bed in the barracks one July night, feeling pretty good about things, when someone knocked on the door. One of the cadre sergeants came in.

"You need to go down to the CQ desk," he said, referring to the "charge of quarters" or administrative desk. When you're told to do that in the middle of the night, it's not going to be good.

I got up and pulled on my pants. "I think my father just passed away," I told the other two guys in the room.

Downstairs, I was handed a phone, and found myself talking to a Red Cross worker. My premonition was right—my father had died.

The next day I flew back to Puerto Rico, still in a fog. My father and I hadn't been that close since he and my mom had split up. Still, he was my dad, and his passing was more than just symbolic. If he hadn't been the perfect man, still he had been good to me in his own way. One link to my childhood was gone. My mother, who was now living on her own near him, was in poor health and fading mentally. Even as a young man, you look to your parents for support, at least emotionally; that was no longer possible.

I was a father myself—had I done right by my own son? I'd certainly done what I thought I could. But my marriage had failed, and between that and the army, I rarely had a chance to see my boy. I had accomplished a great deal in my career, but there had been a cost to my family that I hadn't thought about.

I'm not a brooder, and my father's death didn't make me rearrange my life in any drastic way. But it did leave me more aware of my responsibilities—to my son, to my brother and sister, and to my mom, whom I discovered was entering the first stages of dementia.

For years, I'd focused on incidents that made me surprisingly angry—times when my father was drunk and acted irresponsibly. Now I saw the other side of him, the better and fuller side: a man who had done what he could despite his flaws, a man with a great heart who couldn't always overcome his limitations.

The story of us all, I guess.

We laid him to rest on a sweltering day. I said a few words, talking about the good times. Later at the house, we passed around a bottle of rum, my sadness dissipating in the bitter-sweetness of the liquor.

The next day I went to talk to my mom's doctor to find out more about what was wrong with her. I was the man of the house now, figuratively at least, and the tables had turned—I was her support, not the other way around. The doctor told me about the early stages of Alzheimer's, a terrible disease that steals a person's mind and slowly poisons it against the body. The disease is somewhat better known now than it was then, though huge gaps continue to hinder treatment.

I can still see her sitting there, barely recognizing me—maybe not recognizing me at all.

"She's going to get worse," warned the doctor.

The words were like bullets, wounding me despite the stoic façade I conjured. I made what arrangements I could, still not entirely believing that her brain had given her body a death sentence, then headed back to Fort Benning and the 3rd Ranger Battalion.

Work was a relief. I'd been assigned to a weapons platoon as a section leader, in charge of about nine guys handling anti-tank duties. Carl Gustafs and Javelins were our weapons of choice: It was a great place to be if you like demolishing serious objectives on the battlefield.

The Gustaf is a recoilless weapon, essentially a big tube that fires an unguided missile. It's been in service since just after World War II in different variants. You can think of it as an updated bazooka firing an 84 mm (about three and a third inches) diameter projectile. The only drawback is the relatively close range of, say, 150 meters against armor, though you can use it at a greater distance against bunkers and buildings.

The other drawback is that you don't want to be standing right behind it when it's fired.

The Javelin is a Carl Gustaf on steroids. Not only is the missile it launches bigger, it's smart: You can set a target and it will direct itself to it, within reason. Attack a tank and it will find the weak point on top rather than trying to go through the heavier armed side. It has a much farther range, and within limitations, can be used against moving targets, including a low-flying helicopter. Our battalion was the first to field the weapon in regular operations.

Firing both of these is, literally, a blast. The Gustaf shakes your entire body; there is no mistaking that you pulled the trigger. The Javelin is a little less earth-shaking—the rocket pops out before going full blast. But both are awesome, powerful weapons that give small ground units tremendous firepower.

So training was a blast, literally and figuratively. War itself may not be fun, but practicing for it certainly is. I remember one maneuver where we were working with a special operations unit, supporting them as they simulated a raid on an airfield. Fast-roping from a helicopter, humping to our positions—we were like a football team that had worked our way to the Super Bowl.

There is no unit in the army with a higher esprit de corps than the Rangers. Everyone is extremely physically fit, and the best at what they do. If the standards are high, the morale is even higher. Wearing that black beret—this was at the time when only Rangers had that honor—was a sign that you were one of the best.

And so when I fell from that lofty position, was in effect kicked out of the regiment, it felt as if I'd been pushed down the deepest hole possible.

■ ■ ■

I was at Benning when Irma finally filed for divorce. We'd been separated for a long time, so it wasn't really a surprise. She was living with our son near some of her relatives in Louisiana. Meanwhile, I had my own life and friends in the army. I was determined to keep in touch with my son—I called every week, and saw him when I could—but I'd be lying if I said I was heartbroken when I saw that she wanted to officially end the marriage.

In the meantime, I'd made friends with another soldier and his wife, and we'd all occasionally spend off-duty hours together at bars or what have you. Somehow or another, through a misunderstanding I guess, command got the notion that I was committing adultery with my friend's wife.

Possibly a jealous member of my unit informed on me in a way that made it appear I wasn't doing the right thing morally; maybe it was just a case of people wanting to see fire where there wasn't smoke. In any event, my command believed that I was violating military law by having an affair.

Rangers are held to a high standard, and even *appearing* to violate those standards is reason for dismissal. I was told to find a position outside the regiment.

I fought it. My friend and his wife both wrote letters saying nothing was going on. But the decision had already been made. I was a liability to the unit's reputation, and there were no second chances, let alone excuses. I was given a general letter of reprimand, which stayed in my file and effectively blocked my advancement for years to come.

Desolate, but not ready to leave the service, I decided my best option was to move sideways. I took a slot as a drill sergeant.

I like to think I did a good job. My joes were never the best at drilling, and I wouldn't get too terribly upset if their barracks weren't spotless. But I pushed them harder than anyone at PT and during the physical exercises that I felt would set them up for success on the battlefield. I tried to teach them the rudiments of being a soldier, how to patrol, how to work in a team. I gave them lessons the Rangers had taught me. I passed along things I'd learned the hard way in Iraq and Bosnia.

The wars had put things into some perspective for me. A properly buttoned shirt isn't nearly as critical as an intimate understanding of the capabilities of your weapon. Marching is important not so you look good while parading, but so you have endurance on the battlefield. If my guys were singing when they were jogging, they weren't going fast enough.

I ran with them. I learned who could be pushed, and who had

to be cajoled. It made me a better leader and judge of character—even though it was probably my hardest time in the army.

Getting a general letter of reprimand is not like getting a slap on the wrist. Certainly there are worse things, but if you are career oriented and want to advance, it's like going around with a big "kick me" sign taped to your behind. I had trouble getting assignments, and my hopes for promotion were dashed—over the next several years, I watched a number of my peers move on to E7 and E8 while I stayed an E6.

Being at Fort Benning made things even worse. Whether true or not, I certainly felt that I was an easy target for rumors and innuendo. So when I heard that my old LRS unit in Germany was looking for an E6 who had Ranger and Pathfinder training, I did everything I could to get a transfer. Luckily, they took me back with open arms.

■ ■ ■

The highest praise a drill sergeant can get isn't a commendation from the commanding officer. It's seeing a kid you took under your wing promoted to first sergeant, or hearing a warrant officer call you "Drill Sergeant Castro" years after you've gone on to something else.

Those are the compliments I remember. I cherish each one, to this very day.

4

Crime and Realities of War

Going back to Germany was like coming home from college after a tough semester. A lot of the guys I'd worked with earlier were still there. I knew the mission, and I was blessed with a team that was experienced and capable. The job was a cinch because of them.

I began to enjoy my time off. Knowing the language made it easier to get around. I poked around the little towns, discovered beer festivals and *biergartens*. After exploring Germany I branched out, visiting the rest of Europe—Holland, Austria, Switzerland, Luxembourg, Italy, the Czech Republic, Britain, Turkey, Greece, France. I became a great tourist.

But it wasn't all fun and games. Soon after arriving, our unit was sent back to Bosnia. Within days I was back in Tuzla. This time, we had a well-defined mission: find "PIFWCs"—Personnel Indicted for War Crimes.

We were going after the bad guys.

The United Nations was trying to punish those responsible for genocide by trying them as war criminals. Milošević was the most famous—he would later die of a heart attack while awaiting trial—but he was the tip of the iceberg. Dozens of former military

officers, guerrillas, and terrorists were suspected of killing civilians, and the UN moved to bring them to justice. In many cases,
indictments were handed down without the accused criminals
being in custody. That was where we came in—we were given a
list of wanted criminals and directed to apprehend them.

Without going too deeply into operational details, we generally worked like this: Intelligence would provide us with information on a certain suspect or group of suspects. Besides photos
and other personal information, we would get license plate
numbers and vehicle descriptions. We would then try to set up
an ambush along a road they were suspected of traveling. Even
though they knew they were wanted, many still visited the area,
as they had family and other contacts there.

Our work was secret; not even the other people on the base
knew about it. Among other things, we were assigned to stay in
a secluded area of the camp and obscure our unit patches. We varied our routines and otherwise tried to make our comings and
goings secret or at least unpredictable.

A team of six might leave in onesies and twosies, hitching
rides on the backs of trucks and rolling off in the dark, then meeting up and walking a mile or more to a target area. Our packs
would have enough food and water for a few days. Radios, binos,
weapons—no matter how high-tech the equipment we carried
was, the most important gear was always our own eyes and ears.
Stopping, looking, listening, even smelling—you'd be amazed what
your nose can tell you—were far more important than examin-
ing a map or combing through intel.

One night we were given information that a suspected war
criminal was planning to drive through an area a few miles away.
At dark we headed down to the road, where satellite maps had
shown an abandoned house perfectly positioned for surveillance.
We did a rolling insertion from trucks—we jumped out the back
as they went through a dark patch of the road—then hiked a few
miles to the house.

Going into a building, even one supposedly empty, was always hazardous. We had to check for booby traps as well as am-

bushes; there were still mines all over the place. The least amount of inattention could be fatal. In this case, we cleared the house quickly in the dark—there was no electricity, and in any event lights would have tipped off anyone nearby. We found a room that looked out on the road; rather than using the window, which would have been obvious, we punched a hole in the wall to use as a lookout. I posted security and settled in, not sure what to make of the large piles of rags and shoes that cluttered the floors of nearly every room, or the large blotches of dried paint on the floors.

The place smelled wretched, but that wasn't unusual.

It wasn't until first light that I realized the dark blotches on the floorboards was dried blood, not paint. One of my men called me into a nearby room, and kicked at the rags lining the floor. They were clothes, torn and bloodied. Under them were catheters and IV bags. The nearby shoes were caked with dried blood and mud.

We realized that the house had been used as a makeshift hospital during the worst days of the war. How many people had died there? The floorboards and discarded clothes gave no specifics of the horrors, but we didn't need numbers. I gathered my men and had them take up positions outside, haunted by what we'd seen even as it underlined the importance of our mission.

Ghosts turn out to be a poor substitute for intel, or even dumb luck; the war criminal we were looking for never showed up.

Mosquitos, ticks—insects fed on us throughout the deployment. I wish I could say that we captured a dozen war criminals, but the truth is none of my teams made a single arrest. While we were able to pass along what we were told was good information on several surveillance missions, we never learned whether those led to arrests, either. I came to see what we were doing as almost a matter of faith: We were a small cog in a wheel that was trying to spin justice from chaos and depravity. Even if we did our jobs perfectly, we might never know whether we succeeded.

The usual lot of a soldier in a conventional war is one of blindness and faith, followed by certainty: You fight and fight with only a dim picture of the overall battle, trusting that the generals above are pushing you in the right direction. But eventually you do know, one way or another, how you did—it's either victory or defeat. What we were doing in Bosnia was far more ambiguous, much harder to measure: Even if we had arrested a hundred war criminals, would we have changed the reality of what they had wrought?

That sort of question was way above my pay grade. But if I'd been asked, I would have had a ready answer: *We have a mission, and we'll do our best to accomplish it.*

In the end, that's all a soldier can really do.

Besides hunting criminals, we provided security for the local elections, guarding a polling place by providing overwatch from a nearby hillside. About the only danger we encountered was an open manhole in the road, which I fell into as I ran in the dark when we were inserted. I limped for days afterward, and the guys had a lot of fun with that. I'm surprised none of the jokers put me in for a Purple Heart; it would have matched my purple hip.

5

The Brotherhood of the Elite

We returned to Germany a short time later. Some years before, I'd thought about trying to join Special Forces, the army's elite special operations unit. It was the logical next step for someone who wanted to keep pushing ahead in combat arms. And while my reprimand had set me back, enough time had passed for me to explore that possibility again.

Could I have stayed in LRS and probably Germany the rest of my army career?

No doubt.

Would I have been happy?

Probably.

Would I have been satisfied?

No. For me, real satisfaction came from moving ahead. I always had to feel that I was getting better, that I was achieving the next goal, climbing the ladder to the next rung. Without that feeling, I couldn't be satisfied.

So I set my sights on earning a green beret.

The words "special forces" are often used interchangeably with "special operations" or "commandoes," to mean troops trained for specialty missions. In the army, however, "Special Forces" refers to very specific units—the so-called "Green Berets." (The name is a reference to our headgear. Berets of any color were extremely unusual at the time the group was formed; now they are common.)

Green Berets are special operations troops, and commandoes, but we're much more than that. Special Forces, or SF, was established in the early 1950s at the height of the Cold War. The idea was to create an elite force that could infiltrate behind enemy lines, organize or hook up with local guerrillas, and carry out clandestine missions against the enemy. Special Forces were also given the mission of acting as scouts, providing intelligence to commanders from posts deep inside enemy lines, and training and advising conventional foreign forces.

Unlike conventional units that are organized in battalions, regiments, and divisions, Special Forces is structured into teams, battalions, and groups. There are five active-duty groups and two that are part of the National Guard; traditionally, each group is assigned to a specific geographical area around the world, building relationships in these foreign countries.

A Teams are the basic fighting units in Special Forces. Speaking generally, each A Team or ODA (Operational Detachment Alpha) has a dozen men, all proficient in the language of the area where they are assigned. Each member of the team is highly trained in a specific area—communications or first aid, for example—though as a practical matter between experience and cross-training, most are proficient in just about any skill a soldier might need in war.

Each A Team is supported by a B Team of roughly the same size. The B Team's job is to do anything and everything necessary to help the A Team succeed at its mission. A lot of this is seemingly routine—arranging transportation, making sure the proper ammunition is available—but it has to be done under potentially dangerous and often covert circumstances.

As long as the soldier meets some basic requirements, anyone can try out for Special Forces. You don't have to be an infantryman—I know a cook who made it—but you do have to meet some very rigorous physical requirements. Historically, most successful candidates are at sergeant rank and above—the experience and maturity help quite a bit. (At the time I joined, there was a requirement to be an E4 or above; a special program, though, allowed recruits to come in directly to Special Forces, and earn that rank if they made it. While I'm talking about it, current requirements essentially prevent women from joining, though that will be phased out, possibly by the time this book is published.)

One of the requirements to get into Special Forces is a security clearance. While my reprimand hurt me, it didn't bar me from that clearance, and so I was able to put together a packet and apply for selection without a red flag. I blew out the physical fitness test, got my clearance, and reported to a small post at Camp McCall, ready to be owned for twenty-one days of suck as a candidate in Special Forces Assessment and Selection. It was the first in a series of tests and evaluations I'd have to pass if I wanted to wear the SF tab.

Maybe I should confess to a brief detour I took before starting the course. I went over to Selection with a friend of mine, a combat photographer who also wanted to join Special Forces. By design, we arrived in the States a few days early, checking out the area and acquiring the gear we needed for the course.

A day or so before we were supposed to report, my friend and I investigated one of the local watering holes. In the course of our investigation, my friend made the acquaintance of a young lady on the dance floor.

They were putting the moves on when a rather large fellow pushed his way through the crowd, aiming to have a serious philosophical discussion with my friend's skull.

People began bowing up left and right. The bartender grabbed the phone to call the police.

I took a step forward. I would never let a friend fight alone, but this was a complicated situation: If there was a fight and we were arrested, we wouldn't have to wait for trial. We would fail selection before we did our first push-up.

Something flew across the room—a body, maybe. I sprang into action. Possibly I threw a punch; more likely I simply grabbed my buddy and pulled him outside as fists began to fly.

We weren't quite to the door when a pack of girls spilled in front of us, pulling and punching at one another. Somehow we managed to duck past them and make it to the parking lot. The police arrived as we pulled out; I didn't stop to give them directions or advice.

There's a common misunderstanding about special operations soldiers; people think we like to brawl and are constantly getting into fights. I can't speak for every single member of Special Forces, but in my experience we're a hell of a lot more mature than that. I like to say I'm a lover, not a fighter; war may be my occupation, but I do it on the battlefield, not in a bar.

You need a certain amount of maturity to get through the entire selection process, so that may be one reason SF soldiers generally avoid messing it up. Another is the attitude that comes from the top: *We're an elite force. Act like it.* Most guys do.

My buddy and I reported for selection the next day. They put us up in a tin-roofed shack that had some of the nastiest bunks I've ever seen. But that never affected my sleep—the cadre ran us so hard I could have slept at the bottom of a latrine each night.

The first week at McCall is mostly about the individual. You have a PT test, go out for runs, survive a notorious obstacle course nicknamed the "Nasty Nick." There's a rather long and involved psych review; the fact that I passed it proves that I am sane, or at least was at that point.

All the time, the cadre is doing various things to keep you awake. They can't duplicate the stress you'll see in combat, of course, but by building your fatigue they can see how you react to pressure. A surprising number of guys drop out in these early stages, realizing that things are only going to get harder.

This was 1998; I had just turned thirty-one. That may not

sound old to you—it sounds pretty young to me right now—but it made me the oldest one in the group by a good margin. And on a lot of those runs, I felt every one of those years. I was no spring chicken.

But I wasn't admitting my age, even if the others thought I was an old man. It was a matter of pride—I worked harder than ever. Looking back, I think I was probably in peak physical condition. Maybe my age made me train smarter; maybe my memory is glazing over the aches and bruises. Whatever; it felt like the prime time of my life.

Here's another common misunderstanding I want to correct: The instructor cadre never yelled at us. They were extremely professional, and always correct. "Soft-spoken" exaggerates how loud they were; a lot of times they barely spoke above a whisper. But you listened for every nuance. And they were always watching. If they caught you sleeping at the wrong time, or simply out of place, you were going home rather than moving on.

As time went on in the course, we began working on exercises that required cooperation. We were formed into twelve-man teams and given missions. These were pretty varied—I remember one involving rescuing downed "pilots" who turned out to be sand-filled duffle bags—but the mission objective was always beside the point. The instructors wanted to see how we worked with others. You can't organize a guerrilla movement or train an army if you can't find a way to work with people.

We capped off those first weeks of training with a decently long hike, twenty-five or thirty miles. I remember it as a zombie march: Everyone was dead tired, physically and mentally. But even the guys who were beat physically had the right stuff. I remember one soldier whose feet were covered with blisters and were raw and bloody. You could see the pain on his face with every step he took. The day of that last march, he pulled on his ruck and hobbled into formation.

"I'm not quitting," he muttered as we were ordered to start. "Not quitting."

He was behind me, so I don't know how far he got. Eventually one of the instructors ordered him to stop; he may have been crawling by that point. They moved him on to the next phase—blisters or no, the guy had the toughness it takes to wear the green beret.

Passing selection doesn't mean that you're SF. That just lets you try out for the "Q Course" or qualification training. Of course, if you've gone through those weeks of hell without quitting or being pushed out, you're already fairly certain that you're going to do whatever it takes to make it through Q Course.

Maybe.

In my case, having made it through selection, I was sent back to my LRS unit to wait for an opening.

I was still waiting when my guys received word that they were going to act as a rescue unit in Kosovo. The Balkan Wars were flaring up again. American Apache helicopter gunships were part of a NATO force there; one of our LRS platoons was tasked to rescue the crews if they were shot down. This isn't just a case of driving to the scene of the crash, or even being able to fight your way to it. Rescuers have to know how to do everything from shut off fuel to rig the chopper with explosives so it can be destroyed.

They also had to be expert SPIES.

Not the James Bond stuff. SPIES: Special Patrol Insertion and Exfiltration System. Think very long ropes dangling from a helicopter, clutched by soldiers who are flying through the air.

Wheee. It's fun, but don't look down.

Soon after arriving at our base in Albania, we lost an Apache on a training mission. We were fortunate that the crew wasn't seriously injured. Two weeks later, another gunship went down, again in an accident. This time it caught on fire as the team fast-roped down to the rescue. Thirty millimeter rounds began cooking off—the crew had surely died on impact, but that didn't make it any easier for the men watching helplessly as the ammo percolated off. All they could do was call the mortuary service and wait for the fire to go out.

I stayed in Albania for about three months. Starting to get

anxious about ever getting a slot with SF, I decided to take the initiative. Some soldiers might try to pull strings by contacting higher-ups in the chain of command. I went right to the source: I contacted the clerk who processed my orders and made my case.

Eloquently, with flowers and chocolates rather than words.

I have no idea if that had anything to do with what happened, but you'd have to work hard to convince me otherwise.

▮▮▮

The letter of reprimand could have ended my military career. Instead, I'd managed to work my way past it. I had a lot more work to do if I was going to achieve my goals: The Q Course is not easy, and no one was going to guarantee that I could make it through. But I felt like everything was going in the right direction. Physically and mentally, I felt better than ever. I'd started taking college classes in addition to the military ones I needed for work; now I was the sort of student I hadn't been at eighteen, actually studying.

Then I was hit with something that threatened to completely unravel me: In September 1999, just as I was about to report for SF training, I got word that my mother had only a few days to live.

▮▮▮

This was right around the time that Hurricane Floyd hit North Carolina; just about the whole state was closed for business, and that included the airports. I ended up driving to Virginia and hopping a flight to Puerto Rico from there.

The island had escaped the worst of the storm, but things were chaotic nonetheless—Félix "Tito" Trinidad, a very popular Puerto Rican, had just beaten Oscar De La Hoya and the place was going nuts. You would have thought Katy Perry had come to Puerto Rico and rode through San Juan naked.

The next day my sister, brother, and I went to the nursing home where my mom was. On the ride over, my sister did her best to prepare me, explaining that Alzheimer's had really devastated the woman we all loved. Mere words couldn't prepare me for what I saw when I entered that room. An old woman was tied to the bed, an IV and catheter strung out to the side. The thin hospital sheet barely covered her bony skeleton. Skin hung against the mattress like a deflated balloon.

This wasn't my mother. This was a stranger.

Not my mom.

Not.

I could feel the tears starting down my cheek as I leaned down toward her.

She smiled—I swear she smiled. Somehow through the haze of the disease that had robbed her of her senses, she recognized me.

I kissed her on the cheek. It was one of the hardest things I've ever done: an acknowledgement that this stranger had been the most important person in my life.

"Your baby boy is here," I whispered.

Outside, I told my brother and sister that she wouldn't have wanted to be like this. She was a strong and proud woman, and to live her last days as little more than a vegetable would have galled her.

We left for lunch, then headed home to rest. I don't think we were in the house more than a few minutes when the phone rang. My sister picked it up; I knew what had happened before she even spoke.

"Mom died."

"She was waiting for me," I said. "She was holding on until I could get home to her."

I got back in my rental car and drove down to a funeral home to make arrangements. An undertaker followed me back to the nursing home with his van. When we reached her room, we found that she was still tied to the bed, restrained as if her body might somehow follow her soul to heaven. I undid the restraints and tubes as gently as I could, then the undertaker and I rolled the bedsheet around her and put her on the gurney.

She was amazingly light, this woman who'd given me life.

We buried her near my father, two souls that struggled to find peace together in life. I spoke at the burial service about how strong Mom was, how she was always working, how she spent her entire life trying to achieve. Only now do I realize that was my inheritance: Her example got me working, and keeps me working, on and on.

6

Loss and Love

I'd been flying high. Now I'd fallen low.

I spent some time taking care of my mother's affairs. With about a week or so before I had to report back for the Q Course, and still waiting for some of my mom's final papers and bills to be cleared, I decided to take a brief vacation at a resort hotel in the Dominican Republic. It was a spur of the moment thing, helped by a high school friend who happened to be a travel agent.

I spent the first two or three days there completely to myself, mostly in my room. Finally, feeling a little more energetic, I decided to go out by the pool. It was empty; I lay back on a chair and relaxed, still in a funk.

Sometime later that morning, two older ladies came down, speaking Spanish; I said hello and went back my brooding. Not long afterward, a much younger woman came down and started talking to them. She took off her shirt and shorts, revealing a blue-and-white bikini, and dove into the water.

I couldn't take my eyes off her. I decided to go over and talk

to her but before I could come up with a plausible excuse—or un-
tie my tongue—she was gone.

She took my heart with her. But she also gave me a mission.
That night I prowled the hotel, using all of my LRS skills looking for her or the older ladies. I didn't see them inside or at the
pool, but when I went down to the beach, I spotted the trio standing near a bonfire. There was music, and people dancing. I was
just about to ask the younger woman if she'd dance with me when
the music stopped.

Tongue-tied again, I overheard the older women mention a
disco. I soon made my way over there and after a bit of recee—
aka reconnaissance: I had to use some more of my best scouting
techniques—I managed to locate the two older ladies.

The younger one was nowhere to be found. I was about to
give up when I saw her walk in. She was wearing a spotless white
T-shirt and denim cutoffs; her hair curled down her back, and
her hips swayed just right.

Very hot.

"Would you like to dance?" I asked.

"Not this one. The next one."

I knew a polite turndown when I heard it. I sulked into the
background, returning to my funk. The music continued; I
grabbed a drink.

I was about to leave when I saw her across the dance floor
waving her hand. She was dancing with someone else, but mo-
tioning me to join her.

Really?

Without much hope, I went over as the music ended. A meren-
gue started to play.

We danced. Then we talked. We talked some more. We talked
until they closed the disco. We talked outside until the sun was
starting to come up. Her name was Evelyn. It turned out she was
from the States, and was here with her mom and an aunt on
vacation.

I can't remember what we talked about, but I remember how

beautiful she looked in the night, how her eyes slipped into mine, and through them to my soul. I remember how easy it was to talk to her, and how important it felt to do so. I remember not feeling tired at all, just the opposite.

The next morning—after two or three hours of sleep— someone banged on my door.

"Go away," I moaned.

"Do you want to join us for breakfast?" Evelyn asked.

I jumped out of bed. "Sure!"

From that point on, we spent just about every waking moment of the next few days together. We ventured all around the island, sightseeing and talking. We even pretended to get married at one of the churches.

Evelyn lived and worked in New Jersey; her mom lived in Queens, New York. By the time my vacation was over, we were already planning to see each other as much as we possibly could.

■ ■ ■

Evelyn's memory of that trip and our meeting pretty much parallels mine, though there are a couple of minor discrepancies. For one thing, she claims I followed her around for *hours* before introducing myself. Like a stalker.

Maybe.

She also says my Spanish was pretty rusty that first night. She claims she took pity on me and used English the whole time.

And that may be true, too.

But she agrees it was pretty much love at first sight, and that from that moment on we were inseparable, in thought, at least, if not actually in body.

■ ■ ■

Q Course teaches you a lot—small-unit tactics, navigating in the wilderness, surviving on your own. You learn by doing, and doing again. And again for good measure.

Each time I tested myself, I learned a little more. Could I

navigate in the woods in the dark if dropped behind enemy lines without a GPS? If I could see the stars, I could.

Could I orient myself with a map if I had no idea where I was?

If I examined the terrain, I could. I could stare at the hills around me, listen for a stream, scan the shadows for the break that showed where the road was.

There were dozens of tests like that, each different, each assessing more than the skills they were calling on. They assessed your resourcefulness, patience, willingness to push yourself.

I kept pushing. I saw a goal in front of me—joining Special Forces—and I wanted to achieve it. One more goal, one more achievement. Whatever it took.

Years later, the details of some of the problems and exercises are still alive in my brain. I can see myself in the dark woods, pushing through the thick summer underbrush. I've just crossed Scuba Road and I'm heading toward the Bowling Alley—a long, narrow field that after the woods feels as open as a rec hall. I'm near Puppy Palace—a dog kennel on land adjacent to the exercise area. I can hear the hounds baying as I come up to Four Wire Road. There are miles to go before I reach my objective. . . .

One night we were on an exercise at a place we called Bone's Fork Creek. I crossed the creek and leapt up onto a fallen tree trunk. I slipped off, my lower leg going one way and the rest of my body the other.

Oh . . . damn.

I rolled onto the ground, a little dizzy and in some serious pain. I managed to hobble up the embankment and to the road, where I settled onto my ruck. One of the instructors drove up a few moments later.

"Castro, what the hell are you doing?" he shouted.

There may have been a few other words of the four-letter variety in there.

"I'm busted up," I said.

"Get back out there."

"I will, but I'll have to leave my knee here."

They ended up taking me to the hospital, where it turned out I had torn my ACL, the ligament in the knee that does most of the work when you bend your leg.

Afraid that if I had an operation I would be disqualified from SF, I managed to avoid surgery through stubbornness, a bit of subterfuge, and rehabilitation, pretty much in that order. Even so, I was on the sideline for three months, and spent a good portion of that wearing a low-profile brace under my uniform pants. In the meantime, I was given permission to enroll in college classes. Like civilian employers, the army encourages soldiers to further their education as they advance in their career; a degree isn't mandatory for promotion in the enlisted ranks, but it certainly doesn't harm you. And maybe I figured I'd be a little bored just sitting around waiting to get better. But the biggest factor was my failure years before to finish college. I'd blown it. I'd goofed off and fooled around and didn't study. I hadn't achieved.

Now I was mature enough not only to recognize that, but to make it right. I began taking classes, one at a time, with the long-term plan of finally getting a degree. (I eventually chose business as my concentration.)

Knee healed, I joined another class and went through the program, training as an "18 Bravo"—a Special Forces weapons sergeant. It was more of what I'd already done over the course of my career—a lot more. I was introduced to a variety of weapons from outside the States, from Russian AKs and Markov pistols to German H&K G3s (an older assault rifle). Machine guns, mortars, anti-tank weapons—they didn't teach us how to fly Apaches, but I would have been first in line if they had.

Green Berets and special operations soldiers in general are often asked what their favorite weapons are. Those of us who are trained as 18 Bravos are expected not only to know about guns, but to *really* know about them. And that tends to mitigate emotional favorites. So let me point out that I don't really have one; weapons are tools, and different tools have different applications. Even the best tool for the best situation will have limitations somewhere else.

But . . .

I am partial to Heckler & Koch, the German manufacturer responsible for many classic Western European and NATO guns. Maybe it's because I've spent so much time in Germany. Maybe I just have learned to appreciate the fine engineering that goes into their guns. Whether it's the G3 or the MP5 or even a pistol, I've found myself drawn to H&K.

Of course, if you're taking history into account, there's something special about the M1 Garand. In a lot of ways that was the gun that won World War II for the Americans. Holding it in your hands connects you to millions of soldiers who made tremendous sacrifices to keep our country free. And while I would never call the AK-47 a thing of beauty, I do recognize that its tremendous ruggedness and tolerance for abuse makes it a valuable rifle in the real and messy world of fighting.

Following my specialty phase, I moved on to a massive exercise called Robin Sage, which basically simulated guerrilla recruitment and unconventional warfare. (The order of SF schools and exercises has changed since I went through them.)

We spent some time in classrooms learning and planning our moves. Finally, we did a night jump into the area. I went out clean, had a good chute, everything was smooth . . . until I landed.

The area where we were training had once housed buildings. Apparently some of the foundations or maybe just old bricks were still scattered under the ground. Erosion occasionally scooped away the dirt, exposing jagged hunks of cement and stone to the elements—and to landing paratroopers.

As I landed, my left foot snapped back. Adrenaline and my training kicked in, temporarily blocking the pain. I pulled out my weapon, ready to use it if necessary, then rolled to my knee. I undid my chute and grabbed my ruck, then stood up.

Crrrack.

Seriously. I hear the bones breaking even now.

I fell to the other knee, silently cursing.

It turned out I'd snapped three metatarsals. I was sidelined again. I made things worse during recovery by not using my crutches—when they took the cast off after eight weeks, they discovered that the bones hadn't healed because I'd put my weight on the leg. I was re-casted and spent another eight weeks in plaster. That's what happens when you go macho.

I felt like I was falling to pieces. Once again I put the time to good use, enrolling in more college classes. Still, between the casts and rehab, I lost some six months—and gained twenty pounds of excess weight—before I got back to Robin Sage and Special Forces training.

The washout rate in the Q course isn't anywhere near as severe as in selection—which is the idea behind selection—but you can't phone it in either. Besides training specific to your specialty, there are weeks of guerrilla tactical training and survival tests. There's also language school.

One of the key qualifications for a Special Forces soldier is the ability to learn a foreign language. In my case, that language was Spanish—which I already knew well. And in fact, I scored a 3 out of 3 on the proficiency exam, which meant I didn't have to take the language courses.

Language proficiency is so important that it generally determines which SF group you're assigned to. If you're going to a place where everyone speaks Spanish, for example, the ability to speak Spanish well is, if not an absolute prerequisite, at least strongly recommended.

I wanted to go to South America, and not just because of the language. My relationship with Evelyn was blossoming—having those three months of recuperation greatly sped things along. She had family in Colombia. And 7th Group, the Special Forces unit assigned to South America, also happened to be headquartered at Fort Bragg, which would make things a lot easier for me in terms of living arrangements.

On the other hand, I also spoke German decently and loved Europe. So being assigned to 10th Group, which traditionally has been aligned with that area, wouldn't have been the worst thing in the world.

I decided to focus on 7th Group. So I found the woman who'd

gotten me assigned to the SF course, sent some more flowers and—coincidence or not—I got my wish.

I should mention that, while in my experience the group tends to have some 60 percent or more native Spanish speakers, you don't have to grow up speaking Spanish to serve there. I know a lot of great speakers who have anything but a Hispanic background. And even vice versa.

The day I reported to 7th Group, I thought back to my days as a cadet in ROTC. Some Special Forces guys had come to talk to us. They looked like supermen to me.

I can never be like those guys, I thought.

As I'd gotten older, I realized SF soldiers weren't supermen at all. Yes, they were incredibly well-trained, in great shape, mentally and emotionally calm and sharp. But their biceps weren't made of steel, and they couldn't leap tall buildings in a single bound. They were human.

And now I was one of them.

■ ■ ■

I was also, once again, a married man.

My relationship with Evelyn had grown to the point that I decided I wanted—*needed*—to spend my life with her. She had just finished course work for her psychology degree, so there was nothing holding her back.

On New Year's Eve, 2000, I proposed.

Wanting to do something a little special, I picked out a ring and took it with me when we went out to a club to celebrate the new millennium. We were in Queens, at dinner with her mom and some friends. The waiters had just passed out champagne, and while she was away from the table for a moment, I slipped out the ring and dropped it into her glass.

She came back, and took a sip—without noticing the ring.

All sorts of things flew through my mind, the least alarming being what I would do if she swallowed it. I realized you should only go so far with a surprise.

"Look in the glass," I told her.

She stared down into it. Suddenly, her hands began to shake. "Yes!" she said. "Yes!"

We were a great match for many reasons. Sex—obviously. Just looking at her: beautiful legs, a great smile, eyes that lit up a room . . . just holding her: soft bosom, thin waist, gently rounded hips . . .

That was very important, but there was a lot more. We both valued family, and for some reason could talk and share just about anything without worry or complication. And we were both strivers—even while working, she had decided to pursue her college degree, not an easy thing. She liked North Carolina, where Fort Bragg was located. And she loved to travel, something we did as much as we could once my training was done.

I'd finally found the love of my life.

I don't know how to put everything I felt into words. Love isn't a matter of words, after all. It's what you feel inside, a feeling that grows even in the hardest times. And that's what we had.

What we didn't have was a wedding date.

Truth was, we weren't very focused on planning the event. There was so much else to do. Evelyn looked for and found a job; I settled into mine. Aside from knowing that we wanted an informal event and to have all our friends there, we really didn't put any effort into planning.

Then I got word that I was going to deploy to South America. That presented a potential problem. Even as a fiancée, Evelyn wouldn't have any official status with the army if something happened to me. If there was any kind of emergency, not only wouldn't she be able to help, she wouldn't even be notified, at least not officially.

She brought up that point in June when I came home from work. I was laying back on the bed, hands behind my head, when she walked into the bedroom and asked what I thought we should do about it.

"Maybe we should get married right away," I said. It was still early in the afternoon. "We can go to the courthouse and have a quick ceremony. Have a big smash later on."

"When would we go to the courthouse?" she asked.

I rolled off the bed. "Right now."

I called up some friends and had them meet us there. We filled out the paperwork, bought the license, and stood in a hallway in front of a thick, bulletproof glass window as the judge said the magic words.

You may kiss the bride.

And I did. Evelyn and I were married on June 4, 2001. We kept it a secret for a while, still planning to have a "real" ceremony and party. Little by little, we told people what had happened or they figured it out. Somehow, we never got around to having that big ceremony, but I still smile every time I think about those vows in the hallway.

■ ■ ■

Many of 7th Group's most important missions during the time I was assigned there took place in Colombia. In fact, I ended up deploying there five different times. There were two reasons for all the activity: guerrillas and drugs. Both were major problems the country's military had to deal with.

There had been guerrilla movements in Colombia for nearly a century, largely in extremely poor rural jungles. In the 1990s, the oldest and largest guerrilla group, FARC *(Fuerzas Armadas Revolucionarias de Colombia)*, kicked up activities and recruited upwards of ten thousand men to form a large but decentralized force. These units attacked government posts, police stations, and army bases. They also kidnapped a number of people, including American aid workers. The government attempted negotiating with them at the end of the decade; by 2002 the talks broke down and an all-out war was launched.

The United States supported the government against the guerrillas, supplying equipment and advisors, as well as training and occasionally logistical support. Seventh Group was part of all that.

Despite my rehab, my knee continued to bother me and gradually became worse, until I finally submitted to the inevitable and had it operated on, shortly after finishing the Q course. Coming back to work, I was told I was in no shape to join an A Team. Instead, I was posted to a B Team, supporting two A teams deploying in Colombia.

I was more than a little disappointed. I hadn't joined Special Forces to work as support staff. I wanted to be in the thick of things. But in some ways it turned out to be the best thing that could have happened to me. I learned a lot about supply, how the army and SF work behind the scenes. Later on, when I was finally cleared to join an A Team, I was able to use those lessons and some of the connections I'd made to make sure my team had what was needed to complete its mission.

From ammo to airline flights, there are a thousand little details that have to be taken care of if guys in the field are going to do their jobs. Bullets don't just magically show up when you need them. Someone has to get them there. And that same someone has to know exactly what you'll need, even if you don't know yourself.

But that was in the future. My B Team deployed soon after I arrived, setting up shop at Larandia military base, which is in Caqueta in the southwest mountains. The area was surrounded by guerrillas, and Americans were not allowed to leave the base. At the time, the Colombians were flying cocaine-killer missions from there, launching aircraft that would spray herbicides to kill coca, the raw ingredient of cocaine. The A teams we were supporting were training Colombians troops in jungle and anti-guerrilla tactics.

You wouldn't believe how poor the country and its people were. The lowest ranking soldiers were draftees who served a mandatory one year in the army. They were poorer than dirt— anyone with a few dollars was either buying their way out of the military service or becoming an officer—and they were always looking for a way to supplement their meager income. That meant that anything on our side of the base was likely to be stolen and sold on the black market if it wasn't nailed down. That included weapons and ammo, which undoubtedly would have ended up in the hands of the guerrillas and drug cartels.

Even so, I came to appreciate the sacrifices these young enlisted guys made. They lived in the mud; their barracks looked like a prison. Worse. It was no wonder that the regular army didn't amount to much of a fighting force, and progress against the guerillas was painstaking. These dog soldiers were living worse than literal dogs.

Understanding their hardships was one thing; expecting them to fight was quite another. In one incident I remember, the Colombians dragged their feet rather than pursue a small contingent of FARC guerrillas who had killed two Colombian soldiers nearby. After hours of cajoling by our commander, they finally mounted a patrol, only to promptly sit down on the banks of a river once out of eyesight of the base.

The Colombians had an excuse for everything. They were a complete one-eighty from everything I had seen and experienced in the U.S. military. But it was the norm in Colombia, and in a lot of places that don't have professional-level armies. The corruption and sloth at the lowest levels of society is merely a reflection of what's above.

There were definitely exceptions. Later in my SF career, I got the chance to work with a Tier 1 counterinsurgency force that was every bit as professional as an American unit. But their dedication was the exception rather than the rule.

It was while I was on a B Team and deployed to Belize that I met the rock star Jimmy Buffet.

We were supporting an A Team *waaaay* out in the jungle when one day our sergeant major gave me and another soldier an important mission:

Find beer.

The A teams had been out for something close to thirty rain-filled, mosquito-swarming days, and were in desperate need of a morale boost. So we grabbed a Humvee and started driving. We had no idea where we were going, except vaguely in the direction of civilization. Actually, any direction away from the camp where we'd pitched our tents would have been closer to civilization.

After an hour or two of driving we saw a fancy sign in the brush that pointed us up a path to a high-class resort. What it was doing there I have no idea. Nor, I would imagine, did the resort staff, since the place was almost completely empty when we arrived. There was, however, a little cabana and bar area out back. We sat, and in short order were being served steak and potatoes, the first real food we'd eaten in what seemed like a lifetime.

"Who do we pay?" we asked when we were done.

"Don't worry," said the server. "The gentleman at the bar is taking care of your bill."

We walked over to thank the gentleman, who was alone.

He looked familiar, but not that familiar. We asked who he was.

"Jimmy Buffett," he told us.

Yes, he was *that* Jimmy Buffett. We had found Margaritaville.

We had a few beers with him, and then grabbed as many as we could carry in the Hummer. Back at camp, word quickly spread; in short order, just about everyone was headed to that resort to meet the musician.

Buffett was a great sport. Not only did he treat us to food and beer, he ended up inviting the unit to a concert in North Carolina, where he was playing a month or so later; we all got in free as his guests.

■ ■ ■

Back home one morning that fall, I went to the base for early morning formation and PT, then came home to grab a quick breakfast with Evelyn. It was one of our favorite routines. I had my coffee, got my uniform on, then sat on the couch lacing my boots.

The news was on.

Breaking news: a plane has hit the World Trade Center.

Holy shit!

Evelyn came over and stared at the TV. Our first impression was, *God, a small plane hit the building. It's so sad.*

I got up to go to work. I had just started to back the car out of the driveway when she ran out of the apartment shouting at me.

I slammed on the brakes. "What's wrong?"

"Another plane just flew into the World Trade Center."

I ran back inside, just in time to see the video of the second aircraft hitting the building. Numb, I watched for a few more minutes, not really believing what I had seen. Finally, I realized my place was at work—we were at war.

When I got there, it seemed everyone was as stunned as I was. Guys were taking out guns in the team rooms, all the while staring at the television.

New York: Boom.

The Pentagon: Boom.

Pennsylvania: Boom.

Oh, my God. What next!

We fought through the numbness, telling ourselves we were prepared for anything. All of us checked with family members—Evelyn's mom walked home from Manhattan to Queens that day, but was OK—and we called friends in Washington. It was a day like no other. We rallied ourselves, though as yet we had no orders except to remain on alert.

"We don't know what's going to happen," said one of my teammates, "but we're ready."

In a lot of ways, it was a statement and an attitude that would define my own future. For the immediate future, our assignment remained South America; the war on terrorism and the Middle East in general was someone else's concern.

■■■

After about a year on a B Team, I found my way to an ODA slated for another South American deployment. But even then, I wasn't able to get into the action—I made the mistake of admitting that I was qualified to attend HALO school when the team needed a HALO jumper, and off I went.

HALO stands for "high-altitude, low opening"; it describes what happens when you jump out of a plane way, way up in the air, then fly (and fall) to an altitude where you open your parachute. You start out training in a wind tunnel, learning how to turn your body into an airplane, then you do a series of jumps from every conceivable aircraft under every conceivable condition.

Check that. We didn't jump from the Space Shuttle. But that was about it.

If you're ever in a position to make a HALO jump—and admittedly you may have a hard time arranging that unless you're in the military—the aircraft to choose is the C-17. It is the Cadillac of HALO jumping. You can get the entire team on the ramp and go out together, which makes it a lot easier to hit your mark. There are also a lot of more subtle conveniences, including being able to plug into wall fixtures for your O2. (Yes, that's how high you are when you jump.)

Military jumping, by the way, is a lot different than sky-diving, even from a very high altitude. The chutes are bigger because you're carrying a lot of weight—maybe a hundred pounds between your legs—and you're doing it at night, into potentially hostile territory. You have a weapon, and you sure are hoping there isn't a big crowd waiting for you when you land. But it is still a huge adrenaline surge.

Now HALO qualified, I joined the team two weeks late in Bogota, Colombia's capital. We had a number of projects, including helping to set up a training base near the northern border in Indian country near Venezuela, which was helping the guerrillas. From the air, the region looks beautiful: a paradise of green against white peaks in the distance. But it is anything but paradise. On one mission in Colombia a bit later on, we heard something rattle our helicopter as we flew through a valley; the pilot called back and asked if one of us had accidentally discharged our weapon.

Hell no, we said. *What are you talking about?*

When we landed, we found the compartment riddled with

bullet holes. A bullet had missed one of the team members by inches. We took the flights a little more seriously after that.

The guys who were with that unit remember it as a "dream team." We were all experienced soldiers, but more than that, there was a special synergy between us. We could joke and keep things light, then be deadly serious when the "stuff" hit the fan. For me, I felt like I was coming into my own, putting everything I'd learned throughout my career into play.

Being older than most of the other soldiers can sometimes help in a leadership role, assuming you play it right. I try to put people at ease, show I'm not their enemy, establish a relationship with them. If they want to put my experience to work, great. If they think they have a better way, hey, that's OK, as long as we accomplish the mission.

I'm not saying my way is the only way, or even always the best way. If I know a better way, it's because I've made plenty of mistakes getting to where I'm going. If I can help others learn from those mistakes, then we're all ahead of the game.

As the war with the guerrillas heated up, we continued to advise and support the regular army and elite units that were involved. But our activities were limited; on at least one occasion that I can recall, we were allowed to go out with a unit but had to stay back before the point where they expected contact. As it happened, there was no contact—a lot of patrols in the jungle were like that—but those were the rules.

Between deployments, I went to sniper school. I was a good, solid, but not superb shot, accurate enough to pass the class but no star. The truly difficult part was the stalking, which required you to work your way through various fields and vegetation, take your shot, then return, all without being detected. During one exercise, I found a shortcut—if you ran with all your might as soon as the cadre dropped you off, you could get into the field and take your position before the "target" arrived.

The instructors weren't too pleased when I got my "kill," but no one said special operators are supposed to fight fair.

That training helped me on another deployment to Colombia,

when I set up a military sniper school. Years later I met some of the guys I'd worked with and trained; now I know what teachers feel like when their star pupils look them up a decade after graduation.

■ ■ ■

The year 2004 was an important year for me. For one thing, I finally got something I'd wanted, though maybe not hard enough, as a teenager: my college degree.

Those rollbacks and injuries had helped give me an opportunity to go to school. They also taught me the wisdom of the old saying that if life gives you lemons, make lemonade. It's funny—even just saying that I want to laugh, because it sounds so corny. And yet it's true. I could have given up or even just taken it easy. Instead, I pushed myself to put wasted time to good use. It was an important lesson, obviously one I would have liked to have learned before I hit the beaches as a teenager, but a critical one nonetheless.

In many ways, I'd reached the pinnacle of my army career. As far as I was concerned, there was no better unit in the world, let alone the U.S. Army. The group's mission took me to Colombia, which gave me the chance to see Evelyn's relatives every so often; she even came down a few times to visit. I think the fact that I was deployed to the country where her relatives were made my assignments there a little easier for her than if I'd been sent to Iraq or Afghanistan. The places I was going were not where her family came from, and there was a good deal of danger in some of the things we were doing, but her overall familiarity with the country eased her mind a great deal.

Or at least if she worried, she didn't share her fears with me. Military wives have a difficult "job"—they can't worry openly. And probably like every service member since George Washington, I didn't go out of my way to underline the dangers I faced.

The unit's deployments tended to be shorter than many

others', which may also have made things easier, not just for her but for me as well.

I loved being an 18 Bravo, and if I kept doing a decent job, I could expect to be promoted. Evelyn and I had a house near Fort Bragg. We were even able to save enough money to buy the one next door, which we rented out to other military families. She had a good job with a school that let her take long vacations in the summer; we used that time to travel and visited many places.

I had reached a point in my life when a lot of people might have been content to sit back and start enjoying things. Maybe I should have done that. I'd certainly earned it.

Instead, I decided to accomplish the second goal I'd set for myself as a teenager: become an army officer.

■ ■ ■

Aside from emergency commissions during war—known as field commissions—it has traditionally been rare for an enlisted man to become an officer. Every army in the world has two tribes, enlisted and officer, and as a general rule these classes are separate.

In 1940, Omar Bradley, then commandant of the Infantry School, reorganized and expanded a small program for enlisted men into a formal Officer Candidate School at Fort Benning. The idea was to take noncommissioned officers who were intelligent and experienced but lacked college degrees and train them specifically to be officers. (A college degree is now required for admission.) The U.S. Army's rapid expansion as Europe went to war helped fan the program; more important, the battlefield exploits of the men who graduated as second lieutenants proved the program's worth. Briefly shut down during the post–World War II drawdown, OCS was reestablished at Benning in the early 1950s and has operated ever since. Classes in leadership and military management skills remain at the heart of the program.

I met all the qualifications for the program, and then some. There was only one hitch—I was thirty-seven, and ordinarily the cutoff is thirty-four.

There is a waiver process, and as I worked my way through it, getting recommendations from some of the men I'd served with, they kept coming back with the same question: *Why? Why do you want to do this?*

Part of the answer was easy:

I want to command an A Team. You can only do that as a captain. Which means OCS.

But the fuller answer was harder to articulate. There were definite sacrifices involved. For one, I'd actually be taking a cut in pay, at least at first, as I'd be losing some of the add-ons that came with my present assignment. For another, I'd have to leave the teams for a few years to earn rank—lieutenants don't typically serve on ODAs.

There is also a certain cliquishness to officer country. West Pointers tend to flock together, ROTCers do the same, and so on. Coming from OCS can feel a bit like being the runt of the litter sometimes.

Still, I wanted it.

I went to talk to the commander of 7th Group for my final sign-off. He asked me the usual questions about why I wanted to go, and then asked about my strategy for getting back to Special Forces. I laid it out for him: I'd angle to get into the Quartermaster Branch or Signal as a second lieutenant, getting the logistics experience that would bring me back quickly to SF (as important as they are, these skills are in short supply—pardon the pun). Once with Special Forces, I'd work my way back to an ODA.

I was pretty proud of the way I'd worked out the best way to maneuver through the career ranks, so when he frowned at me I was surprised.

"I'll sign this on one condition," he told me, pointing to his recommendation. "I want you to stay in the mix, pay your penance, before coming back."

What he was saying was this: Become an officer, Ivan, but stay in the infantry. Use the skills you've developed in your sixteen or so years in the army where they can do the most good. Get even more experience in the field you want to excel in, then come back and kick some butt leading the finest small-group fighting force in the world.

Hard to argue with that. Especially when my company commander hooked me up with an officer in the 82nd Airborne, who promised me a slot as a platoon leader when I graduated.

And so in the summer of 2004, I entered OCS. Three months later, after a course that, candidly, wasn't anywhere near as hard as the Ranger and SF training I'd completed earlier, I graduated and headed to the 82nd, a freshly minted second lieutenant eager for battle and ready to show the world that I knew exactly how to lead men into war.

TWO

WAR AND THE UGLY

South Pole Diary:
December 3, 2013
In the cold

The other team members talk about the bleak landscape, and the isolation of the endless blur of light during the Antarctic Day. I can't see that light; I've known only darkness since Iraq. For me, the Antarctic is ice and endless skiing. I ski, listen to my music on my iPod, and think about the past: Iraq, everything that came before, and all that's happened since.

The cold is a strange kind of cold—ski and you're warm, because you're working so hard, but the moment you stop you instantly freeze. The worst thing is to sweat; rest, and you're covered with ice.

The sastrugi, *the frozen waves of snow, continue to confound us. They sap our energy, causing us to work two or three times as hard as we would if the ice were smooth and level. At times you feel as if you're in one of those old-fashioned amusement park rides with moving floorboards.*

The cold attacks my arms and legs, and freezes my face. The worst pain comes from inside. Either because of the air or the altitude or some bug, I've gotten a cough and am having trouble breathing right. It's like I have a cloud inside my lungs.

We've only been at this for three days now, but all my points of reference are already confused. It's hard to know what day it is. My frames of reference are gone. I can't see to make new ones. I ski, I rest, I ski.

Maybe it's harder for the others. They must be used to seeing nightfall, and there is no night here, only day.

I'm not sleeping well. Two or three hours yesterday; the same the night before. I get up early and try to sort myself out, prepare before the others, because it takes me so long to get ready, much longer than them.

The guide from the Commonwealth team had to be taken out of the competition the other day because of altitude sickness or pneumonia. Everyone is dealing with problems—frostbite, hot patches on their feet that turn into crippling blisters, dehydration. Ed Parker, our race organizer, said that to conquer Antarctica we would have to feel pain. He was right about it.

We all feel it. My calf muscles are strained, my heels are sore. My lungs hurt. And the cold, always the cold.

As I ski, as I ponder my own history, I have to wonder: Why am I here? Am I just here for the adventure of going to the South Pole? For the adrenaline of competition? Or am I trying to prove something to the world? Or myself?

I'm here to win, I answer. To be first—in the race, and to the Pole as a blind American. Yet as time goes on, that answer makes less and less sense.

7

War Again

I reported to the 82nd Airborne in June of 2005 to take command of a weapons platoon, AT-2, part of Delta Company, 1st Battalion, 325th Airborne Infantry Regiment.

I barely learned the unit's nickname—Demons—before orders arrived saying we were deploying to Afghanistan by the end of the week.

I was excited. Soldiers don't *wish* for war, but it is what we train for, and sooner or later you want to put what you know to the test. There is no greater test than combat. Put it this way— athletes train for competition, and they want to face the best challenge possible. Whether it's the Super Bowl or the World Cup, the Boston Marathon or the World Series, you want to be there.

I'd been to war before, been shot at and helped hunt down war criminals. But I'd never been the officer in charge, the guy leading the unit. Here I was fresh on the job and already gearing up for action.

There's always a period of testing between the senior NCO of a unit and a newly assigned second lieutenant. Though the officer is nominally in charge, in nearly every case the senior sergeant has a lot more experience in the army than he does. For the young lieutenant, there's a fine line between using that experience properly—as a good officer will want—and losing control of the unit. He has to assert authority without being an idiot about it.

Of course, in some cases, a senior NCO can make the wrong assumptions.

The first day I arrived, I wore a plain uniform, brand-new; I looked like I was as green as green could be. I was mostly busy with paperwork and the usual red tape of reporting to a new command, so my platoon sergeant didn't really have a good chance to take my measure. His attitude, however, edged toward "I can run the show, lieutenant; lay back."

I'm not a lay-back kind of guy.

The second day, I came in with my uniform a little more filled out: my Ranger and SF tabs were properly sewn in place. They were a clear indication that I wasn't wet behind the ears.

"You got me good," confessed the sergeant as soon as he saw my shoulder. "Are you prior service?"

I explained that I had worked my way up the ranks. Having been a noncom, I knew what his role was; I wouldn't be interfering. He and I would work as a team, backing each other up.

"You have your lane," I said. "I have mine. As much as I can, I'll crosscheck you. You do the same."

He was an excellent NCO, and we developed a pretty good working relationship. We shared the same, simple goal: We wanted to be the best platoon in the company.

Under other circumstances, that might have meant months of high-tempo training, a lot of practice with the basics and not-so-basics of combat fighting, and as much PT as the joes could stand.

But we were at war. Everything moved quicker; we would have to pick up things on the fly.

The team had been to Iraq before, but there were a lot of adjustments to be made—on my part as well as theirs. I immediately put together a list of things I wanted to take, including a small refrigerator, a microwave, and a set of DeWALT power tools—items that were not, apparently, on the "normal" equipment list.

The section leader in charge of packing us looked me up to discuss the items. I forget his exact words—they were respectful, I'm sure—but they were to the effect that the platoon really didn't have a lot of space allotted to it, and some of the items I was requesting to be transported were going to put us over the limit.

My response was, respectfully, find a way to get them in.

I was used to deploying with SF, where (within reason) you can ship pretty much whatever you deem necessary for a mission, and necessary includes items that other units may consider "comfort items." I'm not talking about Barcaloungers, but simple things can make a huge difference. The ability to make a good pot of coffee—and share it with your men—helps boost morale, which in turn can make a big difference over the course of several months of grunting and humping.

Give that section leader credit: I don't know how, but he found space for everything.

Evelyn was not particularly happy about the deployment. Afghanistan wasn't in the news nearly as much as Iraq at that point, but it was still a war zone. There had been danger in South America, but it wasn't the subject of news reports. Afghanistan was a little different.

"Oh, it's an easy deployment," I told her. "They just want some boots on the ground. Nothing to worry about."

That's what most soldiers say—*it'll be easy*. Whether it will or not. You want your family to be at ease.

Is it lying?

It might be, depending on the circumstances. But it does no good for your loved ones to worry.

8

Paradise and Other Shitholes

A few days later, we arrived at Bagram Airfield, the large U.S. base near Charikar in the Parwan Province of Afghanistan.

Bagram is nice, as these things go.

Or to use army terms: it's a shithole, but it's not too bad a shithole.

The major problem for us was that we were attached to another unit, which made us orphans—low man on the totem pole when it came to getting supplies and gear. We got the essentials; we had to fight for everything else.

But luck intervened. It happened that an SF unit from 3rd Group happened to be stationed at Bagram at the time. Thinking I might know some guys there, my sergeant and I took a walk over to their camp to say hello. We immediately ran into a couple of guys I'd known from 7th Group.

"Ivan! When did you join the dark side?"

"Castro, you're an officer? Why'd you take the cut in pay?"

"You're with the enemy now?"

Razzing done, they were extremely helpful, asking if we needed anything. They were able to lend us a number of useful items, from gloves and sunglasses to a special computer program that provided satellite maps of the country. Those were the first (and only) detailed maps of our mission area that I ever saw.

That may sound strange, even outrageous, to people who haven't been in the military, and maybe it is. But like everyone else, the army has a budget. Certain units, like Special Forces, have a lot of leeway when it comes to getting what they need for a mission (though I'm sure they have some complaints as well). Others, though, have to scrimp and scavenge, and just because I thought detailed maps of the terrain were critical, the powers that be weren't necessarily going to give them—or even have them to give to us.

We were lucky in one respect when it came to equipment: Being a weapons platoon, we needed Humvees. It didn't make sense to ship ours from the States; instead, we were issued four brand-new up-armored Hummers that had just come to Bagram.

Talk about kids in a candy store. We ripped the plastic off the seats and slid in.

We immediately began customizing them. That was a bit more involved than plastering Demon decals on the sides. We made sure, for instance, that each one was set up to both tow another vehicle and to be towed, and arranged the gear so this could be accomplished within seconds, even under fire. We welded extra mounts to the turret, allowing the gunner not only to work his main weapon but also have a lighter machine gun at the ready.

In the meantime, we trained and got to know one other. We went out to the range as a unit and shot our weapons. We worked up a set of standard tactical procedures, building on some of the things I had learned in Special Forces. Everyone in the unit had to know what to do in an ambush, for example—not just know what they were to do but what everyone was to do. They had to know it in their bones as well as their head. When someone is firing at you, you don't have time to grab a checklist and read through it; you have to react.

I don't want to take too much credit here. The noncoms are

the guys who led the way—that separate lane I mentioned earlier. I marked the lines; they drove the distance.

We took the Hummers through the towns near the base, getting used to the country. The air outside the gate smelled of heavily burnt wood, the main fuel for cooking and heat. And everything looked a hell of a lot different than North Carolina and its environs. The people, mostly men, dressed in loose native clothes, flowing tops that hung down over loose pants, with a beakless cap or turban. There were jingo trucks everywhere, and bicycles.

Jingo trucks—some people called them "jingle trucks"—is a fancy word for the local vehicles that brought supplies to American bases. A lot of them were colorfully decorated and often had chains and bells that clanged as they drove—"jingled." Most troops applied the word pretty liberally, to just about any local vehicle, including buses and flatbeds, usually dressed up in a riot of colors, often with Arabic sayings on tiles that lined the sides.

We were nervous the first time we left the base. It's easy to get bogged down in traffic; the slower you move, the easier it is to be targeted by an IED or a grenade. Worse, we were in full battle rattle—vests, helmets, etc.—and the interior of the Hummers were hot as hell even with the AC cranked. Rolling down the windows was not an option; even near Bagram, that would make the vehicle's occupants too easy a target.

The weight of our equipment put an extra strain on the vehicles, and we quickly learned that they had to be driven carefully so they wouldn't overheat. It was a skill that would come in handy in the weeks that followed.

I spent a lot of time trying to keep the guys at ease, especially the new kids who hadn't been to war yet. I encouraged them to call home, and do things like shower—you never know when you're going to have a chance to take one once you hit the field.

I encouraged my guys to call or write back home. It's important for your family to know how you're doing; it puts them at ease. But many men choose not to call, for reasons I don't get.

Bottom line—if you're overseas, talk to your people whenever you can.

As a young soldier in Iraq during the First Gulf War, my greatest complaint was that I didn't know what was going on. Uncertainty is a terrible enemy. We talk about force multipliers in the military, things that make your force that much more potent. Uncertainty, in my opinion, is a *fear* multiplier. Not understanding what might happen made anything possible. In war, the biggest anything is always death; the less you know, the bigger your fear.

So I tried to address that. I tried to tell my joes as much as I could, about the war in general, certainly, and about what we were doing. I couldn't eliminate fear—that's a personal thing—but I did what I could to lessen it.

The truth was, though, that I didn't have much information to give them during those first few days. I didn't have any definitive information myself. Finally, we received our mission— support a company tasked to set up a FOB, or forward operating base, in the Jalrez Valley. Parliamentary elections were due to be held in a few months; by securing the area, we would encourage people to participate.

■■■

Driving south out of Bagram, I was struck not only by the beauty of the region—vegetation clutched tight to the rocky hills, mountains stretched out in the distance—but by the people. They were modern and medieval at the same time. The most fascinating were the men, who wore some combination of western dress: long robes and shirts topped by the blazer of a business suit. They all wore beards, and something on their head—work caps as well as scarves and *pakol* caps. They lived in collections of little huts clustered tenaciously on the rocky hills and massed in the valleys between them. Every so often we passed farmers with small herds of goats, or camels being used as pickup trucks.

I started to think about the culture, but also the fact that these people didn't know the world I knew. I wasn't thinking that they might or could kill me—though that certainly would have been a possibility. It was more curiosity: How did they live their lives here? And how did I look to them?

An American can't spend time in a place like Afghanistan without realizing how lucky he is not to be a native. Nearly everything I took for granted back in the States was missing here.

Kabul stretched out in front of us as we came down the mountain highway. I was stunned by the sight:

Holy shit, this is a big city.

And surprisingly modern, in great contrast to the arid area I'd driven through to get there. The city itself was a study in contrasts. Large, multistory hotels and office buildings poked up from a vast jumble of smaller cement structures. Satellite dishes vied with minarets for an opening to the sky. As we closed in on the outskirts of the city, the contrasts became even sharper; modern and medieval jumbled together like a time-travel movie gone awry. There were many foreigners here, but you couldn't always tell by what they were wearing; the man in a suit was just as likely to be an Afghani as the one in the *shalwar kameez*, here called a *khet partug*—to many American soldiers, a "man dress," a phrase that carried with it a negative connotation, not always intended.

I should mention that the clothes and terms I use and are most familiar with are *Pashtun*, the dominant tribe in western Afghanistan where we were assigned. Each tribe and area has their own variations, often too subtle for an untrained American to decipher upon first arrival. Later on, you realize that a certain style of cap may actually have different variations depending on the wearer's origin. The subtleties were not something I mastered, or had to, during my stay.

South of Kabul, we passed the hulks of Russian personnel carriers, damaged in the 1980s war and left to rot. Our vehicles began kicking up what we called "moon dust" from the road—a fine layer of sand and tiny grit that caked on our sweat and quickly covered everything. It permeated the air, and caked on your body.

A few hours later, we came upon two dilapidated cement buildings just off the road near a small mountain village. We'd reached our new home.

Apparently built by the Russians and used as some sort of administrative center, the buildings were fixer-uppers to the max. Both had gaps in their walls as well as their roofs. Debris and dirt had accumulated over the years, and the best word I can think of to describe the interiors is "nasty." Home may be where the heart is, but a big dose of disinfectant never hurts.

We checked and fueled the vehicles, making sure they were ready to roll in case we were attacked. Then we set a guard and went to bunk out in the building that seemed the least beat up. Finding a spot to put our bedding on became an art.

Night fell quickly. Checking on security and the vehicles, I looked up at the sky. It seemed as if I could see every star in the universe. The mountain air had a fresh, invigorating energy; it was hard not to admire the natural beauty around me. I wondered if they were the same stars that I looked at when I was home. And I wondered if they were the same ones my loved ones back at home were looking at now.

But beauty in a war zone is a distraction. I put my eyes where they belonged—on the terrain nearby, on the road, on possible points of attack and ambush. I focused my attention on the sounds around us, filtering out the jets and helicopters in the distance. We were alone in our little compound, and yet not really alone.

There were no attacks that night, and none in the days that immediately followed. But I didn't sleep well. There was too much to do when dawn rolled around.

We had been with the spearhead of the force; most of the rest of the detachment began arriving the next day. Headquarters company unceremoniously kicked us out of our "dorm," telling us they needed them and we could sleep in tents.

Which would have been fine, except we didn't have any yet.

Vehicles poured in—not just Hummers but transports with Quadcons and other equipment. Quadcons are large metal boxes that can be opened from two parallel sides. They can be attached together and are easy to transport via truck, ship, or even aircraft. They're sturdy if not indestructible, and hold up well to the environment and travel. They are ubiquitous in Afghanistan and throughout the army in general.

A small group of contractors arrived to begin building up the base, putting in Hesco baskets around the perimeter, setting up generators, making the buildings usable, and, slowly, setting up tents. (Hesco baskets—technically Concertainer or HESCO Bastions, both trade names—are large containers made of wire mesh that are filled with sand and/or rocks to form a barrier. They're used in the States for things like flood control; in Afghanistan and Iraq they became the main building blocks for walls to protect camps and other vulnerable areas.)

As an attached platoon, we were still the low men on the priority list, and after three or four days of taking turns sleeping in the Hummers, I realized it was time to show some junior officer initiative and get us some housing. I took out my DeWALT tool set and called over a couple of my guys.

"Here's what we're going to do," I told them, handing out the tools. "First of all, guard these with your life. Give them to no one. If a general comes over and gives you a direct order to turn them in, do not obey. These tools remain in your hands at all times. Clear?"

It was.

I told them that they were going to go and help one of the contractors as he erected the next tent on base. They would learn how it was done by training on the job.

After that?

"You come and erect ours."

That was how we got our two tents: We scrounged and built our own. But once we had them, we encountered another problem: the heat. There was a solution to that—AC units. I found one that wasn't being used and had it installed. But getting another proved nearly impossible. I finally had to "borrow" the AC unit assigned to the chapel, in exchange for allowing the tent to be used for services.

Having two tents let me split the platoon in half; the NCOs and I had one tent, the privates the other. I set up my microwave and told everyone they could use it; the fridge held cold drinks (soda and peach-flavored iced tea). A discarded wooden spool that had been used to cart electrical wire was set in front of the NCO tent and became a makeshift dining table. Camo netting doubled as an awning: al fresco dining.

The good life, Afghani style.

Our furnishings may have been primitive, but we were in an area of extreme beauty. The valleys were green, with low trees and sprinkles of ground cover, especially near water sources. Above them, jagged stone poked at the sides of the hills and mountains, pushing through the scramble of dirt and rocks. Grass grew in stubborn clumps; tall mountains peered in from the distance, postcard backdrops.

We weren't here for sightseeing. Once we had the FOB set up, we got to work establishing patrols through the area around the base. Command divided the region among the various platoons; we were given three districts in Wardak Province: Jalrez, May-dan Shahr, and Nerkh. I'm not sure what the total population was at the time, but the most recent sources put it at well under a hundred fifty thousand people. Whatever it was, it was well spread out; the biggest village would barely rate a gas station and a traffic light back home.

The population was primarily Pashtun, the dominant ethnic group in southwestern Afghanistan, and the largest in the country as a whole. Most, but not all, are Sunni Muslims, itself the most populous variant of Islam. Ethnic identity is further compli-cated by the large number of tribes; just because you are Pashtun does not mean you are necessarily from the same tribe, though it was a good bet out where we were. Larger tribes have their own subdivisions, which may mean different dialects and cus-toms as well as rivalries. Tribes, subtribes, and significant clans total over four hundred, depending on who's counting. So call-ing someone Pashtun, while useful on one level, is like saying a person from Boston is American—he certainly is, but that may not mean he likes the same baseball team or worships at the same church that a Baptist in Georgia does.

I knew none of this when I landed in Afghanistan; I didn't even know what Pashtun was. While there wasn't much time to get ready before we deployed, even a few hours' lecture on the local culture as we flew toward Kabul would have helped prepare me better.

What I did know was that the areas I had to patrol had very few hard-packed roads, making them ripe for ambushes. Many ran through small, narrow valleys, perfect for hit-and-run attacks. The Hummers could handle dirt roads fairly well, but get too far off the beaten track (literally) and they could easily bog down, making them death traps in an ambush. The goat trails that dotted the country were simply too narrow, too rocky, and too dangerous for us to use. The limited options made the main roads even more dangerous than they would have been otherwise, which was pretty dangerous.

We varied our routines as much as possible in a bid to increase safety, but it was only a partial answer; there simply weren't enough roads through the area to never use the same one twice in a row. On top of that, we had to patrol a lot—all units were expected to mount four patrols a day, no matter how big or dangerous their territory was. The only practical way to cover our responsibilities was to split my group in half, which left each half to run two patrols a day. We'd vary our times, but generally this meant one in daylight and one at night or close to sunset.

We were a small group, but we weren't working entirely alone. We had A-10s and other air assets at our beck and call if we needed them. There were also two Afghan military units that could help. Theoretically, at least.

Technically, it was the other way around—we were helping them. But whenever they accompanied us on a patrol or mission, we were the ones who led it.

The first unit was part of the Afghan army. They were, in a word, useless. The first day I went to meet the commander,

I found him lounging in bed. He was fat and lazy, and wanted to know how much food and money I could give him.

None was the quick and easy answer.

I felt truly sorry for the troops under his command. They were a wretched lot. They could have used food, to say nothing of better leadership and rudiments of discipline. It wasn't that they hadn't received training—a veritable parade of trainers, some from the U.S., some from other allies, had worked with them over the years. But rather than instilling cutting-edge techniques and a serious store of tactical knowledge, the sheer number of trainers had left them with a hodgepodge of different ideas and procedures.

Not that it really mattered, as their leaders were loath to actually have them do anything.

The other group was entirely different. They weren't an official force as we would understand the concept in the States, but they had far more authority than the regular army unit.

They were also a bit of a mystery. I first encountered them on our first patrol. I had all four of my vehicles with me that day, unsure of how safe the area was. We'd been driving for a short while on a hard-paved road—"hardball"—when we spotted a pair of Toyota Hilux pickup trucks driving parallel to us in the distance. Both were moving quite a bit faster than we were, even though we were on the hardball and they were on the sand and rocks.

Armed men filled the truck beds. They weren't a serious threat—even if we were outnumbered, firing at us would have been foolish, as the guns atop our Hummers would quickly devastate the lighter pickups—but we were wary nonetheless as they sped past.

We kept driving, not sure exactly what to expect. Maybe a half hour later, we came upon the two trucks stopped off the road. The men had stopped to pray. I decided to stop a short distance away and see who they were.

They weren't shooting at me, so I figured they were friendly.

We didn't always have interpreters or "terps" with us on patrols; in fact, it was probably the exception to the rule. But I happened to have one that day. I took him with me as I walked over to the men. We managed a stilted, stunted conversation. They told me they were part of a militia group that answered to a local tribal leader.

Or, to look at it from a slightly different direction, a local warlord.

I came to think of the men as part of the Northern Alliance, the guerrilla group that had successfully kicked the Taliban out of the country, with U.S. help. But I never knew their true identity, and it was unlikely that they were part of the actual Northern Alliance; the group generally operated in other areas. The important thing for me was that they considered the Taliban their enemy. That made them my allies.

A few days later I arranged to meet their leader at his headquarters, located in a building a short distance up the road from our FOB. He introduced me to two of his lieutenants, who commanded the groups in the field. One was tall and well built; he wore a sports coat but his pants were baggy. I'll call him Rambo here. The other was a smaller guy, just as tough in the field but a pretty sharp dresser who favored Western-style suits, even when fighting; I'll call him Dapper Dan. (Given the state of things in Afghanistan these days, actually identifying them could conceivably put them in danger.)

Rambo and Dapper Dan conducted their own regular patrols of the area we covered, and we started going out with them on occasion. We developed a good enough relationship that they came to the FOB to share intelligence and to ask my unit to accompany them. Unlike the Afghan army, even the most junior members of the militia unit moved with a purpose. They were aggressive, very disciplined, and clearly well trained.

They also looked, to an American eye, like homeless men. They didn't wear uniforms, except for odd pieces collected here or there; vests, tunics—pretty much nothing matched. Their main weapons were AK-47s, and not particularly new ones; if you told me that the Soviets had left them when they gave up Afghanistan in the 1980s, I would believe you. If you said they dated from the fifties, I wouldn't argue.

The theory behind our mission was that our presence would make Afghanis feel confident enough to vote in the election. Besides random security patrols, we met with district leaders and tribal elders in an attempt to establish rapport. Basically, I was driving around and waving at people, occasionally stopping to shake hands, then driving around some more.

In addition to the leaders, we would visit the local police stations, which were often Taliban targets. The quality of the police varied greatly, but as a general rule they tended to be about as effective as the Afghan army, and far less gung ho than Rambo and Dapper Dan. They were good talkers, though.

One day we went to investigate an attack on a police station. According to the police reports, the station had been overrun by hundreds of Taliban fighters; despite a brave stand, the cops had had to retreat. At that point, the station had been burned to the ground.

What I saw when I arrived didn't exactly match what the police were saying. For one thing, the police hadn't sustained any injuries, not even a bruise. There was no expended brass in the smoldering ruins, which you'd expect if guns had been fired there. Nor were there signs that a large force had been involved in the attack: A hundred men, even on foot, leave quite a trail no matter how careful they are, and there was no such trail here.

Puzzled, I went back to the chief. "How many Taliban attacked?" I asked.

"*So* many."

"You have a number?"

"Hundreds."

"From where?"

"All directions."

The local police had lost all of the weapons in the attack. Maybe all of the weapons had been in the station when the attack started and the police there had run away?

Hmmmmm.

In an effort to turn things around—or at least get the locals to be a little more cooperative with us—my battalion commander and I met with the town officials. After tea and pleasantries, we told them that we wanted to prevent further attacks. It was important that they help us by providing intelligence against the enemy.

Things were courteous but indirect until it was my turn to speak.

"Are you guys in charge?" I asked. "Because it seems to me that the Taliban is in charge. They hit the police station and everyone ran away. If this is not a good village, then you're not going to get any money from the government. You won't be able to dig your wells or build the school you want. Either you start telling me where the bad guys are, or tell the Taliban to fight us. I challenge them for a fight. Tell them to come out and fight."

Judging by their faces, my speech didn't make them very happy. But they did start to give us information; almost every time we came into the area, someone pointed out a cache of weapons supposedly hidden by the Taliban.

Most of these were small stashes—a few RPG rounds, a sniper rifle. The militia group tended to find larger, more valuable caches in the same area, which they would lead us to. Caves dotted the hillside; this was country designed for hit-and-run attacks, small-unit operations, insurgent campaigns that could continue for decades—something that history made obvious.

We carried a lot of firepower. That didn't make us invulnerable, but it did lessen the chances of an attack. If the Taliban were active in the area—and the weapons caches and the attacks on the police station made it clear that they were—they followed a very safe and even prudent strategy. They never got drawn into a prolonged firefight where our weapons could devastate them. They watched and they waited.

We made sure they knew we were there. At random points, we'd stop and test-fire our weapons—all of them, very loudly.

Whether that scared them away or not, actual encounters were very, very rare.

One day while on patrol I heard a pop and saw a puff of smoke, telltale signs that we'd been targeted by an improvised explosive device or, as we called it, an IED. These bombs came in all shapes and sizes, ranging in size from little more than a hand grenade all the way up to a dump truck stuffed with artillery shells. IEDs could be detonated by remote control, timers, trip wires, or similar devices.

We stopped and took up defensive positions, expecting an ambush—according to what we'd been told, IED attacks often signaled the start of one.

We were ready for a battle. I wanted one, in fact—I wanted a chance to beat the Taliban and show the locals what we could do for them. I looked across the surrounding farm fields, expecting a charge, or at least some gunfire.

All I could see was a single man approaching us from across the field. If it was an attack, it was a small one. He didn't appear to be armed, or wearing a suicide vest. Rather than shooting him, one of my guys ran up and grabbed him. He made the mistake of struggling as my guy tried to search him for a weapon, and within seconds we had a dog pile on him, pinning him in the dust.

His wife came running from a nearby building, screaming. Because we had no interpreter with us, we had no idea what either she or her husband were saying, but we eventually figured out that they wanted us to believe they were friends. We wanted to believe that ourselves, but we were hardly in a position to take any chances. Unable to understand what they were saying and aware that they weren't a threat, we let them go and went back to the vehicles.

There were wires on the side of the road near the small crater left by the exploding IED, and something else seemed to be buried under the road. I called the Quick Reaction Force and demolition experts to check it out. In the meantime, a pair of A-10A attack planes came down to support us in case of an ambush.

(A Quick Reaction Force or QRF is a unit that is held back at a central location in case another unit is attacked. They are reinforcements, to use a metaphor from another war, the cavalry that rides to the rescue. Unfortunately, given the distances and geography, "quick" was not always an accurate description.)

A small crowd gathered as we waited. I guess they were just curious, but if there was an IED in the road, they were in far more danger than we were. We motioned to them to stay back, but they just kept pressing forward. Either they didn't understand English—likely—or curiosity had stuffed their ears like thick wax.

Finally, I got an idea. I picked up the radio and talked to the Hog pilots.

Air Force A-10As—Warthogs or "Hogs"—are low-flying attack aircraft that can carry a lot of bombs and missiles. They mount an awesome 30 mm cannon in their nose that sounds like the devil's sewing machine when it fires. The aircraft are awesome support planes. While they are slow compared to the likes of F-16s and F/A-18s, their ability to fly at very low altitude is a great morale booster or psychological weapon, depending on which side you're on.

In this case, the Hogs didn't actually fire any weapons. Instead, they lit some flares as they did a low pass, warning the crowd to stand back.

That was a language anyone could understand. We had no more trouble with crowds that day.

The sun had set by the time the Quick Reaction Force and the explosives experts arrived. They discovered a massive device buried under the road—apparently the bomb that had gone off was a fuse meant to ignite the larger weapon. Something had gone wrong: Lucky for us.

We were maybe two hundred meters away when the EOD guys blew it. (EOD stands for "explosive ordinance disposal" and the word "technician" is added at the end in the technical manuals when referring to the brave souls who disarm IEDs and other devices. But nobody uses the full title; it's always EOD.)

That's a pretty good distance—two football fields. But it wasn't quite enough. Debris showered the trucks. When the dust settled, I walked down into the crater; the road surface was at my chest.

You get a bit edgy after something like that. You think twice about going back to the same place. But you have to go back.

Now when you look at the people, you wonder what they're thinking. You see resentment—or do you? You see sympathy—or do you?

You see potential ambushes and booby traps everywhere. That you definitely do see.

Riding through the countryside in a Humvee, you realize how little you can really see. You realize that in a lot of ways you're riding in a coffin, with little slits that distort and contract your view. You can't possibly see the big picture of what's going on, or even a good slice of it.

Yet you desperately want not to overreact. The last thing you want to do is kill innocent people.

I replayed what had happened for days afterward. That guy who had walked toward us from the field. Was he innocent? Had he simply seen us stop and decided to find out if he could help?

Or was he surprised that we weren't dead? Was he coming to ignite the bigger bomb somehow?

We were in a complicated position in Afghanistan. The army was supposed to be winning hearts and minds—that was the slogan—but at the same time, we were expected to kill the enemy. It didn't pay to be naïve. A lot of the village elders who met with us were interested in American money—they saw us as dollar signs. At least a few of them probably saw us as the enemy as well, though they were smart enough not to make it obvious.

Junior officers have exactly zero influence on American military or foreign policy. And yet, it's drummed into them that they can affect relations, negatively, by making a mistake:

Quick on the trigger . . . next thing that happens, the news is filled with stories about a U.S. force mowing down innocent villagers.

The last thing I wanted was for one of my guys to get hurt. But the *next* to last thing I wanted was to kill someone who was a civilian, even though at the same time I absolutely wanted to kill bad guys. Had I focused too much on any of those things, I would have gone nuts.

Gradually, our paranoia eased. The days settled down into something out of the movie *Groundhog Day*. The highlight of the week was Wednesday—surf and turf at the mess hall. It didn't matter what else was going on; I made sure to get my guys back to the FOB for that dinner.

Three or four weeks in, I began organizing informal classes, both to train the guys and to break up the monotony of the deployment. Subject-matter experts would talk for a half hour, an hour, whatever it took to explain the subject of the evening. The classes varied, but always had something to do with the job. For one class, a medic gave some pointers on first aid—and we ended up jabbing each other with needles to see how to use catheters and open up IV lines. We had classes on how to call for fire—the military term for calling artillery or air support. There were sessions on dealing with unexploded ordinance, a big problem in the area. We practiced calling in air support and medivac, entering and clearing buildings—anything we needed to know, we made sure we knew it backward and forward, upside down and right side up.

As time went on, we got better cooperation from some of the local officials. But intelligence was always a big problem. Part of the reason was that there had been no American presence here before. We were an unknown quantity to the elders, and they were an unknown quantity to us. It takes time to build up sources, let alone trust. The connections that SF has with friendly forces in foreign countries have been built up over decades and depend on a lot of personal contact and continuity. That was far from the situation here.

The gaps were obvious. We'd get a list of key Taliban leaders in the area—but no picture or even identifying marks to go with them. Just deciphering the local names was a challenge.

It was a problem for *all* American units, not just mine. The Afghans had their share of troubles as well—Dapper Dan and Rambo came up a few towns short one night when they were trying to head off an attack on a police station with our help.

How do I know we had the wrong town? We were set up around what we thought was the target when we heard gunfire a few kilometers away; we mounted up and raced over, far too late to do anything, much to the Afghanis' dismay, and our frustration.

Even when we had decent information, a lot could go wrong. A few months into the deployment, command developed strong intel on a bomb maker who had been terrorizing the area. He was tracked to a distant town; we were assigned to set up an ambush there.

While we were waiting for him to emerge from whatever building he was in, more intelligence arrived—the suspect wasn't there at all. Instead, he was riding a motorcycle, heading toward another town.

We picked up and headed out, getting ready to do a direct action there—only to get a new lead: He was back in the first town. We went there and searched the streets, looking for a motorcycle, but couldn't find one.

The search was about half over when fresh intel put him in a third town. We played this game for going on forty-eight hours before we arrived at a small village. We hit pay dirt here: We spotted the motorcycle.

Then we spotted another and another and another . . . the place was Biker Town. There must have been a thousand bikes in the place.

I'm exaggerating, but not by much. After five days of back-and-forth, the operation was a bust.

History buffs will probably note that our role in Afghanistan was a lot different than the mission airborne units traditionally train for. The 82nd Airborne was "stood up" just before World War II, trained to perform dangerous parachute jumps behind enemy lines. Members of the division dropped into Sicily and played an

important role cutting off German reinforcements as they attempted to counter beach landings; they harassed enemy supply
lines and made it difficult for the Italians and Germans to coordinate defenses. The division played a similar role in Normandy in
June 1944; it is at least arguable that the invasion would have
stalled without the paratroopers of the 82nd and its sister division
the 101st (formed with a core of 82nd personnel and at the time
airborne, rather than air assault). And while the 101st has gotten
most of the ink, the 82nd played a critical role in the Battle of the
Bulge, where its paratroopers shored up the northern front of
the bulge, stopping the German advance and ultimately allowing the Americans to mount a counterattack that threw the
Germans back.

Our mission in Afghanistan was very different than any of
those assignments. We weren't dropped in by parachute, and we
weren't operating behind enemy lines. We never faced massed
enemy units. We were more roving targets than the tip of the
spear. Our interactions were more like diplomacy than combat.

An army has to adapt to the needs of the times, and the battle.
Like the rest of the army, the 82nd has adapted its capabilities,
and these days is as capable of handling humanitarian missions
as it is cutting off an enemy retreat. In a lot of ways, the entire army
has moved closer to the sort of capabilities that Special Forces
has, countering insurgencies. That was our primary job in Afghanistan: Work with the local authorities, fight the insurgents
if they appear. Admittedly, regular army units are not as well
equipped or trained as SF teams; they have a much higher turn-
over rate, and little opportunity to create lasting relationships
with foreign armies. They simply aren't designed to operate at the
same level that SF does. But they continue to evolve in that direction, as they must.

That's my take, though admittedly I kept it to myself during
the deployment. I had far better things to do than get philosophical about the use of military units in the middle of a deployment.

We kept going out, meeting local leaders when we could, and

occasionally working with the Afghans. The FOB came under rocket attack twice. One morning I was shaken from bed by a loud boom. I bolted upright, pulled on my boots and grabbed my gun, racing to the vehicles.

Yes, without my pants. I didn't have a shirt either, just my Afghan PJs: black nylon running shorts.

We rolled out, hoping to pursue the Taliban guerrillas who'd shot at us. A spotter had seen action in a cemetery not too far away; we raced there, hoping to catch our attackers.

Nada.

But at least my uniform, or lack thereof, got some laughs when we came back to the base.

■ ■ ■

Sometimes the problems you face as a commander are clear-cut; sometimes they're subtle. Balancing the needs of individuals versus the overall mission can be surprisingly tricky.

One morning when we were going out on patrol, one of the Humvee turret gunners in a rear vehicle had what we call a "negligent discharge." That means that he fired his gun accidentally. The strong official language is a tip-off of how serious the army takes this, and for good reason—a few rounds from any weapon, accidental or not, can do serious damage to property, let alone people.

In this case, no one was hurt and nothing was damaged; the soldier had apparently been loading his weapon and, following proper procedure, had it pointed toward a safe area. The incident was very quick, and in fact I didn't even hear the discharge when it happened, since I was riding in a vehicle in the front of the convoy.

To the soldier's credit, he told me what had happened when we returned from the patrol. Granted, I probably would have picked up the scuttlebutt about it sooner or later, but it was very much to his credit that he owned up to what had happened on his own.

But that gave me something of a dilemma. By regulation, he had to be punished. Yet it didn't seem fair—no harm was done, and he had been completely honest and apologetic.

Could I let it go? How would I enforce that rule later on if I did? And what if command found out that I had broken the rules myself by not reporting it?

I ended up going to my commander and telling him what had happened. I recommended that my soldier be disciplined at company level—which meant, not coincidentally, that there would be no permanent record of the infraction in his file. I also recommended his punishment be corrective training: He was to become the subject-matter expert on every weapon in our unit.

My recommendation was accepted. The soldier not only became the expert on every weapon we had (if he wasn't already); he gave our guys several lectures on each, improving our overall knowledge level.

He was a good soldier who made a dumb mistake, proving not that he was dumb, but that he was human. I'm happy to say that he went on to the officers' course and, last I heard, is now a captain.

9

Home Fires

The Afghan elections finally arrived. The day passed inconspicuously. Despite rumors of planned attacks, our three districts were quiet.

A few weeks later, we started packing to go home.

Homecoming is an emotional time. It's pretty chaotic as well. I always found it a bit of a pain as an NCO; I had to take care of any number of minor things while champing at the bit to leave. Now that I was an officer, I had even more responsibility, which translated into more things to do the moment we hit the tarmac. So I told Evelyn not to meet us when we got back to Bragg. I saw no point in having her wait around for up to ten hours as I ran around making sure we accounted for everything, from men to weapons. I like to have everything squared away before I go off duty; having her there would have just been a distraction.

It was getting dark when I drove out of the gate and headed up the road to my house down the road. There was a surprise waiting: a big sign saying WELCOME HOME.

I'd never seen anything so beautiful, but that was topped a moment later, when I walked in and saw my wife waiting to hug me.

So many things you miss when you're away. Not the big ones so much as the little ones, things we all take for granted—a couch, porcelain toilets, real silverware.

Back home, you learn how to walk again without body armor. You remember that driving a car is not the same as driving a Humvee. You realize that your wife really is sleeping in the bed next to you, and you're not dreaming.

We took a vacation to Aruba, enjoying our time together. We began talking about the family we wanted to start. It was a great week.

Then it was back to reality. I was still adjusting to life as an officer.

Not all the adjustments go smoothly, or work in your favor. One of my guys was nailed on a driving-while-intoxicated charge within a few days of our getting back. It was a bogus charge in my opinion—he'd been moving a car in a parking lot—but that didn't get him off. A minor matter in the civilian world, the charge would have had a serious impact on his career in the military, and so he decided to leave. We lost a damn good soldier because of a few drinks at a party.

There were other adjustments, guys coming in and out. My platoon sergeant went over to the Rangers to become an instructor. I got a promotion to first lieutenant, and then a new assignment: head of the 325th's scout/sniper platoon.

The platoon consisted of twenty-seven guys, give or take. (Like a lot of units, our exact head count varied because of vacancies and transfers.) Besides myself, the platoon sergeant, and a radio operator, I had three two-man sniper teams and three six-man scout or reconnaissance teams. The basic structure could be varied depending on the mission; members of a scout team might be assigned to provide security for a sniper team, for example, or we might attach a sniper team to a scout team during a reconnaissance.

Despite the platoon's mission, not all of our snipers and spotters had gone to sniper school and officially qualified for their role. This wasn't uncommon, however. There's a lot more to being a sniper than just being a good shot, and in an ideal world we would have had at least six guys fully trained and qualified, three acting as snipers and three acting as spotters. But that's a perfect world. In this case, only two or three had gone to school, but I had confidence in everyone on the team.

It wasn't that the guys were lazy or thought they knew it all. The deployment tempo was so heavy that there hadn't been time for the men who wanted to go to school to do so before we deployed. Even if there had been more downtime, few people wanted to volunteer for a school that might take them away from home for months at a time when they were likely to be called to war soon afterward.

By the same token, units could hardly afford to lose guys when so much work had to be done in a short time. So they weren't encouraged to go to school. Our battalion was short of guys who'd been to Ranger school, and I wouldn't be surprised if the shortage extended across the entire army. That was a sharp contrast to what I'd seen years before as a scout and Pathfinder— going to Ranger school was considered a must for anyone who wanted to be a member of an elite unit. There were many shortages; qualified jumpmasters were few and far between, even in the 82nd.

There was an upside to the tempo—experience. My snipers may not have gone to school, but they were good enough to be selected as testers for the M110 sniper weapon. The important mission was an honor.

At the time, the army was considering using the M110, a semiautomatic 7.62x51 mm rifle made by Knight's Armament, as its main long gun, replacing the M24. We spent two weeks jumping from every conceivable aircraft—the *Spirit of St. Louis* may even have been in the mix—landing and then using the guns on the range. It's always good to jump and shoot; if you're airborne, you can't beat it.

The M110 is similar to the SR25, which was used by Navy SEALs and other special operations soldiers. In the field, my snipers typically used M24s and the Barrett M107 50-caliber, weapons I had trained with years before. The M110 was being considered a replacement for the M24. (The Barrett, whose lineage derives from a 50-caliber machine gun, fires a bigger bullet and has a longer range, but it is fairly heavy to carry and not as adaptable to some combat conditions as the M24, which has evolved from a hunting rifle.)

We liked the M110. It withstood a beating in the field, was relatively easy to carry and use, and was versatile enough to handle most missions a sniper would face. As a semiautomatic, it had certain advantages in pressure situations. I can't tell you our entire assessment, but the army eventually adopted the M110. (It has since been updated; other designs are also in service.)

Most of our training missions were much more routine. I tried to keep things loose, even as we worked to sharpen our skills. There was the time we maneuvered to a certain point and captured the objective—a veritable vat of Kentucky Fried Chicken, secreted in a cache by an anonymous enemy courier who looked suspiciously like Evelyn. Even in the army, it's possible to mix business with pleasure, or at least barbecue sauce.

Not long after completing that mission, we were told to stand by for something far more important: We were headed to Iraq, barely four months since coming home from Afghanistan.

During the height of the troop surge against terrorists in Iraq, a great number of missions were conducted by special operations units, including the Army's Special Forces, Navy SEALs, and the like. Under ordinary circumstances, the Ranger regiment would send units to support and participate in many of these missions. But the pace of operations had worn some of the Ranger units down, and SOCOM—the Special Operations Command—turned to us.

It was an honor, a sign that we were among the army's elite units. It was also very serious business. Operational Security—known as OpSec in the military—was very high. Among other things, that meant we couldn't give our families too many details about what we were up to. I could tell Evelyn where we were going, but little else.

I was very familiar with the routine, having been in SF. Evelyn was as well.

She was even less enthusiastic about my going to Iraq than she'd been about Afghanistan. Iraq was in the news, and not in a good way. Whether she had been worried before or not, I think it's fair to say that she knew this was going to be a different deployment than any of the others I'd been on. A hard one.

My right knee, injured years before, had been giving me a lot of trouble. The doctors had examined it and recommended surgery. Evelyn suggested, strongly, that I go ahead with it.

"When I get back," I told her. "How can I not deploy with my men?"

She knew better than to make much of a fuss. There was no way I was going to let my unit go overseas without me. I don't think any soldier worth wearing the uniform would be happy doing that. A lot of guys deploy with a lot more to worry about than a tweaked knee.

We went through the usual predeployment routine. At the base, I had my platoon's "comfort items" packed on the pallet, ready to go. At home, I looked over my will and my power of attorney. I made sure my bills and bank accounts were all in good shape.

I wasn't worried about Evelyn. Not only was she an old hand at running the house while I was gone, her mother was now living with us and could attend to any business that needed to be cared for. That was a perfect situation for us: We'd talked a bit about having a baby; maybe, we both thought, we'd get a chance to do that when I got back.

Two, actually—Evelyn wanted a boy and a girl.

The quick turnaround was a lot tougher on our young guys than it was on me. A few had been expecting to leave the army as their enlistments ran out. They'd made detailed plans, only to be held up by what are known as "stop loss orders." That's a provision in the regulations and your enlistment terms that allow the army to keep you if you're about to deploy or are already overseas. It's understandable from the army's point of view: Having to replace men in the middle of a deployment is not going to increase the odds of success. But that doesn't make it any easier for the guys who have lined up admission to college, or planned to get married, or lined up a new civilian job.

The day we were scheduled to ship out, the families gathered at our base to say good-bye. Wives, girlfriends, moms, and dads came by with their soldiers to meet some of the other families and give their loved ones a nice send-off.

I went around shaking hands, making jokes. What I was really doing was reassuring them that their husbands and sons were going to be looked after. There are never guarantees in war, and I'm sure everyone knew that. But I also wanted them to know that I personally was going to do everything I could to get them home safely.

I can still see Angel Mercado's wife, eight and a half months' pregnant, resting on the chair outside my office. Angel, a fellow Puerto Rican, was in our weapons section in another platoon, but I knew him well. He could have used his wife's pregnancy as an excuse not to deploy, but he felt that doing that would be letting down the rest of his unit.

I can see Heffley's dad smiling in the hallway when I say, "You're the father of this cutup?" Mundey's mom is laughing. Turner's girlfriend looks so pretty, and so young.

So many things I can still see . . .

Evelyn, coming in and sitting behind my desk. She was wearing green Capri pants that hugged her hips just right. Her hair fell down past her shoulders, splaying across the vest she was wearing—green, matching the pants.

Her smile.

I wanted to say good-bye in the office, rather than out on the field waiting for the plane. I wanted to say good-bye in private.

Evelyn waited with her mom while I made the rounds. I came back, closed the door, and hugged her in front of the desk.

We kissed.

I stepped back, impressing her image into my brain, not

knowing when I would see her again—not knowing that it would be never.

■ ■ ■

We have a photo of that day, of Evelyn and me. I see it in my mind sometimes. It's a perfect picture of a perfect moment. A wide future spreads out in front of that couple. All things are possible. All things are good and happy.

10

Return to Iraq

Flights to war are no different than flights to anywhere else. There's a lot of hurry-up-and-wait. We were at the hangar for going on four hours before it was our turn to board the KC-110 shuttling us over to Kuwait. I talked and checked on guys and gear and talked some more, but mostly I waited, half excited, half anxious to begin.

Finally the plane came. Hours later, my body started to cramp.

Did fear take hold of the muscles? Or was it just the fact that I was sitting with little to do for so long?

There's an old saying about idleness being the devil's workshop. I don't know whether that's true or not, but I do know that activity can push away idle fear. There was no way for me to be active on that flight. Sleep was only a partial escape.

By the summer of 2006, America had been in Iraq for three years. While the number of American troops in the country was declining slowly, violence against them as well as civilians was increasing. Unlike in Afghanistan, where the insurgency could be identified as a single entity, the Taliban, the situation in Iraq was more a civil war, with Sunni and Shia Muslims targeting each other as well as Americans. Civilians were caught in the middle, either regarded as legitimate targets because of their religious affiliation or simply seen as acceptable collateral damage. Shiite militia often worked with government forces in the eastern part of the country, targeting innocent Sunnis as well as Sunni fanatics; in the west, foreign fighters sponsored by al Qaeda joined with former Saddam loyalists and so-called mujahedeen (soldiers of God) to target Shia holy places and populations along with Iraqi government posts and American bases.

Our mission was to support special operations units as they struck high-value terrorist targets. Such targets would typically include terrorists who manufactured IEDs, weapons caches, and top terror-cell leaders. This was before the so-called "Iraq surge" or the counterinsurgency plan advocated and implemented by General David Petraeus in 2007. Even so, the basic strategy of neutralizing such high-value targets essentially remained unchanged from the early phases of the war against the insurgency.

We landed in Kuwait, hung out for a few days, then loaded up in a C-17 and headed north to Iraq.

A sure sign that we were in this thing for real came about twenty minutes later, when the crew chiefs told us to get our body armor on. A few moments later, the aircraft prepared to land by nosing into one of the steepest dives I've experienced. We hung on for dear life, and I'm sure more than a few of us thought for sure we'd been hit. Suddenly the plane jerked horizontal, pounded hard on the runway pavement, and screeched to a stop. We piled out, making way for the other three aircraft and their men, which were following behind. A short time later, we were led through the pitch-black to buses waiting to take us to our new home, a small corner of Camp Speicher, one of a number of American bases in and around Tikrit in northern Iraq.

Tikrit is an ancient city on the Tigris River, whose history includes numerous sieges stretching back at least as far as Babylonian times. More recently, it was the capital of the area where Saddam Hussein was born; following the war, it was a hotbed of

Sunni terrorist activity, primarily organized by Baath Party members and others once loyal to Saddam Hussein, generically referred to as mujahedeen.

A former airfield, Camp Speicher was outside Tikrit, a little more than ten kilometers from the Tigris River. A hundred and seventy kilometers from Baghdad, it had been captured by American forces early in the war and used as a base ever since. A long list of units called it home.

Our camp was set off from the main part of the base. Security here was high; unlike our last home in Afghanistan, the base and facilities were already well established. We spent a few days sorting ourselves out. My platoon received vehicles here, but these were far from new. They had a lot of battle damage—not only numerous repairs and shrapnel wounds, but bloodstains and even discarded dressings.

"Holy fuck," I said to my platoon sergeant, Cliff Burgoyne, when I saw the first vehicle. "These guys must have been in hell."

"*We* are getting into hell," he answered.

The trucks needed a lot of maintenance. Some of it was routine, a lot of it not. Bullet holes and bent metal were routine. Blood-spattered interiors were part of the décor. Oil leaked hard from one or two of the engines, and all of the vehicles were difficult to start. While in my previous platoon simple maintenance would not have been that big of a deal, scout platoons were not typically assigned vehicles. So my new platoon lacked the tools needed even for the most basic tasks. We made do, getting two of the vehicles in working order while we waited for the battalion mechanics to fix the others.

In the meanwhile, I went to meet the unit we would be working with. It turned out that our liaison was an old friend from LRS. I also knew his radio guy and two of the other senior members of a unit that was supporting us. We spent a week getting up to speed before finally getting our first mission, a patrol and search of an area where terrorist activity was high some miles away.

Our op (operations) order called for my entire platoon to work with a larger unit composed of airborne and special operations troops. We'd fly to the objective, roughly twenty or thirty minutes away, participate in the patrol, bed down for the night, then return the following evening.

Piece of cake. Always assuming, of course, that nothing went wrong.

We geared up and went out to meet the helicopters designated to take us to the patrol area. The aircraft came in, and right away we saw there was a problem—there weren't enough choppers to take everyone.

I did a quick consultation with the mission commander, who decided that only half of my platoon would be needed for the mission. So my first command decision was who to send.

I opted to split the platoon in half. Since I'd seen a bit more combat than my platoon sergeant, I acceded to his wishes to go and decided I'd stay back with the rest of the unit. After seeing them off, I went back to the TOC or tactical operations center to watch what was going on.

The TOC is a high-tech command center where commanders can process different information and issue their directives. In World War II, commanders did that from tents and lean-tos on the side of a hill. Today's TOCs range from air-conditioned tents to elaborate bunkers stuffed with high-tech gear.

Contrary to what people might think from watching movies, commanders don't always have the "luxury" of real-time imagery of an operation. There are only so many UAVs (unmanned aerial vehicles, also known as drones) and other reconnaissance assets to go around. In this case, though, I was able to watch an overhead feed of the landing zone as my guys came in. They landed without opposition, and hustled to their first objective, a residential building thought to be occupied by suspected terrorists.

When most of us think about Iraq, we think of vast deserts. There is quite a bit of vegetation near the rivers, however, and in this case my guys had to work their way through what amounted to a swamp. But they made it look easy—at least on the TOC's video—and took up their positions without enemy contact.

The house turned out to be empty.

Eventually we lost "eyes-on" coverage, but I was able to follow things via radio communications. With everything working well and no resistance, they bedded down for the night. I took a break and went to check with the half of my team that had stayed home.

"They're looking good," I told them. "Get some rest now. Sleep. You never know when we might be called out."

I took a nap, only to be woken up a short time later by the heat. Back at the TOC, I learned that things were going slowly, though I suppose positively—there had been no serious problems overnight.

The next day, we ran into a foe no army can neutralize: the weather. The sun was relentless, and the heat and humidity gradually took a toll on the men. Scouting ahead to a second objective, two of my guys were seriously dehydrated, and our lack of water became acute.

After a brief rest in one of the local houses, they began moving out. They were just setting up on the objective when three Iraqis ambushed them from maybe fifty yards away.

Chris Turner, one of our snipers, managed to shoot one of the attackers, killing him. The other two ran off but were later apprehended near the second target.

Then came the ridiculous part of the operation. Even though the barrels on the Iraqi AK-47s were still warm, the American troops were ordered by command to let them go, since no one could positively identify them as the two men who'd taken part in the ambush.

The rest of the night passed uneventfully. The heat continued to take a huge toll; it was a struggle to get water into the area. With no new enemy action apparent, command decided to end the operation the next day.

My guys had done a good job. We were ready for whatever the Iraqis threw at us.

Roughly a week and a half before the end of August, we were given a second mission. This one had a specific target—a container yard next to a thermal power plant in Sadr al Yusufiyah that, according to intelligence, was being used by al Qaeda and/or mujahideen to store weapons and create large IEDs. Our initial assignment was to help secure the area, preventing anyone from going in or out while it was swept.

The container yard was huge—maybe a half-mile wide and another half mile or so long. There were railroad tracks for moving the equipment and containers, and a jumble of shacks and discarded gear that made for good hiding places.

Roughly twenty miles southwest of Baghdad, the plant squatted next to the Euphrates in an area known for violence. Downriver from Fallujah and at the edge of Iraq's main population center, the region sat between Sunni and Shia domination; there were countless attacks there during the American occupation. The town of Yusufiyah, some twenty-five kilometers north of the power station, had seen severe fighting earlier that year, including a battle where terrorists managed to shoot down an American helicopter. The enemy in the Sunni area around Yusufiyah and the power plant was said to be aligned with al Qaeda; the group was still active in the area despite numerous American raids against them during the spring. (Many Shia lived in the nearby area, and Shiite militia groups were also operating at different points. Following the withdrawal of American troops in recent years, the region has generally become primarily Shia, and has been a flashpoint in the conflict with ISIS.)

The power plant had been started years before by the Russians, who stockpiled equipment and machines in a nearby yard; work on the plant had been abandoned and everything left to rust and rot. While much of the surrounding area was desert, the land close to the water had vegetation and some small settlements scattered around. Given recent history as well as intel indicating the site was active, we expected resistance.

My platoon—all of us, this time—boarded two Black Hawks and headed south, landing some fifty meters from our objective.

So far, so good. We hustled to our assigned position and set up a roadblock in front of the container yard, laying out road spikes along with signs in Arabic that warned people away. Then we waited in the pitch-black for something to happen.

I'm not sure how long we were there—hours maybe. I scanned the terrain with my night vision binoculars, looking for movement. Suddenly, they went white.

It took a moment before I realized what had happened: a Spectre gunship flying above had lit its IR light, looking for enemy movement.

The Spectre is an Air Force AC-130, a heavily armed, four-engined Hercules that carries everything from 7.62 mm machine guns to 105 mm howitzers, depending on its exact configuration and the age of the aircraft. (Technically, only one variant of the AC-130 is referred to as the Spectre, but it's common for ground troops to refer to any AC-130 as a Spectre or "Spooky," an older name first used during the Vietnam War. I'm not sure which type was flying above us that night.)

Knowing the Spectre was above put me at ease. The guys flying those aircraft are badass; they can hit a quarter on the ground and give you change. While the aircraft are not invulnerable, their ability to provide support in a firefight is legendary. Not even a main battle tank can withstand their fury.

I stayed up all night, watching as the main force moved into position to begin their sweep of the container area. The power plant itself sat quiet, some two hundred meters to the north, looming in the dark over the abandoned containers and nearby river.

Late at night on August 23, soldiers from one of our sister units came upon a group of insurgents as they moved through the compound. As I heard it later, Specialist Thomas J. Barbieri was walking with other members of his platoon when they were surprised by a pair of terrorists who'd been hiding in the shadows. Leveling his SAW, Barbieri pushed his platoon sergeant out of danger and began firing at the terrorists, allowing the other men in his unit to take cover. Barbieri killed one of the attackers but was killed himself, taking a bullet meant for his sergeant. (The other members of the unit killed the remaining Iraqi.)

Geared up and ready for action, pre-injuries.
(All photos family collection, unless otherwise noted.)

I was a terror on wheels as
a three-year-old.

Mom and dad in happy times.

Here I am as a teenage cadet,
already with my wings. There are
many paths to maturity; the Army
is one of the best.

Going to work in Afghanistan. Just your typical commute—IEDs, hostile neighbors, anxious warlords.
(All photos this page, A. Lyon)

We think this is the last photo of me before I was hit.

What we saw from the tower. The mortar shell most likely came from beyond that cloud of smoke, or off to the left out of sight.

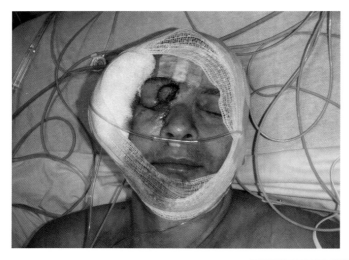

This was taken in Bethesda Naval Hospital, weeks after getting hit—believe it or not, I'm actually pretty cleaned up here.

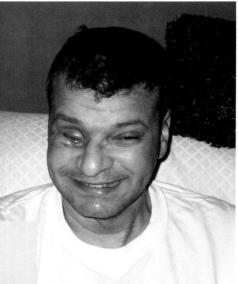

Happy just to be alive.

A more recent photo of me as a captain. My wife says I look pretty good.

My recovery has been a marathon—well, many of them. Here I am, number 4011, with Chet Grayson at the Bataan Death March Marathon, at the start of my running career.

Fred Dummar and I running in the Air Force Marathon— he's been my partner on maybe half my races.

Recovery from my injuries led to many speaking requests, including this early one at the Naval Academy. I'd never spoken before a large group before.

The midshipmen wanted to run before the talk, which was fine with me. But when I told them we do PT first, they balked —hey, it's the Army way. Just kidding; they were great guys ... for sailors.

The South Pole turned out to be one of my greatest challenges. We had to team up to make it through.

Cold much?

Prince Harry and I, joking before the race.

I beat Santa home, but not by much. My son and daughter, my wife, all my family mean so very much to me.

All dressed up and ready for dinner—me in my *very* formal Blue Mess
Uniform. I'm more comfortable in a track suit, believe me.
(*Photo: Darlene Budzinski Matos*)

Buried in Arlington Cemetery, Barbieri was awarded a posthumous Silver Star for his gallantry under fire.

Outside, we heard a few rounds of gunfire, then nothing. Barbieri remained in the compound, where he died of his wounds.

Dawn came. We received orders to push out a little farther, increasing the secured area around the container yard. I located a little shack farther down the road to use as a command post, and was listening to the rest of the operation around midmorning when I heard the first whistle of a mortar round, flying overhead.

Incoming! Disperse!

We spread out, realizing that the shack might be targeted as the mortar barrage continued.

I can't say how long it lasted, or how command responded; our job was to keep that blocking position, and without seeing the enemy there wasn't anything we could do about them. Later on in the day, we noticed cars pulling up in the distance, well out of rifle range, obviously scanning our positions. Too far away for us to target, they weren't doing anything overtly offensive that would have allowed us to fire anyway, according to our rules of engagement.

But . . .

Without a vehicle, we were in no position to go and question them. I called my suspicions in to command and kept my frustrations to myself.

Ordered to move into the container yard as the operation continued, I kept a small force on the road and moved inside with the rest of my platoon. It wasn't long before some of the guys discovered a car that looked to be in working condition.

Too bad we don't have a key.

I watched one of my guys unsuccessfully try to hot-wire the car to get it going.

"It's not going to work like that," I told him finally. "Let me take a look."

I took out a Leatherman tool (a combination pliers, screwdriver, and knife) and went to work on the ignition switch on the steering column. A corkscrew twist and a little pop left and right—the car started right up.

It might have taken a little more work than that, and I'm not detailing where I learned the technique—all I'm saying is the car was running when I was done.

The guys loved it. They draped a VS-17 panel on it so we wouldn't get shot up, then used it to drive around the compound. (The US-17 panel is a piece of material visible to aircraft pilots and used to identify friendly vehicles.)

I made my headquarters in a small, one-story, three-room building. There was a crane in the yard, and one of our sniper teams climbed it so they could use it for overwatch. That evening, one of the units at the other end of the yard came under fire. My guys returned fire from the crane; they think they got one or more of the Iraqis, but I wasn't in a position to see it myself.

Searches continued the next day. Everything in the yard was old and rusted. The Russian and Arabic inscriptions on the containers were chipped, worn off by the friction of the sand and wind.

Once more we saw cars and Iraqis in the distance that we were sure were scanning our positions. Nothing came of it: We flew out that night; as the helicopters circled away, charges that had been planted on a stash of IEDs discovered in the yard exploded below. It was a massive display, better than any fireworks I'd ever seen.

■ ■ ■

We returned to Tikrit.

Barbieri was the first soldier in our company that we lost in the deployment. Every death hits you hard, but the first one especially. There was a big turnout for his memorial.

His boots sat on the ground, his helmet propped on his rifle, a photo of him next to them on a tripod. One by one we went to the picture and saluted, bidding farewell.

Soon after, the colonel commanding the special operations unit came by to offer his condolences on the loss of our man.

He also told us we were going back to the site, this time to hit the power plant itself.

Once more they expected opposition, and we carefully planned the mission. A mock-up of the plant was prepared, and we drilled our landing and our immediate moves, planning and coordinating how we would hit the target.

A large square roughly a kilometer long and nearly as wide, the compound was dominated by an unfinished power plant near the center. The building was several stories high and looked more like an office building in the first stages of construction than anything that could make power. Walls and windows had not yet been erected. Pipes stuck out and girders were exposed. A large, equally unfinished smokestack stood nearby.

The power building was the biggest structure in the complex, but not the only one. A one-story administrative building sat at one corner. Though also not quite finished, it had been used at some point before construction was suspended; there were windows and even furniture inside.

Smaller, more primitive buildings were scattered across the grounds, along with piles of dirt, debris, and construction equipment and materials. The entire complex was surrounded by a wall and, in some parts, fencing roughly ten feet high. The Euphrates meandered past on the western perimeter, while the container yard we had hit a few days before was to the south.

The attacks we'd experienced had all come from the east, where there was a canal, some farm fields, and a few houses scattered around. The area directly to the north was mostly open, with some houses here and there. An urban area, or at least something much less rural than the area immediately around the plant, lay to the north and east; Baghdad itself was some twenty or so miles farther in that direction.

Helicopter transport was limited and, unlike the earlier missions, our job this time was going to be limited to sniper overwatch. That meant we'd only send the three teams, along with personnel for command and security. One was tasked to the north side of the complex and two on the east. I opted to go as command and control, leaving my platoon sergeant and the others home.

It was only fair—they got to go on the first mission while I had to stay home.

■ ■ ■

The few hours before leaving on a mission can be maddeningly short or horribly monotonous. This time was the latter—we were prepped and ready, but had to wait for the sun to go down.

With nothing better to do, I decided to go over to the PX to take the first steps toward fulfilling a lifelong dream: buying a boat. Step number one was getting a pickup truck big enough to haul a trailer. I'd found one on the Internet—a brand-new 2005 Dodge Ram pickup. I handled the paperwork on the computer, then signed out and returned to my tent.

The boat, and I guess the truck, were actually substitutes for a motorcycle, another dream possession I'd long lusted for. But when I'd told my wife, Evelyn, that I was planning to get one, she balked. Bikes were too dangerous, she said; why don't you get your boat instead?

So that was what I was going to do. I bought the truck on the Internet, with plans to get the boat as soon as I got back home.

■ ■ ■

The chaplain held a service before we left. I have to confess that I was a poor churchgoer, but I went to the service that evening. So did a lot of other guys: It was standing room only. Barbieri's death had made us all a little more conscious of our mortality.

Service over, we hustled to the pickup area and got into PZ Posture, the formal name for readiness before a helicopter mission. A big Chinook, blades whirling on both ends, settled down in a storm of dust and we hustled aboard.

While I had gone to Special Operations Target Interdiction

Course and was technically qualified to use the long guns as a sniper, I was not there to shoot; I was there to command. Practically speaking, I was a buffer between my guys and the force commander, implementing his orders while at the same time seeing to the needs of my men. It was the concept of different lanes I'd explained to my first platoon sergeant—the guys on the guns had their job to do, and I had mine.

Not that I wouldn't use a gun if the situation called for it.

Somewhere in the middle of that flight, I started singing "Ridin' Dirty," Chamillionare's rap about, well, riding dirty. It was our ritual, our game song. The guys joined in. We were tight. We were going to rock this mission.

As our Chinook approached the southern end of the complex I leaned toward the rear of the helicopter, getting ready to launch as if I were back in high school running a race. I threw myself onto the ramp as it lowered and began running straight to the wall, racing to get there as quickly as I could. My guys were all around me—we all wanted to get there first.

Truth is, it was kind of wrong—as a platoon leader, you shouldn't be leading the charge. But adrenaline had taken over and I was too torqued to care.

I scanned the sector, looking through my NOD. My gun was high.

The Chinook, now empty, pulled overhead, its big blades pounding air and grit against the earth—and us. We reached the entrance to the compound and went in, quickly but carefully, clearing the immediate area to make sure no one was lurking in ambush.

Inside, my sniper teams split up, each heading for a different post. I ran with the team headed by Sergeant Brian Mundey. Mundey was from Texas; a stud who'd been through Ranger school and was as good-looking as he was capable.

Mundey was one of the guys who had been "stop-lossed" before we deployed, declared by Uncle Sam as too valuable to lose for this deployment. Despite the major monkey wrench the army had thrown into his life, he was joking that day, showing off his customary sense of humor. Lyon was our platoon RTO; he had my radio. Our shooter was Ortiz; "Red" was his spotter. (He's still on active duty, so I'm using a nickname I made up.)

Our objective was a large fuel tank near the entrance. Empty and not in great repair, it was circled by rickety metal decking and stairs. I reached the bottom ladder and stopped, waiting for the others to catch up.

I didn't wait long. Mundey took the lead and I followed, climbing as the metal shook.

If this thing falls, we're going to die.

We reached the top. I looked toward my second team, which was climbing another oil tank nearby. Then I started scanning the area and watching as the main part of the assault unit came in and entered the complex.

Some forty or fifty feet off the ground, we had a good view of the area to the east of the complex. Aiming lasers danced across the night, but we saw no tracers and heard no gunfire. The resistance we expected—people inside the compound, maybe, or an IED, or some sort of attack—didn't materialize.

Not that anyone complained.

Our position was relatively secure from attack. The rickety stairs were the only way up, and their sorry state of repair was an effective early warning system—put one step on the bottom rung and we'd know you were coming.

The night moved along slowly but without enemy contact. We took turns on the fifty (the Barret 50-caliber rifle) and the M24; I did a stint on the latter, relieving my guys so they could rest. In the morning, a detailed search of the building and grounds began. The early sun was ferociously hot; I could have fried an egg on the top of that tank. We took our ponchos and rigged them with our rucksacks so we could get some shade on the metal decking.

There were thousands of potential hiding places for people and weapons within the unfinished construction site. The shell of the plant was only the most obvious. Construction shacks and half-started buildings, abandoned footings and piles of pipes and metal girders littered the compound. Sandy roads wound past scrub vegetation and construction debris. The place looked like something out of an apocalyptic movie set, covered with grit.

Sometime shortly after the sun came up, we spotted a van riding up and down a road out to the east. We were too far to get any sort of view of the people inside the van, even through binoculars; we were sure, though, that he was watching us, or maybe had a mortar in the back of his truck.

An air force combat controller—the guys who call in air support during combat—came up to join us. He tried getting an aircraft above to take a look at the van, but the plane was too high to get a visual. Maybe it was innocent, most likely it was not, but there was nothing to be done about it.

A short time later, mortar rounds began sailing into the compound. I leapt up, trying to see where he was firing from.

I also closed my armored vest and pulled on my helmet.

"Oh, shit!" yelled one of the guys a few moments after the brief shelling ended. "That shack is on fire!"

I turned around and looked down into the compound. Flames leapt from a small, one-story structure made of wood and tin near the cement building at the far corner of the complex. Seconds later, men ran in and began pulling people out.

Members of the battalion's mortar section attached to the operation had taken shelter inside the building with their gear and ammo. Their rounds were now in imminent danger of exploding.

I soon realized I knew one of the men working to get the survivors out—Sergeant Ralph Porras. Ralph, who'd served with me in my first platoon at the 82nd, should have won a medal for valor that day. Even as the fire grew, he helped people scramble to safety and then began hauling out unfired mortar rounds, making sure there were no large explosions and further injuries. Ammo cooked off but he kept at it, until finally the building was clear of people and large munitions.

The direct hit on the shack effectively took out the entire mortar section—killing one, and wounding or stunning the rest. The man who died was Staff Sergeant Angel Mercado, the Puerto

Rican native whose wife, eight and a half months pregnant, I'd seen outside my office just before we left.

The shack kept burning, the fire reaching the small-arms ammo inside. Bullets popped and fizzed all through the day, and well into the night.

Somewhere during the mortar barrage, I cut my hand on the railing somehow, undoubtedly when I took cover from the fire. I only realized it later on; a quick bandage and a glove and I was good to go.

I looked up when I was done and saw two tiny bugs growing rapidly into birds and then helicopters low on the horizon. The Apaches swooped in, circled, then popped smoke, clearing a Black Hawk medivac helicopter inside to pick up our wounded.

That was around noon. The rest of the day passed slowly, the heat continuing to build, adrenaline and sweat, boredom and tension as thick as the humidity.

A special operations sniper section was watching the eastern side of the complex from the roof of the building right next to the shack that had been hit. That evening, right around dusk, they called the battalion commander on the radio and said they wanted to come to my position.

"Great, no worries," said the battalion commander. "Tell you what, Ivan, switch with them."

I looked at Mundey; he looked at me.

"That's the stupidest thing ever," I said. "Why the hell would we do that?"

Let me explain that a little further.

While they had told the commander that they wanted to move because of the vantage, it seemed obvious to me that the special operation team had decided that the corner was not a safe position. And it wasn't: The building right next to it had been hit by a mortar earlier in the day. It doesn't take a skilled mortarman to adjust the weapon to strike a target near one he's already hit.

The area the other team was covering could have been covered from our tank, which was higher than the building. Or it could have been covered from somewhere else. It just made no sense to put another unit on the building.

In fact, *all* troops should have been ordered away from that corner completely, but weren't. The only thing I can think of was that command didn't expect another attack, or had thought that the first strike was a wild fluke. It's possible he just couldn't see the exact situation, or knew exactly how close the buildings were.

But the problem was, I'd been given an order. I couldn't argue with it over the radio, especially without an alternative.

"We're not going to argue," I told Mundey. "We'll go there tonight, then move in the morning."

The Iraqis were not known to attack at night; I had plenty of time, I thought, to come up with an alternative plan. We went across the compound, walking through the dark.

The entrance to the building opened into a hallway that ran left and right. These halls formed arms around a central courtyard. The arms didn't quite meet at the back, leaving an open space facing the walls. The rooms were intended as offices, and in fact some had been set up and still had books and papers as well as furniture; maybe they'd been used somehow during construction.

Made of concrete or some similar masonry material, the building was one story high; to get up on the roof you had to use a makeshift ladder inside the open central area toward the back.

The stench of burnt explosives from the earlier fire hung heavy in the air. I was surprised to find some men on the ground outside the building, getting some rest. Inside, there were still more, also trying to sleep. Despite the earlier attack, the hallways and rooms were filled with soldiers trying to rest; the building was the most solid structure around.

Ortiz and Red went up to the roof to take a shift. Lyon, Mundey, and I went to find a place where we could get some rest. We finally found a corner of the building unoccupied. While they were grabbing some shut-eye, I hunted down a medic to clean my hand, which was looking pretty ugly after baking in the heat all day. He cleaned it and dressed it, and I went back to my guys. Exhausted, I collapsed and slept until early dawn.

The sun was already up and hot when I woke. I grabbed my bag and started packing it so I could move as soon as I got permission. Somebody had a camera, and they took my picture.

September 2, 2006. I'm smiling, ready for action. I look great, or so I'm told—I've never seen it myself.

It's the last photo that shows me with two eyes that can see.

■■■

Mundey was with me as I climbed up the makeshift ladder at the back of the building and looked around. It was still early morning.

In the corner of the roof, there was a solar panel that was being used by some soldiers for shelter from the sun. Near the corner we had a gun covering the outside of the area. I sent my two guys down and told them we were leaving, then started looking for another place to go. While I was looking, I saw Ralph Porras nearby on the roof.

"Hey, Ralph," I said.

"Hey, Lieutenant."

"You guys see anything?"

"Nah, it's pretty quiet."

"Really?"

"There was one guy on the other side of the canal in a house," interrupted one of the other soldiers. "He keeps going in and out, and I think he's got a cell phone."

I picked up my binos and looked out. Just then someone spotted an old man walking toward the compound. He was unarmed, at least as far as I could tell from where I was. Ralph hopped off the rooftop, then together with another soldier, went and apprehended the man and brought him in.

Ralph was one of those guys who always took action. He was a leader. In a few minutes he had the old guy inside, where it turned out he had information for us about possible attacks. Someone went to get an interpreter; Ralph climbed back up to the roof. Mundey got a warning about a vehicle approaching the gate; suicide bombers and vehicle IEDs were a known hazard. He tracked it, ready to take out the driver if it attacked.

In the meantime, I found the lieutenant in charge of the other men on the roof and told him I didn't think it was a great idea for the men to stay here; the building had been bracketed by mortar fire the day before. Then I went to work looking for a new sniper post. The best spot seemed to be the half-built energy plant, which I'd rejected earlier. It was back a little farther than I wanted, but it still had a good view of the area we had to cover. It was the best option, if we couldn't go to the tanks.

A few hundred yards away, Chris Turner was on his Barrett sniper rifle, watching as an Iraqi equipped with a set of binos and cell phone swept our positions.

The man was clearly a spotter—a scout who calls in positions for an attack. Chris called his team leader for clearance to fire. He was given that clearance, but as he lined up the shot, an officer jumped on him and prevented him from shooting.

"What the hell?" said Turner, or something to that effect.

The officer told him that battalion had commanded the man not be shot. Apparently there was some question in the commander's mind about whether the man was *really* a spotter.

Turner argued. Eventually he was given permission to take a warning shot, firing over the man's head.

No, that's not army sniper doctrine. The man ran off.

Meanwhile, I'd rehearsed what I was going to say to the battalion commander. It had to be assertive and confident, yet not insult him or seem too cocky.

This is Sierra Six, I'd like to move my unit to a higher structure . . .

I brought the mike to my mouth. Just as I went to press the button, a mortar round crashed through the air a few meters away. It landed in front of the building.

I can't believe how close that was! I can't believe that missed us!

"Get off the roof!" I yelled. "Get off! Jump!"

The words were still in my mouth as the next round landed on the roof, five feet away.

There was a flash of light, a boom . . .

From there on, and forever, the world became black—not black as I'd known it, not black as a color or shade, not even as the absence of light, but a walled emptiness difficult to comprehend, much less communicate.

THREE

NOT WORTH LIVING

They gave me a timeout.

I've been coughing pretty much since we got here. With the injuries mounting, the organizers have started taking a harder look at our health. About two hours into racing today, our guide listened to me cough and told me I had to see a doctor before continuing.

I have to admit, I've felt better. Between the altitude and the cold and whatever I can't cough out of my lungs, it felt as if I had an elephant on my chest.

But I have felt a lot worse. A lot.

I wanted to keep going. Anywhere else I would have. I would have crawled to the finish line.

Except you can't do that at the South Pole. And doing it in a race like this wouldn't affect just me. It affects my team.

Still, I'm pissed off. I'm angry with the guide, I'm angry with the organizers, I'm angry with myself. There were six miles left to the end of the stage. I don't know what the hell is going to happen now.

I just feel like an utter failure.

11

Blinded, and Worse

What I remember after that flash on the roof of the Iraqi building is fighting.
Me fighting. Not shooting, not punching, not waging war in any
of the conventional or normal senses of the word, but fighting
as desperately as any human can fight. I was physically unconscious, but on some level I was engaged in a primitive, vicious
battle to stay alive, to stay me, to remain Ivan Castro. It took everything, that battle—every piece of energy, every muscle, every cell.

I fought to breathe. I fought to pump blood through my body.
I fought to get the giant clamp off my head.

Imagine being punched and having the wind knocked out
of you. Imagine at the same time that you have been suddenly
plunged into a deep vat of very hot water, or maybe oil—not burning or boiling, yet somehow as hot as that.

Imagine that this vat of water has no light and no possibility
of light.

Imagine that something has your legs and chest and head, and
is pulling them downward. Imagine you struggle upward, but
can't escape.

Imagine that someone is sucking the life from you.

That is what it was like.

At some point, I started hearing voices. I don't know what time it was; it was surely hours and probably days after I'd been hit. I believe that by then I was on my way back to the States. But wherever I physically was, mentally I was stuck in the middle of a long, distorted dream. I was a prisoner, chained by a wild succession of bizarre thoughts and sensations I couldn't comprehend.

That incoherent cloud and the body that contained it was eventually deposited in a hospital bed at Walter Reed Army Medical Center in Washington, D.C. A few things poked through the confusion. Mostly these were voices: familiar ones—my wife and her mother—and unfamiliar ones, an alien mishmash of medical personnel.

I tried to open my eyes, but all I could see was dark.

I tried again. I tried for hours and then days and then weeks and months.

12

The Known Unknowns

Over the years I've asked everyone who was there, my guys, the medical people, and Evelyn, especially, questions about what happened. I've pieced together a picture of the moments and days after I was hit, first in Iraq, and then back home during the roughly two weeks I spent unconscious and in a medically induced coma. What to me was one long slog through an ocean of confused and occasionally painful nothingness, to them was a succession of discrete events, quick actions, and undoubtedly a lot of sorrow and prayer.

I still don't know exactly what happened to everyone else who was on that roof or in the building, who took care of me, whatever happened to the attackers. Nor do I know what happened to me at every hour that followed. So there are gaps in what follows here.

I fell on the roof, my body badly torn. Mundey and some of the other guys happened to be near enough to or under, the large panel that they were somehow spared the worst of the mortar blast. But Sgt. Porras and PFC Justin W. Dreese, a twenty-one-year-old from

Northumberland, Pennsylvania, were killed by the blast and died that day, September 2, 2006.

Ortiz, my sniper whom we'd relieved, was one of the first guys on the roof after the round hit.

He ran over and saw three bodies down.

"Where's Lieutenant Castro at?" he yelled.

I was lying at his feet, my face so bloody and wrecked that he didn't recognize me.

The guys who'd been on the roof when the shell landed were either in shock or too wounded to help; most of them probably couldn't even hear because the concussion or sound of the blast had wiped out their hearing.

There happened to be a Skedco up there—a kind of combination stretcher and sled that can be used to move injured bodies. A couple of guys grabbed it, put me on it, and dragged me to the edge of the roof.

Strapped onto the stretcher, I was lowered to the ground and then carried inside. "Doc" Landers and a physician's assistant named Acosta heard the explosions and bolted to the building. They immediately began working on me. They took scissors or a knife and cut my clothes and boots off, stripping me naked. They stopped some of the bleeding and undoubtedly saved my life.

In the meantime, they pulled Ralph and Justin down. Both of them had been hit by huge pieces of shrapnel, which tore massive holes through their bodies.

Ralph and Justin are with me now, always. We were brothers in pain and death—near death for me. I wear their names on a metal band I wear around my wrist every day. I've worn out that band twice, and quickly replaced it.

Ortiz went down with me and stayed while the doctor and medics worked. I was moaning but completely unconscious. My sunglasses had been blown into my face, embedded so deep that they had to be pulled out with a pliers. I had an open bone fracture of the humerus, the arm bone. I had trouble breathing because of a collapsed lung. Part of my right index finger had been chopped off. There were gashes and cuts all over my body; I was awash in blood.

A medivac helicopter came soon after the attack ended. My guys carried me outside the complex to the field and loaded me into the helicopter. They admitted later they didn't know if they'd ever see me alive again.

Probably they didn't think so at all. I wouldn't blame them.

They took me to Balad Air Base, about forty miles north of Baghdad. It happened that my platoon sergeant, Cliff Burgoyne, had been up there standing by in case he was needed as part of a reaction force on the mission. When Cliff heard that I'd been hit and was coming, he went over to the hospital where I'd been received.

The sergeant found a doctor and asked if I was there.

"Yeah, he's on his way to Germany," said the doctor.

"Is he going to be OK?"

The doctor waited a moment. "We hope so," he said, then turned and went off to another patient.

About the time I arrived in Balad, Evelyn was driving with her mom to do some shopping when her cell phone rang. The call was from a good friend of mine, Matthew Smith, who was in the 82nd but stationed at Fort Bragg as part of the rear detachment. It was the day after Labor Day.

"Evelyn, I have to tell you something," said Matt, his voice cracking.

"What?" she asked.

Matt started to choke up and couldn't answer.

"What, what?" Evelyn demanded. "What's going on?"

She pulled over to the side of the road.

"Ivan's been hit," he told her.

"What? What's happened to him?" she demanded.

Matt started to explain, then choked up and couldn't talk. But it was enough: My mother-in-law, sitting next to her, burst into tears.

Someone in the office took the phone from Matt and finished what he couldn't, telling Evelyn that I had been severely hurt by a mortar round.

She sat there in the car, paralyzed. Someone pulled up in a pickup behind her and got out to see if she needed help. He thought her car had broken down.

Somehow, she forced herself to tell him that she was OK.

"My husband has been hurt," she stuttered. "But we're OK."

Evelyn turned around and went home. There, she called Matt again to ask more questions.

Where is he?

How bad is he?

Is he coming home?

Matt couldn't answer; he didn't know.

"Listen," she told him. "The next time you call me, call with all the answers."

"I will."

"I need the answers to all of these questions, Matt. Please."

"I know, I know."

The brigade surgeon called her soon afterward, but he didn't have much information yet either. Evelyn started fielding calls from a number of people trying to offer comfort. Friends started arriving at the house, a swarm of them, who passed the word to others. One of my best buddies, reached at the beach where he'd taken his family for vacation, got off the phone and told his wife to pack up the kids; they were going back to help Evelyn.

At the time, Evelyn thought the most serious injury would be the loss of a finger.

How is he going to shoot? she thought. *He's a sniper, and now he can't shoot.*

Odd thoughts pass through your mind in a crisis. The lack of information frustrates you, and yet more precise information rarely comforts you. And it couldn't have in this case; the only thing that would really have calmed her would have been news that it was all a mistake, that I was perfectly fine.

And of course that wasn't the case.

Eventually, Evelyn found out that I was on my way to Germany. She called the hospital there and somehow managed to find a military doctor not only involved in my care, but who came from Puerto Rico. The cultural connection was somehow reassuring.

"Do I have to fly out there?" she asked.

"No, we're stabilizing him and flying him to the States," he told her. "It won't be long."

The doctor went into great detail with her, cataloging the injuries, including the fact that the fluid around my brain was swelling; they were extremely concerned about a traumatic head injury, which at its worst could kill me or leave me a vegetable.

Evelyn found out they were taking me to Walter Reed. Two of our close friends, Colonel Ricardo Nieves and his wife, Evelyn, went up with her, dropping everything at a moment's notice.

When they got there, though, I wasn't there. The doctors in Germany had determined that I was too bad off to fly, and it took roughly two days to stabilize me. In the meantime, unsure what was going on or how long it would be, Evelyn found a guest house on the Walter Reed base and took a room there.

The halls smelled of mildew and tears, haunted by years of families waiting and hoping for their loved ones to get better. Some of the facilities for families there have since been improved and renovated; at the time they were pretty beat-down. I'm not sure how much Evelyn noticed, if at all, but the surroundings didn't add much to her morale.

Eventually, the doctors decided I was stable enough to fly. I hadn't regained consciousness; the world around me was still a vast blank. But I believe now that as I went up the ramp of the C17, I started hearing voices, as if I were in a dream.

People were talking. Medical people.

Jet engines wound up. I smelled JP8, jet fuel, a smell you don't forget.

We were moving.

Everything suddenly felt familiar, yet strange at the same

time. I was in the back of a C17. How many times had I jumped
from one of these?

Something made a pumping sound, a distant rhythm, a deep
huff that repeated over and over, bass to a rap song, or a drum, or
breath: the ventilator.

I felt as if I was tied down. I was tied down. I had to escape.
I have to fight. I have to get home. I have to ask for help.

"Take it easy," said a voice above. "Calm down. Calm down!"
I have to fight! I need to get home!

"This guy needs some more morphine. Now!"

I blacked out again. Maybe it was all a dream, or maybe I had
started to come out of the coma. I'll never really know for sure.

Several hours later, I landed in America and was rushed to
Walter Reed, at the time the army's chief medical hospital on the
East Coast. (Military care has since been reorganized with many
facilities closed; Walter Reed has since been integrated into
Bethesda Naval Medical Center and is called Walter Reed Bethesda;
they were two separate facilities when I was hurt and immediately
afterward.)

They put me in an intensive care ward and at the same time
notified Evelyn that I was there. Shown into the room, she was
overcome with grief when she saw me. Ric Nieves and Evelyn
dropped to their knees and began to pray.

Covered with a sheet but nothing else, hooked up to a ventilator, surrounded by miscellaneous medical equipment, I must
have looked as if I was at death's door.

Beyond that, more likely. My fractured arm was in an exter-
nal fixation device—a kind of metal cage that to Evelyn looked
like a medieval torture device. Every part of my body had swol-
len as it fought infection and the wounds; my testicles, Evelyn
said later, were the size of Perdue chicken breasts. My skin was
still covered with dirt and grit.

The nurses began reeling off the long list of my injuries: *shattered nose, broken arm, collapsed lung, amputated finger, enucleated eye . . .*

Enucleated eye is the medical way of saying my right eye had been blown out of its socket.

My left eye was still there though, at that point, heavily bandaged.

As difficult as it must have been for Evelyn to hear and see all of this, she found some sort of strength to hang in. And more: When two men came in to adjust the device that was aligning my broken bones, she rolled up her sleeves and went to work helping them, handing them equipment as they adjusted the device.

"Are you OK to do this?" one of them asked. Even they were having a hard time.

"Do it," she said. "Whatever you need to. Put everything where it needs to be."

The Nieves had to return home; another friend from SF, Robert, came up. Robert's wife was in Korea at the time; he dropped his kids off at an in-law's and drove up to D.C. from North Carolina to stay for a few days.

While my shattered arm and my missing eye were the most obvious injuries, I had plenty of others no one could see, including a pulmonary embolism, torn nerves, muscles, you name it. But the most serious was a bilobed aneurysm in my neck, which could have killed me at any moment. In layman's terms, an aneurysm is a large bulge in an artery that could burst at any time. If that happened to me, I might easily bleed to death. I could also have a stroke, a heart attack, lose brain function—you name the bad stuff and it probably was on the list, if not because of the aneurysm then because of some other complication.

The aneurysm had to be treated by a specialist, and the best available one nearby worked at Bethesda Medical Center, the navy's hospital a few miles away. The team supervising my care decided that it would be most efficient to take me to that hospital for the operation. I was sent there for the operation . . . and never went back, thanks to Evelyn.

Bethesda is a short distance from Walter Reed—maybe fifteen minutes by car—but the wards were a world of distance when

I was there, at least as far as Evelyn was concerned. Walter Reed was crowded and run-down. The entire atmosphere, not just in the hospital but outside, seemed heavy with pain and fatigue. Bethesda, on the other hand, seemed very hopeful. The doctors and nurses who worked there seemed far more positive and energetic. Whether the care was actually better or not, it absolutely seemed like a more positive place.

The surgery for the aneurysm went well. But as I was coming out of it, they saw that I was having trouble breathing. The doctors then discovered that I had a pulmonary embolism, another serious matter—more surgery, with a special filter put into my body to catch any clot before it reached my heart.

Right after the operation, the general in charge of the 82nd came to check on me at the hospital. He found me at Bethesda. He spoke to Evelyn, assuring her that he would do anything he possibly could.

"Let Ivan stay in this hospital then," she told him. "Don't transfer him back to Walter Reed."

Actually, I think it would have been more along the lines of: *Oh, yeah? Well why don't you put those two stars to work and get Ivan transferred here full-time.*

The general put his two stars to work. He was as good as his word: I stayed at Bethesda.

Evelyn says now that she had already convinced the doctors and the hospital administration to let me stay anyway. I'm not so sure. For one thing, it's not the standard procedure. While my medical records make it clear that at first the doctors were extremely concerned about the aneurysm and follow-up care— surely enough reason to leave me where the specialist and his team was—that soon ceased to be a critical concern. As far as I can tell, I was the only army guy in the ward; everyone else was navy or marines. Draw whatever conclusion you want; I've seen that woman in action and nothing can get in her way.

Evelyn and my mother-in-law spent pretty much every day with me, arriving in the morning and leaving late at night. Once it became clear that I was going to be in the hospital for a long time, Evelyn arranged to take a leave of absence from the school where she worked as a speech therapist, having gone back to school for a masters in the field. Eventually, she would end up giving up her job to stay with me.

Evelyn had the day shift; my mother-in-law had the night. Once I was moved from ICU, I was placed in a room with two beds. As luck would have it, the other bed was empty. Mom started sleeping there, which meant I had round-the-clock family care supplementing the nurses and doctors. That was an extremely unusual situation, and one extremely beneficial to me. I doubt most hospital patients, let alone wounded servicemen, have that luxury.

Days slowly ticked by. I was still unconscious, though occasionally I drifted toward a semidream state where I could hear voices. Meanwhile, I had contracted an infection, and despite all the medication the doctors gave me, neither it nor its fever would go away. Low-grade at first, it gradually seemed to get worse, but no one could figure out why. Finally, while taking X-rays of my busted nose, they discovered two pieces of cotton gauze that had been placed deep in my nasal cavity at some point immediately after the explosion, presumably to help stop the bleeding.

The pieces of gauze were removed. The fever soon broke, and from that point on, my recovery accelerated.

I wasn't exactly Lazarus, springing up from the dead, fully healed. It was a long and bumpy slope upward, first toward consciousness, then toward something like primitive functionality: the ability to talk, walk, hope.

The one constant through it all was pain. I was on a panoply of drugs, including painkillers, and yet I felt plenty of pain. But from the medical records, it looks as if I rarely or never admitted it to the doctors or nurses caring for me. Instead, my wife and mother-in-law would notice and plead for more medicine.

The first words I spoke when they finally took me off the ventilator were profound and worthy of a great intellect:

Can I spit?

At least according to Evelyn. I don't remember.

She went and got a cup.

The brace that had been supporting my neck was removed. Evelyn shaved me, removing several weeks of growth. My sister came to see me. My uncle, aunt, and cousin came to see me. I went in and out of consciousness; my memory of that time is a checkerboard of tiny pieces of sounds and sensation, each surrounded by black squares, empty holes where continuity fails.

"You're back in the States," Evelyn says. She's on my right side.

Ralph Porras and Justin Dreese are dead.

You lost an eye. You have a fragment in the other eye. They're going to pull that fragment out. We're going to surgery.

After my condition had stabilized enough for eye surgery, they took me in to examine my remaining eye and remove the fragment that was lodged in the iris. The fragment was only part of the problem, though admittedly a large part. If the nerves had been severed, then even if the fragment was successfully removed, there would be no hope of my ever seeing. And there are pages of dense prose in medical books and journals describing all of the other possible injuries when the eye is damaged by an explosion.

The medical reports assessing my eye are clinical in their language, never entirely ruling out the possibility that I might be able to see, at least partially. But even before the operation, the doctors were not optimistic. They explained to Evelyn that, while it would be necessary to remove the fragment to prevent an infection, the odds of my seeing were not great.

I know to some extent Evelyn blames herself now for approving the operation, when really she had no choice. Rationally speaking, her decision to let them operate had no bearing on whether I would see or not. But she's told others that she blames herself. That's a ridiculously heavy burden she doesn't deserve. The fragment had to go; an infection could easily kill me as well as destroy the eye. And the operation wasn't entirely without any hope—during an early exam, the doctors believed I reacted to light, so there was some basis to believe that, with the fragment gone, I'd be able to see something.

Evelyn waited as patiently as she could while the operation proceeded. When it was over, she walked with me as I was pushed back to the room, hoping for the best and praying against the worst.

One of the harder things for her, as I went through operation after operation, were the organ donor forms. Long before I'd been injured, both my wife and I had decided our organs could be used for others in the event that we died. Now each time I went into the operating room, she was handed a form to sign reaffirming that decision.

As much as she wanted to honor my wishes, the whole idea became revolting.

"You're going in thinking you may fail?" she said finally.

She kept signing, but it was one more thing that took a toll.

Little by little, my mind swam back toward normality. Or at least something close to it.

One day Ric came to see me. I leaned close to him, as if plotting my escape. In a whisper I told him, "This is a special place, for special people." Another day, the general who headed my division came to see me and present me with a Purple Heart. His wife came, too. I don't remember talking to him, but I do remembering mumbling to her.

"Your husband has a tough job," I said.

Another time, drifting out of a dream, I heard the ventilator.

"Turn off the bomb," I told Evelyn. "Turn it off."

You have the most messed up dreams under sedation. I had a dream that I was in Vietnam as a prisoner of war. I was held captive and tied down. There was beeping and radio equipment— another prisoner was trying to send a signal back to America to get us out.

There were dreams with aliens, people in space suits come to abduct me. I saw two guys in chem suits hovering near my bed.

Two guys.

One time I came out of a surgery and was convinced, absolutely convinced, that I was aboard an alien spaceship. I began screaming at the top of my lungs for my wife.

Evelyn! Evelyn!

Everything was in that scream. I was fighting for my life. The only thing I wanted was Evelyn. I needed to get back to her, and it was impossible.

The doctors and nurses grabbed me, holding me down.

"Calm down," said a nurse.

I grabbed her hand. I wanted to break it.

Evelyn, who'd been sleeping at the Navy Lodge, a hotel on the base grounds, somehow knew I was in trouble and came over to the hospital. They rushed her in as I continued to scream.

Ivan! Ivan, I'm here.

As soon as I heard her voice, I was calm again. The nurse hit me with more meds, and I drifted back to oblivion.

Separating the world into reality and dreams took time and effort, but it came eventually. Ordering reality was harder. I didn't have the cues I was used to, not even light to tell me when it was day and when it was night.

But I did make progress.

"Ivan, do you know where you're at?" asked a nurse every day.

"I don't know," I would answer.

"Bethesda Medical Center."

"Uh. OK."

One day, starting to get my wits together, I answered. "Fort Benning, Georgia."

"No," said the nurse. "Bethesda."

"Uh. OK."

The next day: "Do you know where you're at?"

"Fort Bragg, North Carolina," I answered.

"Well, he's coming north at least," said Evelyn. "He'll be here soon."

"Ivan, do you know where we're at?" the nurse asked the next day.

"Listen," I said. "If you don't know where we're at, and I don't know where we're at, we're fucked."

"He used profanity," said Evelyn approvingly. "He's good."

They began weaning me off the pain meds and my consciousness gradually improved. The eye doctor examined me at intervals, still keeping my eye under wraps.

"When do we take the dressing off?" I'd ask.

"Soon," he'd answer.

One day I put my hand to my face, feeling the empty space.

"Evelyn, what's wrong with my hand?" I asked.

"Your finger is amputated."

"What? My finger is amputated? When were you going to tell me this?"

"I thought—"

"Stop! Stop right now. I want you to tell me everything that's wrong with me. Do I have legs?"

"Yes, you have legs."

"Do I have both arms?"

"Yes."

I made her list each injury. To me, when I knew I had my legs, the eyes were my most serious wounds. I knew my right eye was gone, but my left eye was still there, and I had faith that I would be able to see when they took the bandages off. If only they would hurry up and get it done.

Soon, Ivan. Soon.

SOCOM—Special Operations Command, which oversaw the special ops unit we'd been working with as well as the Special Forces group I had once been part of—took an interest in my case and started tracking me. Two SF medics—I called them the Thompson Twins—acted as liaisons, tracking my care and making sure that Evelyn was getting everything that she needed. My old SF team came in and visited. So many friends stopped by that even if I had been fully conscious I'd never have been able to keep track.

The one visitor I wish I hadn't had was my son. He was thirteen at the time. I know why my ex-wife brought him; no one was sure I was actually going to live, he wanted to come, and a son has a right to see his dad, no matter.

But seeing me helpless and beat up must have hurt him badly. He fainted, and had to be carried out of the room.

I was unconscious at the time, but maybe not completely—they say my heart rate jumped during the commotion.

Every day seemed to include an operation or test. The procedures ranged from simple wound cleanings to putting a filter in my heart. I believe I saw every department at the hospital, outside of Labor and Delivery.

Although maybe they snuck me in there while I was unconscious.

Days went by. I asked Evelyn when they were going to take the dressing off of my eye.

"I want to see," I told her. "I want to see. When is that going to come?"

"Be patient."

As I recovered, I eventually became strong enough for physical therapy. My banged-up body and neglected muscles needed to be taught to move again. One day a woman named Katie showed up with a wheelchair. Brusquely introducing herself as the therapist, she wrapped a belt around my waist, then unceremoniously slid me into the wheelchair next to the bed.

Then she left.

Evelyn and her mom looked at each other.

"Where did she go?" I asked.

Evelyn went to look for her but couldn't find her. An hour, maybe more, passed. Finally we decided I might as well get back into bed. As Evelyn and her mom struggled to lift me, I leaned and pushed as best I could, finally making it. It felt like I'd climbed Mount Everest.

The next day, the therapist returned.

"What happened to you?" I demanded. "You were supposed to give me physical therapy yesterday."

"I did. You got back into bed, right?"

"Yeah."

"That was your first session."

Talk about tough love. Boy, did that bitch push me. I hated her.

Obviously, that was the idea, and somewhere deep inside I knew that then, just as I know that now. But it didn't make the strain any easier.

I still couldn't see. Getting the damn bandages off my eye became my top goal in life. It was everything. I couldn't wait, even if it seemed never to come. Then finally one day the doctor came in and took off the bandage on my left eye.

He flashed the light.

"Doc?" I asked.

"Your eye isn't reacting."

"So?"

"I'm afraid—you're not going to see."

"No," I said, angrily. "You don't know what you're talking about. I'm not going to be blind."

"Ivan, I'm sorry."

Evelyn was silent. She already knew. When the doctors had checked the bandages, they had also checked for light reaction. We were well past the point of any hope, though I didn't know that.

"There must be another specialist," I insisted. "You don't know what you're talking about."

"Well, we could bring someone over from Walter Reed."

"Yeah, bring him over."

The next day, another doctor came. We went through the same routine; he shined a light in my eye, I looked up and down.

"No," he told me. "You're not going to see."

"Get out," I said. "I'm done with you."

■ ■ ■

My retina or the nerves or both had been damaged beyond repair and my body's ability to heal. No matter what I wanted or wished or did, I was going to be blind for the rest of my life.

Evelyn found a national expert on eye surgery at Johns Hopkins hospital in Baltimore. She managed to get an appointment.

We were going to pay out-of-pocket, but Sharon Henderson happened to be visiting the day Evelyn got the appointment and she mentioned it. Sharon was chief operating officer of the SOCOM Care Coalition; with her was Admiral Eric Olson, the head of SOCOM.

"Pay out-of-pocket?" asked Sharon. "Don't you have a referral?"

"No," I said. Just as with many civilian insurance plans, the military would pay for outside experts if properly referred to by a doctor. But we had no idea that even existed, let alone how it worked.

In a matter of maybe two hours, we had a referral in hand. The Thompson Twins volunteered to get us to Baltimore and back.

We drove up there. It was well after my operation but I was still hooked up to an IV and a catheter.

Another exam, just like the others.

"I hate to tell you this," said the doctor, "but you're going to be blind for the rest of your life."

"Those are the only tests you're going to do?" I demanded.

"Look, your eye doesn't react even to light. Nothing is getting to your brain. You guys are a beautiful young couple, and you will survive this, but you will be blind forever."

The doctor rose and left the office. We got up slowly, and made it to the hallway, where Evelyn broke down in tears.

It was the first time I had heard her cry since I'd regained consciousness. I wanted to hunt that doctor down and beat his ass. Not because he told me I was going to be blind, but because he made my wife sob.

The ride back was the longest, most silent car ride ever. Only then did it sink in that I was going to be blind.

■ ■ ■

Evelyn spent endless hours in the hospital library doing research on eye injuries and reconstruction. A lot of work has been done with stem cells; it's possible someday doctors will be able to grow new tissue, repairing nerves and critical organs. She found some experiments in China that seemed to be promising, but when we discussed them with one of the doctors, he said they were very unlikely to yield results, and could easily endanger my life.

And so I remain blind.

Evelyn thinks someday that research will not only help the blind see, but that I will be among them. She thinks the day isn't far off.

Personally, that's not something I waste my time considering. I did so much of that in the hospital—whole days and weeks praying for a miracle—that I feel I've worn those wishes out. I have to deal with what's in front of me, not what will probably never be.

Evelyn also blames herself for allowing them to operate. She is convinced that the operation was what robbed me of my sight.

She's wrong. The mortar round blinded me. And she had no choice but to let the doctors do what they needed to do. I'd be dead as well as blind. Alive is better.

13

Hopelessness and Grace

I didn't think that at the time.

Every night I prayed that the next morning a miracle would happen and I would see. I would pray so hard.

I'd wake up and look around, up and down, look for light . . . I would strain.

No light. And then my mind started to play with me. I knew what Evelyn looked like. She would come in the room, and I would see her.

I see you!

And I would describe what she was wearing.

You have your hair down and those little Capri pants and that pretty jacket . . .

She'd get all excited and happy—then realize that I'd described something wrong, her hair or her pants or her shirt. I was having phantom vision, a common problem for those who suddenly lose their eyes.

My nightmares got worse. Things happened around me and I couldn't move. I was in a car and it would career out of control and crash and I couldn't move. I was carjacked.

The dreamscape wasn't war, but the psychology was pretty obvious—things would happen and I couldn't move, couldn't save Evelyn, couldn't help myself. It was directly related to my being in bed so long, restrained and sedated, but it was also metaphorical: the injuries, blindness especially, rendering me helpless.

Helpless meant impotent. Impotent meant worthless. Blind meant all of the above.

As the days went by and I couldn't see, I despaired. What was I going to do? I was a worthless piece of meat.

I can't drive, I can't see, I can't even eat. I can't walk on my own. I'm not the man I was before.

I'm not a man.

My dreams and goals had been yanked away. Bouncing grandkids on my knee—that would never happen. Our family—that would never happen.

My career as an officer was over. The great times I'd had in the army would never be repeated. I'd never watch another fight on TV. I'd never see my wife's smile.

I was afraid Evelyn would leave me. I expected her to. I was jealous anytime anyone was around her. I was sure they would take her away—what woman would stay with a blind man?

All I knew about the blind was this: They walked with canes and had guide dogs. I knew nothing beyond that, except that I wanted neither a dog nor a cane.

I replayed the attack over and over, a million times a day. And a million times a day I wished I was dead. I wished that the mortar round had taken me out. It had done something worse: It had robbed me of my spirit, my soul, myself.

I was angry, mad with the world and with God. I cursed Him and pushed my faith away.

I sunk deeper and deeper in my chair each time Evelyn wheeled me around the ward. I was done.

"What's wrong with you?" she snapped at me one day as we returned to the room.

"I'm blind."

"You don't understand," she said. "Every time I wheel you

around there are people watching you, parents. If you could only
see their sons. They're kids. Kids. They don't even look old enough
to vote. There is so much damage—traumatic brain injuries,
missing both legs, an arm and a leg. They can't eat. They're in
comas. Guys that have never been married. The parents—to have
their kids just be blind—they would trade places in a heartbeat
with us. The parents look at you and wish their loved ones could
have what you have."

What did I have? I could breathe on my own. My left arm
was messed up but rehabilitation would bring it back. My hand
was usable. My legs were weak but still worked. I could hear.
My memory was intact.

My only problem was that I couldn't see.

I was ashamed of myself. I was ashamed that I was willing to
despair, rather than fight.

"I'm going to turn it around," I told Evelyn. "I'm going to turn
it around."

■■■

Pulling yourself out of a deep hole involves more than just a decision to do it. Pulling yourself out of a depression is many times
harder, and more complicated. There was certainly more to it
than that one moment, even if for me that one moment sparked
the beginning of my climb.

I had a son who loved me, a wife who'd given up her job to
take care of me, a mother-in-law who was acting as a night nurse.
I had an army of friends who came by whenever they could. I had
others still in combat who were all pulling for me. All of those
things played in the background of that spark Evelyn ignited
that day.

My faith certainly helped, as did the lessons and examples my
parents had given me.

One other thing, one other spark, ended up driving me, pulling me out of that metaphorical blackness.

At some point in October, not too long after Evelyn scolded
me, I found myself between one of my doctors, Dr. Fick, and a

nurse, Hannah. They started talking about the Marine Corps Marathon.

I sat listening as they talked about the race and the experience.

You know, I used to run. I used to enjoy it.

The next time Dr. Fick came into the room, I interrupted his examination.

"Hey, Doc, I heard you talking about the Marine Corps Marathon. You run?"

"Yup," he said.

"Can anybody run?"

"As far as I know."

"I'm going to run in it next year. You think I can?"

"Yeah, you can do it," he said, going back to the exam.

Today, it's not particularly unusual to see people with prosthetics in races, and there can be several blind people running as well. But at the time, competing with *any* disability was practically unheard of.

Undoubtedly he thought I was on drugs. Well, I *was* on drugs. But I was as clearheaded as I'd ever been in my life.

I could barely get out of bed, let alone walk, but in one year I was going to run a marathon. Blind.

FOUR

BLIND MAN RUNNING

South Pole Diary:
December 7, 2013
In the tempest

I'm back. I only missed a few hours. My cough was nothing. Clean bill of health.

But that's not the real news. The expedition is in serious trouble. We're losing people. We're not going to make it to the Pole the way we're going. Some of us may even die. The conditions are too extreme.

So things have to change. The race leader called us together and, after laying out the situation, said we have two options:

Give up, or try something else: Instead of racing with each other, we band together and help each other to the Pole.

Prince Harry seconded the idea. "Sacrifice the race for the purpose of the cause," he said. The cause—bringing attention to the worth and dignity of the wounded by reaching the Pole— is more important than beating each other.

It's noble sounding, but I have trouble letting it go. Why am I here if not to race? Where's the achievement in just getting to the Pole?

Maybe I'm being stubborn and unkind. Maybe it's crass to think like that, when it's a matter of life and death. But I can't stamp out that competitive streak. It drives me. A race got me out of bed when I was at my lowest. Races have kept me going.

Is that an ugly truth? Would I let others die so I could say I won? So that I was "first"?

No. I care about everyone I am with. Deep down, inside, I want everyone safe and sound. I've trained with these guys for a year. I love them. That's more important than a race.

I voted to ski on, despite my doubts. The only other option is to quit, and I'm not a quitter.

14

How I Lived

Let me make this clear:

In any other war, I'm dead.

The immediate care I received, from a doctor and a physician's assistant, along with at least two medics, was in many ways a stroke of luck—it's rare that you have that level of expertise close by during battle. The quick medivac to a larger facility, new tools and techniques for dealing with extreme trauma—all of these things played a role in keeping me alive. From quickly stopping my bleeding to discovering and treating the aneurysm to combating my infections—remove any one of those elements and I surely would have been a dead man.

Move me a footstep closer to the shell and I would have been killed outright, like Ralph and Justin. Some 2,536 men and women died during Operation Iraqi Freedom, including those two men, including Angel Mercado, including Thomas Barbieri. Six hundred and ten died of their wounds—they were still breathing when they were taken for care, but died sometime after that.

To avoid that statistic, to escape with my life, means I was incredibly lucky. Even if I don't feel that I was.

The numbers are humbling. But they're not a consolation, and they didn't point me toward a goal.

The idea of running in that marathon did. If I could run, achieve something—hell, if could just get out of bed and prove that I wasn't worthless, then maybe I could go on, lucky or not.

The marathon was an impossible goal. Even if I hadn't been blind, running a marathon—running a quarter mile—would have been a huge accomplishment. I was weak and way out of shape.

Maybe its very impossibility spurred me on. It was so far in the distance that I didn't have to think rationally about it. I could concentrate on the little steps in front of me, literally at first.

If I was going to do something, it had to be fast and furious. It had to be now. Every soldier has to have a mission and a plan.

Mine was that marathon. I started doubling up on my physical and occupational therapy sessions. They brought me to a gym and got me on a stationary bike.

"Hey man, can I stay ten more minutes on the bike?" I'd ask.

Sure, they'd say.

Maybe they were rolling their eyes, maybe not. Whatever. They let me stay . . . and for more than ten minutes. I rigged my bed up with resistance bands, and began exercising in bed.

Most hospitals have terrible food, but Bethesda's was excellent. Too good, in fact. I'd lost a lot of weight following my injury, and when I was finally able to eat solid food, I started to make up for it. But as I got stronger, I realized I'd gone too far— I was pushing 220 pounds, way over my normal weight. So I began watching what I ate. No more pastries, no more desserts. Every morning I had coffee, just coffee. No more Boston crème donuts, no more croissants and butter.

I was being cared for by a large medical team that included a group of brand-new Navy nurses, all ensigns or O-1. All were lovely and dedicated. Gradually, I started making friends.

Of course, this did bring some dangers to my new regime.

"What would you like for breakfast?" Gabrielle from Boston asked me one day.

"Oh, I would love bagels and cream cheese and smoked salmon," I told her.

The next day she came in with exactly that. Oh well—just another half-hour's worth of exercise, right?

Gabrielle from Boston is in my heart forever. Nurse Robin, Nurse Hanna, Nurse Nancy the Civilian, and Red-headed Katie (I have my sources)—they were all Ivan's Angels.

I'm sure the nurses would have been kind to me no matter what, but Evelyn had taken out an insurance policy by plastering the walls of the room with pictures of me before I was injured. Everyone who visited was asked to bring a photo. The idea was that when a new doctor or other provider would walk in, I wasn't just a wounded man lying inert on the bed, but a man with a life and a family and friends. She spread other hints around as well: an SF blanket at the foot of the bed, challenge coins on the nightstand. (Challenge coins are specially minted coins commemorating different military units; receiving them is an honor.)

Evelyn rallied friends for more than photos and mementos. I got letters and e-mails from people I hadn't heard from in years. Friends as far away as Korea got in touch. All the attention cheered me up—and on. I couldn't give up on all those folks. I had to keep going.

I needed to run that marathon. For them.

My body began responding to the workouts and healthy food. There were still operations and tests, and little problems, mundane things. Like constipation.

At one point I realized I hadn't gone to the bathroom in quite a while—probably a side effect of all the painkillers. The medical staff saw it, too.

I took stool softeners, suppositories . . . nothing worked until an enema.

Saying that worked is like saying the nuclear bomb is an explosive device. I went from my bed to a special chair nearby and sat there, on that throne, naked and sweating, for hours. I filled the pan twice. They actually weighed what I produced: fourteen pounds of relief, some sort of record, I'm sure.

In the first days after the attack, the doctors feared I might have experienced some brain damage. That proved untrue, fortunately. My memory came back, and at times it even surprised me. One day, walking down the corridor with Evelyn and my mother-in-law, I heard someone greeting them.

I instantly recognized the voice.

"You prayed over me," I said, pointing in the direction of the speaker.

"That's right," replied the priest, surprised. "You remember?"

I did remember, even though I hadn't been conscious at the time, and in fact couldn't have remembered that incident until that very moment when I heard his voice and it flooded back.

You wonder sometimes whether everything that happens to us, around us, is stored in some way in our brains. Even if the retrieval system is broken, maybe it's still there, waiting to be used, or perhaps being used in a way we aren't even conscious of.

The mental adjustments to my injuries and new reality were more than the physical. I was used to working out; I wasn't used to not seeing the world with my eyes. I started telling my relatives and friends that I was blind, and there was no hope of seeing. My sister listened to me explain over the phone what the situation was, but it didn't quite make sense.

"No," she said. "Believe in God. Have faith in God."

"It has nothing to do with faith," I explained.

"I'll donate one of my eyes."

"No, Olga. Thank you, but it's a nerve. I'm not going to be able to see."

"I love you."

None of the conversations were any easier. Evelyn, of course, had prepared most people, but I still felt responsible to tell them. They had to hear it from me, and I had to tell them, to make it real for both of us.

I was still taking an array of pills—something like a dozen or so three times a day—so many that I had trouble swallowing them and asked to have them put into pudding. The doctors kept adjusting the meds, the pain pills especially. There were so many sources of pain: the original injuries, operations, reconstructive surgery on my face (which continues to be checked), adjustments to my arm, even the catheters—just getting an IV line in could be a struggle, as my veins were calloused and traumatized. I struggled with the pain for weeks, veering between wanting relief and rebelling against the haze that descended over my brain because of the pills. Eventually I decided I had had enough: I went cold turkey, or close to it, on the pain medication, striving to get back to normal, or rather the new normal, whatever that was going to be.

By mid-October, roughly seven weeks after being hit, I was walking around easily. As the days went on, the possibility of being released and going home became a reality.

I had my first wife bring my son back up to see me. This time, I made sure I was cleaned up before he came in. I put on a fresh gown and sat up in bed, willing not just strength but confidence into my manner.

"Just Ivan and me," I told the others when they brought him in.

He sat down next to me.

"I'm always going to be your dad," I told him. "I know you saw me when I was really bad, and obviously I'm going to be blind, but no matter what, I'll be your dad. I'll always love you, and I'll always be there for you. Us Castros, we're as hard as woodpecker lips. No one can take us down."

He was quiet.

"Don't be ashamed of having a dad who's blind," I said.

"I'm not."

"Good."

He was sad, though he tried hard not to show it. I know he felt a lot of loss at that moment. I hope at some point he looks back and finds that from that loss he nonetheless gained some measure of strength as he moved on. And I hope he always knows the great love I felt for him that day, and all days.

For Halloween, I decided I'd give my nurses a surprise. Evelyn went out and bought me some things to make a pirate costume—I had an eye patch already, so it was a natural. We took candy and went to all the rooms nearby, kind of a reverse trick or treat. With the help of a wheelchair, we rode down to the ICU and greeted all the nurses who'd worked on me when I arrived. They were overjoyed that I had made it and remembered them. It was Halloween and Christmas, rolled up in one.

In a lot of ways it was a pregraduation party. I was ready to go on to the next step in my recovery: *Blind School.*

That's not the official title, but it is how I thought of it. I had to learn how to be blind: how to go out on the street without being run over (if possible), how to find out what time it was, how to use the Internet. Things I had taken for granted all my life I now had to relearn.

Occupational therapy for blinded servicemen—aka "blind rehab"—is not handled by the military itself; there aren't that many soldiers who become blinded while on duty, so it wouldn't make sense for the army or other services to staff an entire facility. Even the Veterans Administration does not have many programs for the blind; those that they have are relatively small, and cater mostly to older people who are either partially blind or slowly losing their sight.

My best, closest choice at the time was a facility in Augusta, Georgia: the Charlie Norwood VA Medical Center. We left Bethesda with no fanfare, no band, no ceremony, just heartfelt words of thanks and good-bye from the staff we saw. Suddenly released: an anticlimactic ending to the worst weeks of my life. There were a lot of moments like that in the days and even years that followed: points that should have seemed momentous, yet were subdued and almost nonchalant at the time.

As eager as I was to leave, I was also nervous. I was going out into the world blind. I didn't know if I could survive, let alone what the future might hold.

Evelyn and I drove down from Maryland, stopping at the house in North Carolina for the weekend. Walking in, I knew where everything was, and yet I didn't. I made my way cautiously, feeling around the furniture and walls.

Watching, Evelyn felt something clutch inside her chest. It was only then that she *really* realized how much different our lives were going to be. It was only seeing me, arms extended, feeling my way across the familiar space, that she began to understand the depth of my loss, and hers.

We continued on the next day, both of us quiet for most of the ride.

Georgia was not a happy place for me. In retrospect, I appreciate the efforts of the staff, but at the time learning to cope with being blind was largely about learning to give up my independence, something I was extremely, fiercely, reluctant to do. I know that's the wrong way to think about it: The training actually gives you much more independence than you would have otherwise. But I was at a point where I didn't see that.

See.

I didn't use that word as a pun, or even as an ironic note. The concepts of sight=knowledge, sight=understanding, sight=reality are so embedded in our everyday lives that it's impossible to use "neutral" words.

You see?

Even I use the word all the time, saying I "see" something when I don't mean that I am physically using my eyes. It's so embedded in our consciousness. Now I had to learn how to remove it, and still get on.

The rehab facility is part of a large facility in Augusta that features a wide range of programs and includes a rehab unit for active-duty soldiers, where I was admitted. The hospital, which has two campuses, does everything from treating heart attacks to counseling soldiers with PTSD. It also provides training for medical students from the Medical College of Georgia.

We got off to a bad start at the facility when there was no one at reception to process me when I came. The people who initially checked me in seemed far more interested in their own red tape than my specific needs. And it didn't help that the hotel Evelyn ended up having to stay at was frequented by drug addicts and hookers; I worried about her constantly. (Eventually, Evelyn was able to get a room at a nearby Fisher House, one of some sixty-five facilities around the country that provide temporary housing for military families whose loved ones are being treated at a nearby medical facility. The nonprofit organization doesn't charge the families for the rooms.)

Some of my complaints will seem petty, I'm sure. The gym designated for active service members had very old equipment, and not much of it. A lot of the staff weren't particularly enthusiastic when it came time to work with patients. The food was bland at best. Not one nurse checked on me the first night I was there, nor the next two.

But it wasn't just the staff. It bothered me that a lot of people in the ward didn't seem to be pushing themselves. They weren't making an effort to get past their wounds, at least not that I could tell. That wasn't my problem, of course, but it irked me.

After a few days, I was transferred to the blind rehab ward. I was surprised to find that most of the people in the program were not actually blind—not yet, anyway. The majority were losing their sight because of disease, diabetes especially, but could still see, at least to some degree.

Most were old, as well—there were a lot of World War II veterans. A lot didn't have families to help care for them, or push them. It was easy for them to beg out of the sessions, staying in bed instead and watching TV. I don't necessarily blame them, but it made for a less than invigorating environment.

The program had only eight beds. Because of that, there was a long waiting list to get in. With Evelyn staying nearby, I thought they would welcome the chance to open another slot if I gave up my bed at night and stayed with her. They eventually let me do that—it was harder than you'd imagine, even though the sessions were all during the day—but they kept my bed empty, rather than giving it to someone else on their list.

The programs were supposedly aimed at giving me daily skills for living—everything from doing the laundry to getting around on my own—and what were called manual skills. A number hit the mark. Others didn't.

Manual skills started with a lesson on how to make a belt. I have no idea what the purpose of that was supposed to be. Then I was supposed to put a clock together from a kit. Last time I checked, there wasn't much call for blind clockmakers, kits or no kits.

"I'm not going to do that," I told the instructor. "I want to learn woodworking and plumbing. And work on small engines. This way at least I can take care of small repairs around the house."

He ended up agreeing to give me a test to prove that I could deal with some of the basic skills those early projects supposedly covered. I aced the test and moved on. I learned how to put together a water faucet and fixed a toilet—call me if you have a leak.

I worked on electrics, doing some circuit-board work and putting a switch together. I'm not an electrician, but I do understand the principles, and can do more than change a lightbulb in a pinch.

How do I know if the lights are on? They hum, they give off heat—you train yourself to tell. I also have a device that will tell me whether it's dark, and another that can read colors.

There was a state-of-the-art woodshop at the facility. They weren't out to make me a carpenter, but I did get to work with the tools without taking off any of my other fingers.

"What do you want to build?" the instructor asked the first day.

"I love wine. I'd like to build a wine rack."

I built a huge one. It was nice enough that eventually I gave it to a friend.

Living skills were more immediately useful. Some things were easy to master. Some were hard. It didn't always work the way I expected.

Shaving was easy. Let's face it—a lot of us are half-asleep when we shave in the morning anyway. So I mastered it pretty quickly without cutting myself.

Walking on the street was a different story. Learning to do it safely by using a cane was an ordeal.

I couldn't just walk down the middle of the sidewalk, slashing my cane back and forth. I had to learn to tap my cane on the pavement in a specific pattern across the front of my body, left to right and right to left, listening for the sound of the taps, feeling for the edge of the sidewalk. I couldn't walk too fast—I had to walk to those taps, walk behind that touch. I had to learn to walk slowly and deliberately, squelching the natural hop in my step.

A speed walker has a certain rhythm to his body as he moves. Elbows, chest, legs, head: everything moves in a coordinated dance designed to get you ahead. Speed and endurance, those are your highest values. You don't think of obstacles on the track.

■■■

Walking as a blind man is very different, harder to learn. Speed is an enemy. Speed makes you miss things, distorts the sounds you need to focus on, dulls your sense of touch. Your pace becomes more deliberate, almost robotic. And no matter how much you push it, no matter how much *I* push it even now, as an experienced blind walker, I can never safely break into a trot, let alone a sprint, unless I have someone to guide me. So even the most independent person undertaking the simplest act of independence—walking—must always consider the possibility that he will need help, become dependent. Loud noise, a car horn, an unexpected crowd, or an inadvertent jostle: The smallest things loom large on the street when you're blind.

I don't always walk with a cane. Frankly, I prefer not to. Inside my house or in a familiar building, I use a different technique: hand railing. Basically that means I feel my way along a wall or rail with the back of my hand. In my house, of course, I'm familiar with everything along the way as I go from one room to another, but I can pick up quite a bit even in a new room. Staying in a hotel, the first thing I do in my room is check out the layout, working it into my head so that the place is familiar, or at least reasonably so.

The sessions with the cane were tedious and frustrating to the max. Using the cane inside in a controlled environment was one thing; outside was quite another. I'd walk along the sidewalk pretty well, then suddenly miss the turn and find myself on the grass—or the curb. Patience, never one of my virtues, came slowly and with great difficulty. It must have taken me six months, mostly on my own or with Evelyn, to really learn how to walk properly with the cane.

Uneven sidewalks are a bane to the blind; it's very easy to trip. Sidewalks aren't straight, aren't level. People put things on the sidewalk all the time—garbage cans, flowerpots, signs, you name it. The blind have to navigate around those. Other people walking think they have the right of way and don't get out of the way. Not used to dealing with blind people, they freeze or simply get in the way.

Driveways can be an adventure. Low-hanging branches can pick you off. But you're lucky to have sidewalks at all in many places.

The instructors also taught me Grade 1 Braille, a very basic system that keys patterns of raised dots to single words; it's a basic literacy scheme. On my own, I learned how to type—something I wasn't very good at to begin with, and still can't exactly brag about, even with dots pasted on the keyboard to guide my fingers. I did much better with a screen reader, which reads the computer screen.

The man who taught me computer skills was a guru—and blind himself. Not for nothing, he was probably one of the best instructors there.

No matter what else was going on, the best parts of every day were my workouts. I was still in terrible shape, but I managed about thirty minutes of cardio every day, along with stretching and some very light PT, including push-ups and sit-ups.

Then I graduated to machines. The first time I got on a treadmill, I piled pillows around the machine and tied large elastic bands to my waist to help keep me centered on the runway.

It was horrible. The best thing I can say is that I didn't fall.

I got rid of the pillows and bands, eventually. I ran as well as I could, one hand on the machine, slowly at first—v-e-r-y slowly.

There was an elliptical, the machine that works your arms as well as your legs, a bit like cross-country skiing. That was actually easier to use in a way, since there was no chance of drifting off the treads.

The other patients probably shook their heads watching me, but I kept at it. There was an all-in-one weight machine in the gym; you know, the jack of all trades, master of none type. I made do, gradually increasing resistance.

The physical progress I was making was encouraging. But if I was going to run the Marine Corps Marathon, there was one thing I absolutely had to do:

Run.

How exactly do you do that when you're blind?

Damned if I knew.

I returned home for Christmas and New Year's. I spent weeks after the holidays going back and forth to Bethesda for a series of tests and surgeries—to be honest, I don't even remember which procedures they were, let alone the order. Maybe one was on my knee, maybe one was to remove calcification on my arm (a byproduct of the stress of recuperating from my wounds). Maybe another replaced my ulnar nerve. Maybe the doctors did something to fix my nose or my cheek. Or to check on the embolism. I was getting so many operations and procedures, they blurred together.

I was back at Bethesda, both as an outpatient and an inpatient, for a month and a half, maybe a little more. At some point, I asked one of my doctors if I'd be done with all my surgeries by the end of the year.

"Ivan, this is something you can't dictate," he told me flat out. "You don't have control over how your body is going to heal."

That sucked. I wanted to put a close to that chapter of my life. But there was no easy closing. Even today, I still occasionally have to get procedures, though they're minor by comparison.

What kept me sane were my workouts. They were my job

and my passion. When I finally got back to North Carolina, my mother-in-law took me every day to the gym. She got to the point where she knew every machine I needed and could steer me through the two- or three-hour workouts.

I was there so much even the maintenance guys knew me.

Looking for a way to get more leg work in without putting too much stress on my knees, I started taking a spin class with Furman Hammonds at the Pope fitness center. One day, Furman asked if I'd be interested in riding on a tandem bike.

"Hell yes! Let's do it."

Furman arranged for Bob Miarer, an older guy who belonged to a local bike club, to take me out for a spin in his tandem. I was hooked within a block. I'm sure I got Bob a little worried when, after a few minutes, I told him we should go faster.

We did.

"You're burning it, man," he told me.

We started riding regularly. He had an older tandem cruiser with wide tires and a heavy frame. We changed the tires, got new handlebars, and made some other adjustments, but eventually decided we needed something lighter, a bit faster with narrow tires but built for long distances and serious riding. An organization called Operation One Voice supplied me with a Trek touring tandem through their Wounded Warrior Bike Rehab & Fitness Program. (In their own words, Operation One Voice is a program designed by police officers, firefighters and community leaders to raise funds to help support the immediate needs of children and families of wounded and fallen Special Operations forces.) The bike has taken me many, many miles.

15

Where There's a Will, There's a Way

But how to run?

Today, there are a decent number of us blind runners, hopefully providing a range of examples and how-to tips. But back then, if there were other blind guys running, I didn't know about them.

Realizing that I couldn't just start out on a city street, I figured a track would make the most sense as a starting point—there's a pretty set pattern, after all, and while there are often other runners around, there are no cars or even bikes to get in your way.

I also knew that I would need a guide. But I had no practical idea of where to get one, or how to run with one. It happened that another SF soldier, Matt Johnson, was trying to come back from some leg injuries and was gradually working himself into shape at the same gym. I knew Matt; he had taken over as captain of the A team where I'd served before becoming an officer. It seemed to me that we were a good match because of our backgrounds and our common need to rehab.

I have no idea what Matt thought of that. Probably he thought

I was a little crazy—but then, being another Special Forces guy, I'm sure he understood the drive to succeed at the most difficult task. Anyway, somehow I talked him into running with me. We met one early evening in the gym lobby near the track at Pope Air Force Base (now part of Bragg). It was close to five o'clock but still pretty hot when we walked out onto the track.

I knew we needed some sort of tether to keep us close. A rope? A rubber band? Maybe one of those resistance bands used in rehab?

It was Matt's idea to use a shoestring. It sounds a little goofy in retrospect, but it actually solved a pair of problems. A shoestring meant we would have to be relatively close to each other as we ran. It was light and easy to hold, which meant it was also easy to let go of. There was no question of one of us pulling the other down. Think of being pulled by a rope tied to your belt and you see the potential for trouble.

But that's not to say that the shoestring turned us into a synchronized pair of runners. We started out haltingly, and things got worse from there. It was comical.

Now it's comical. *Then* it was painful.

Figuratively for me, literally for him. I was all over the place, bumping into him, losing my balance. Matt's legs were still pretty messed up and every step hurt—and would have hurt even without the added pressure of keeping me upright and on the track. I think we managed one whole circuit—four hundred meters or about a quarter mile—before stopping. If you told me it was less, I wouldn't be surprised.

Matt's beat-up leg was exhausted, but his brain was revving.

"We should tie the shoestring in a loop," he said. "It'll be easier to keep it taut."

We gave that a shot, walking rather than running the second time around the track. Tying the shoestring into a loop gave us about sixteen inches of clearance, which surprisingly turned out to be perfect.

Ideally, when my guide and I hit our stride, we look like contestants in a three-legged race, coordinating our inner legs and arms as we moved. It's a lot trickier than it may sound. The guide has to match my pace but can't let me pull him off course. I have to match his pace and pull just enough so that the shoelace is taut, not tight.

It's a Zen thing, I guess.

Matt was exhausted at the end of the lap, but I knew the concept would work. A simple shoelace, relatively long, ends tied to form a loop, became the answer to my prayers.

The "blind running device" remains a mandatory part of my running equipment. There are two versions: BRD-Whiskey—Blind Running Device, white, and BRD-Bravo—black.

Matt turned out to be too injured to run with me again. But I found a true training partner in a young woman named Lynn Salgado who was in my spin class. Lynn, in her early thirties, noticed one day that I was training pretty hard and asked why.

"Because I want to run in the Marine Corps Marathon," I told her.

"Really?"

"Yeah."

"I've run marathons," she told me. "Would you like to train with me?"

Would I!

We started working out together. Slow and easy at first, then faster and faster. I'm so grateful to her, and Matt, for taking time out of their own lives to run with me. Without them I never would have been able to go on.

■ ■ ■

My guys had come back from the deployment where I'd been injured, but had barely gotten through the holidays when they were assigned to go back, part of the leading edge of the "Surge," the 2007 increase in troops and change in strategy meant to help bring some stability to the country.

I had no idea of what was going on—though still on the 82nd's active rolls, I was way out of the command loop, and even gossip rarely reached me—until one day I was working in the gym at

Pope when someone mentioned that my scout platoon was over at Green Ramp, a short distance away.

I quickly grabbed my things and had my mother-in-law drive me over there so I could see them off. It was the first time I'd been with the whole platoon since the attack. I'm not sure how they took it—were they happy to see me, glad that I had made it through? Or did I remind them of how dangerous it was there, of what might happen to them over the next few weeks and months?

Maybe a little of both.

There was a bit of grousing among the guys about having to go back so early. It struck me the wrong way.

"Don't feel sorry for yourselves," I told them. "You signed up for this. Feel sorry for your families, your wives, your kids. They didn't volunteer. You have a job to do, one that needs to be done."

It was a kick in the pants, I guess, but no more than the kick I gave myself every day. Tough love.

"You're in my thoughts and prayers," I added, smiling and patting backs, shaking hands. Then I left; it wasn't my time to be there.

I put off going back to blind school, even though I was still due more classes and rehab. There were so many operations that it wouldn't have made sense to break up the sessions. What I did do, though, consistently, was work out. I ran with Lynn. I trained in the gym. Every day, without fail. It was my fix; I was an exercise fiend.

I grew stronger physically and mentally as winter turned to spring, and spring gave way to summer. Don't let me mislead you. I didn't begin to *like* being blind. I didn't really *accept* it either. What I did was focus on pushing myself, focus on being who I was, blind or not. It was and is a strange mix of independence, of will, and surrender to the need for help. My wife, my mother-in-law, my friends—each was a source of strength.

And, at times, resentment. I didn't resent them at all—I resented having to depend on them. I resented my injury. If I took it out on them at times, and I'm sure I must have, with crankiness and anger they didn't deserve, I do deeply apologize.

In May, a ceremony was held to honor soldiers who had died on missions connected with special operations. Justin and Ralph's names were to be inscribed on that wall; I was invited to help honor them.

It was a difficult day. There are a lot of names on that wall, and I knew more than just those two.

Evelyn and I arrived early that evening. The minute we parked, an officer came to walk us to the pavilion where the ceremony was to be held.

"Ivan," he said, surprised. "I served with you in 7th Group."

He had been an SF team leader some years before, just randomly assigned to escort me. We walked to the building, where another officer met us—he, too, was someone I'd served with.

I found out later he choked up when he first saw me, and had to take a moment to shake it off. I don't blame him—and I never realized it then; he was too professional to let on.

I don't want people to be sad because I've been injured. Worse, I don't want them to pity me. From my perspective, I'm lucky: Things could have been a lot worse, as Evelyn pointed out that day in the Bethesda ward.

I want people to be happy around me, and treat me normal. Not easy, I know, if they focus on my injury rather than the rest of who I am.

Walking up to our chairs in front of the memorial, I joked and tried to put my escorts at ease. Evelyn and I had seats near the center. I sat, waiting patiently to be called on. My role was simple: I had only to say the names of my brothers who died next to me:

Pfc. Justin W. Dreese. Died September 2, 2006
Serving During Operation Iraqi Freedom

Army Sgt. Ralph N. Porras. Died September 2, 2006
Serving During Operation Iraqi Freedom

Afterward, we went inside and had some beers. Lieutenant General Stanley McChrystal, commander of the Joint Operations Special Command, came by and shook my hand. We stayed a while, talking. Finally, tired, I went home, worn down not so much by the day but everything that had led to it.

■ ■ ■

That summer I faced a milestone that would have been bittersweet even if I'd never been injured—my fortieth birthday.

Numbers are just numbers, age is all in the mind—no matter what cliché you use as a defense, we all calculate our lives by numeric milestones, arbitrary and otherwise. Looking forward and looking back, we have signposts that give us meaning as well as track time, tick marks noting our journey through the world.

Looking forward is always different than looking back; expectations are always more arbitrary than real life. From the vantage of my thirties, forty always seemed like it would be a significant achievement and a passage, a time for planning ahead, maybe starting to think about life after the army, and certainly a point for planning a family of our own.

Forty turned out to be a remarkable achievement, but for none of the reasons I thought when I was thirty or thirty-five. The very fact that I was alive to notch that mark was remarkable.

I wanted a party. For years I'd told Evelyn I was going to plan a huge bash with seventies music—I just love funk, say what you will about disco. But as the day approached, everything felt out of synch. A big party didn't necessarily feel right. Then as I called people asking if they'd get together with me all I heard were apologies. It was a weekend, and everyone was going out of town or had some impossible relative coming or had to go to some wedding or, I don't know—they were all legitimate excuses.

"Don't worry," said Evelyn. "We'll celebrate ourselves, just you and me. It'll be low key."

All right. Damn.

I worked out that morning, got changed, and then Evelyn and I headed out to get some lunch.

By that time I'd gotten to the point where I could tell where I was when we were driving, as long as we were in a familiar area. Maybe it's an innate sense of direction, or the orienting and land navigation courses I took as a soldier. Maybe when you're blind you pay more attention to your surroundings, picking up whatever odd clues you can, desperate to institute some control on the world, or at least render it less chaotic.

Whatever. I usually know where I am and where I'm going if I'm being driven in the area around my home and Fort Bragg.

But I have to give Evelyn a lot of credit, because that day she managed to distract me to the point that I didn't know where I was. Between small talk and errands and turns and different things, I lost track.

"Where we going?" I finally asked. "It seems to be taking a long time."

"Oh, it's a special place."

Evelyn parked and we got out. Two steps later, we were at the front door.

"How'd you manage this?" I asked. "You have us parked at the front door?"

"I got lucky."

"Not in a handicapped space." I hate parking in those spots.

"No. Just luck."

I pulled open the door and took a step inside.

"Surprise!" yelled about a hundred of my friends.

They got me. Evelyn got me. She had rented a nightclub in town. Disco music blared from the speakers. The whole place was decorated in 1970s style. People were wearing bell-bottoms, platform shoes and flowered shirts with huge thick lapels.

Evelyn had purchased a John Travolta–style suit for me, and naturally I was commanded to change immediately and join the party. I danced for hours. I've never partied so well. All of these people had seen me at my worst, had held my hand and prayed. Now, they shook my hand in celebration.

It was a true milestone. And a good one.

16

Mission imPossible: Staying In

I was still assigned to the 82nd Airborne, but I had little contact with the division, let alone command, during those months. Every so often, people would pop their head in quickly, ask if everything was going OK, then head off.

I'm guessing that they felt they had to focus primarily on their mission, and had enough to do worrying about the guys who could help fulfill that mission. They didn't need a blind, bedridden paratrooper. Even when I was up and walking around, from their point of view I was of little use. I hadn't been in the unit long enough to make deep connections when I got injured.

As far as I remember, to that point my battalion commander—the guy who put me on that roof—never visited, never sent a letter, never stopped by to see how I was.

Avoiding me? I can't speak for him.

The division probably assumed that, like just about every other soldier severely injured in combat, I was headed out of the army. Typically, severely injured soldiers stay on the rolls while receiving treatment; then, once they have gotten to the point where they're stable and don't need operation after operation, they are given a medical discharge. The procedure is a lot more complicated and bureaucratic than I'm describing here, but the end result is the same—the wounded are let go.

With the first phases of my recovery now more or less over, I was rapidly reaching the point where, under "normal" circumstances, I would have been discharged. But I had no intention of leaving the army.

In the meantime, the Marine Corps Marathon was coming up in October. While I'd run with Lynn on roads around the base, I had not run in an actual race. I decided I needed some sort of competitive event before taking on the marathon. I settled on the Army Ten-Miler in Washington, D.C. It was an army event, there would be other wounded there, and I was comfortable with the Washington area, especially the Navy Lodge where I arranged to stay. Running in the same area where the marathon would be was a plus.

Lynn couldn't come, so I needed a guide. I called Phil Young, a friend of mine who had been my A Team leader and was now based in the Washington, D.C. area. He was also an excellent runner, far more accomplished than I had ever been.

I called and asked, "Would you take a chance and run with me?"

"Hell, yes!" he answered. "Let's do it!"

Evelyn, her mom, and I went up a few days ahead so I could do a practice run with Phil. The early arrival also gave me a chance to visit the wards at Bethesda and Walter Reed. I had started to reach out to other wounded soldiers, blinded ones especially, sharing a bit of my story and what you might call "blind lore"—everyday things that matter to people without sight, like talking watches. It was a little like being a member of a new club, even though it wasn't one I'd ever wanted to join.

Phil and I did a training run in the parking lot of the Pentagon; we progressed to a longer run around the Potomac on the nearby trail, getting used to each other's pace and the intricacies of the BRD, or blind running device, aka, shoestring.

After one of the sessions, I went to Walter Reed and visited with some guys who had lost their legs in the war. At some point, one of them mentioned that he was part of a group that was going to run in the race, too, and suggested I join them. They called themselves "Missing Parts in Action," and they were both organized and serious about running. I said I'd love to run with them, if they'd have me.

The next day I got a phone call from someone at the local ABC television news affiliate, asking if I'd agree to be interviewed.

Why not?

A reporter came by the next day and asked a few questions. If I recall correctly, *Are you crazy?* was not among them; probably the correspondent was too polite. It was never very clear to me how ABC found out I was running in the first place; to be honest, I didn't ask. I was too focused on getting ready for the race.

The morning of the race, Evelyn, her mom, and I went to Walter Reed, planning to board a bus with Missing Parts and ride to the race. When we got there, we found a dozen or more guys with prosthetic legs standing around in sweats and running gear, waiting—the bus had somehow gotten lost. After milling around a bit, most of us decided to make our own way to the starting point a few miles away.

It was a madhouse when we got there. Evelyn twisted through the traffic to drop me off near the start line. Her mom helped me find Phil while Evelyn parked the car. Shucking off nervousness, I stretched and loosened up, walked, got ready, stretched again, and waited.

We were just about to line up when familiar arms wrapped themselves around me. Evelyn had run all the way from the car to give me a kiss and wish me luck for the run.

I hadn't realized how much the race meant to her as well as me. In a lot of ways it was her achievement as much as mine: She'd nursed me and pushed me and carried me here, leading me out of the darkness of my depression into this brave if hard new world. Without her I would have been dead by now.

Instead, I was running.

"Ready?" asked Phil.

Bang!

I didn't even get a chance to answer. We were off.

Literally thousands of people, men and women, run in that race; it attracts upwards of thirty-five thousand contestants, along with several times that number of spectators, helpers, and race officials. The start is a stampede of footsteps, rubber soles hitting the pavement, arms flailing or windmilling in time.

Phil and I quickly fell into a good, steady pace. The run felt a lot like our training sessions, just longer. Our time was a hair under eighty-seven minutes.

If you break that down, that's eight and a half minutes per mile, for ten miles. Not a world-record time—for my age a good showing would be under an hour—but phenomenal for a blind guy who hadn't run since college. (I knocked ten minutes off the next year. Yes, I am a bit proud of that.)

Crossing the finish line was an incredible achievement, but it wasn't a moment with fireworks or loud bands. To me, it was a warm-up to the marathon, another step along the path.

What happened next, though . . . that was special.

Reporters swarmed me at the finish line. They couldn't believe I'd done it. They couldn't believe that some thirteen months before I'd been blown apart on a roof in Iraq, humped to a medivac chopper, flown to Walter Reed, and then taken to Bethesda, more dead than alive.

But I had done it. I had. And that fact was about to change my life, almost as radically as the mortar shell had.

■ ■ ■

The evening after I ran, Evelyn and I were lying in bed at the Navy Lodge, watching one of my favorite news programs, *ABC World News* with Charlie Gibson.

The show was wrapping up. It got to the last segment—and all of a sudden, they were interviewing me out near the Pentagon, right after the race.

"I'm on *ABC World News!*" I shouted.

I liked the show before. I loved the show now! The next day, I was swamped with calls from reporters.

I wasn't expecting the media storm that followed that race. Up to that point I had no idea that anyone would care. Being hurt in a war is not a news story. Being blind doesn't get you on the news. Struggling to climb out of a hospital bed and live a normal life isn't exactly front-page stuff.

But, here I was. *Stars and Stripes* did a story. The local newspaper did a story. Wire services did stories. My head could have blown up. My ego certainly might have.

They didn't—or at least I don't think they did; that may be for others to judge—because I had another race—the Marine Corps Marathon, coming up in two weeks. That race, longer and far more demanding than the Ten-Miler, was my obsession. I'd say "focus" but that's too weak a word for the amount of mental and emotional real estate it occupied.

I had been aiming for the marathon for an entire year. It's said you can feel some things in your bones; this I felt in every strained ligament, in every bruised muscle in my body. I was not only going to run that marathon; I was going to kill it.

Figuratively, of course.

There were suddenly a lot of distractions. A few days after I returned to North Carolina, George Mannes from *Money* magazine got ahold of me. His angle wasn't the race, exactly, though that may have brought me to his attention. His focus was much more serious—he wanted to write about the financial hardships that families face when a soldier is injured in war.

It was a hard decision to make. To do the story, we had to divulge all of our finances—our mortgages, our car loans, our savings accounts, budgets, everything. But the cause convinced us to do it.

People don't realize that soldiers don't make lots of cash. As a first lieutenant with considerable experience before the injury, I was making roughly $70,000; Evelyn had gone back to work and made in the area of $40,000. Together that was not a bad income, but even so we lived paycheck to paycheck, like most service families. If you're in that situation and one of you gets hurt, disability won't make up the difference. (In my case, it would have been only about a third of my original pay.) And many wives of injured soldiers find they have to quit their jobs to care for their husbands—Evelyn had to do that, and even with her mom around and no kids to raise, it was incredibly draining.

If you're in a situation where you have a lot of debt, the situation is even more pressing. Parents, siblings help out—so one injury affects maybe half a dozen families.

There are payments, including life insurance. But, first of all you only get that money if you have a very severe injury. Lump sum payments—I believe I got a $100,000 insurance payment to cover my injury—are one-time only. Whatever doesn't go to immediate bills, or to help you set up your house, car, or whatever to immediately deal with your injury, has to be invested wisely—you're not getting another payment. And you have to somehow budget and plan to cover a lifetime of diminished income as well as diminished abilities.

George happened to be a marathon runner. He decided that, besides interviewing me at home, he would run with me and interview me while I was running.

OK. Why not?

Lynn Salgado, who'd been training with me since the winter, invited a friend of hers to run with us. So we had a little group when we joined the start line at the Pentagon on October 28, 2007. (Unfortunately, I've forgotten the friend's name, as well as those of some of the others who were wishing us well that morning.)

The gun sounded. Lynn and I took off running. I was pumped with adrenaline and over-caffeinated with excitement, so much so that I didn't keep my pace; I just felt strong and ran. I realize now that was a mistake—I started out too fast. It was a beginner's mistake, and I was definitely a beginner.

Lynn and I ran hard up Route 110, climbing to Rosslyn and Lee Highway, turned on Sprout, hit the George Washington Parkway. We headed downhill through crowds, yelling and clapping and cheering us on, all through Georgetown.

Somewhere around mile ten, in the vicinity of the Lincoln Memorial, Lynn told me she had to go to the bathroom.

"OK," I said.

She handed me off to her friend and ran up ahead, aiming for one of the porta-potties stationed along the race route in D.C. We kept our pace, figuring that we would meet her as soon as she was done. But when we got there, a sea of people surrounded the relief area, and we couldn't find her. After a few moments' pause, we decided to keep going, with a little slack in our stride, hoping she would catch up.

We reached the next set of porta-potties. I took a break myself, then looked for Lynn, but still couldn't find her. There were crowds of people, cowbells sounding, music from bands—it was a madhouse.

We started running again. We reached another set of porta-potties without finding her.

"I guess you're it," I told the friend, and we set off again.

We ran steadily until roughly the twenty-mile mark. Now it was her friend who had to hit the restroom. George took the BRD and she took off ahead, running to the next porta-potty spot after promising to meet us.

Naturally, we didn't see her when we got there.

I called her name. Nothing.

"Well, George," I said finally, "not only are you going to do an interview, but you're going to take me to the finish line. Let's go."

George and I took off, passing over the Potomac. The crowds got louder and louder as we went. My energy surged. We dropped the hammer and nailed those last four or five miles. The end was an uphill climb but I was only feeling power, breathing good, legs strong as we looped toward the finish line at the Marine Corps Monument. I cruised near the graves of our war heroes at Arlington National Cemetery as we came to the end, marking some 26.2 miles in 4:14.11, or just under four hours and fifteen minutes.

You don't stop when you cross the finish line. You've been running for hours, and your legs and body need to wind down slowly. The organizers also want you to get out of the way of the people behind you. George and I each grabbed a banana and some orange juice, walking off the exertion until we found a place near the statue of Iwo Jima to get our photos taken.

Sometime later, we met Lynn and her friend there. Both had gotten sick along the way—maybe because I'd pushed them too hard in the beginning—but both had finished.

Everything that came out of that race was positive—with one exception. Unfortunately, when I was interviewed immediately after the race, some of my comments made it sound as if Lynn and her friend had dropped out. Because she wasn't right there when the reporters caught up to me, I don't think she's ever gotten the credit she deserves. If it weren't for her—and her friend, who selflessly volunteered to guide me through the middle of the race—I never would have finished. Actually, without such a great training partner, I might never have been able to compete in the first place.

■ ■ ■

There had been a lot of media after the Army Ten-Miler. There was even more—a lot more—after I finished the Marine Corps Marathon. I'm not sure that I was the first completely blind runner to run in the event—there certainly were people with limited sight who had run before—but I was definitely considered a novelty because of my wounds and service.

I decided that I was going to use the publicity and attention to deliver my message: *No matter what life throws at you, no matter what obstacles or adversity you face, make the best out of it.*

It's become my mantra ever since. I don't ever say it's easy, or even that you have to smile through it. A lot of times, you can't smile. Even frowning is an effort. But you can push your-self. You can still achieve.

You can still be who you are. You can still help others. In-spire them, maybe; push them, maybe.

Whatever. You can still keep going. Give one hundred percent.

It was a message my parents had given me. It was a message the military had given me.

It was who I was.

17

Running (Blind) Man

Running suddenly became who I was: the blind marathoner.

Running was many things—exercise, a way of pushing myself, a way of explaining that blindness wasn't the end of the world. From the media's perspective, it was a message: *You can achieve anything if you try.* The message itself was an old one, but here was a new package for it, a new spin: Blind Guy Running Marathons. It made me a little famous—even emphasizing "a little"—a term I was and am uncomfortable with, even if it is a fact.

I hadn't started running to get that message out. And while I was aware of all those things, I was still running primarily because I loved it. I loved the way my body felt as I pushed myself. I loved having a physical goal: Finish the race. It was something that tested me and gave me meaning—not to mention sores and the occasional bruise. But if the media was going to stick a camera in my face, I'd make the most of it.

I was blessed that I was given another chance to live when Justin and Ralph had been taken. I was running for them, too.

After the rush of news reports came offers to run in other

races. There were requests for me to speak, and even offers of support—people wanted to help me in my recovery. A few days after the race, a member of Operation One Voice in Duluth, Georgia, contacted me, asking if there was anything they could do to help me.

"I'd love a tandem bike," I said.

Done. And by the way, would you like to participate in a relay bike race from Duluth down to SOCOM headquarters in Tampa, Florida?

"Sure," I told them. Bob Miarer, the buddy of mine who had first introduced me to tandem biking, rode with me, all the way down to MacDill Air Force Base. It happened that Admiral Olson, the head of SOCOM and a former Navy SEAL, was standing nearby when we were congratulated and interviewed by the media. They asked what was next; I told them I wasn't sure. Maybe I'd try running in the Boston Marathon someday.

Admiral Olson had been with Sharon Henderson when she met me in the hospital and arranged to help me see specialists for my eyes. I didn't remember any of that, and I certainly didn't think that one of the country's most important officers, the boss of the military's special operations troops, had the time or inclination to pay even the slightest attention to me.

But . . .

A few weeks later, my home phone rang.

Evelyn checked the number. "It's Florida," she said, with the sort of tone that meant, *Who would call you from Florida?*

She answered. An Eric Olson was on the line. *Admiral* Eric Olson.

"Admiral Olson?" Evelyn turned to me, unsure why a navy guy would be calling me.

I took the phone.

"I overheard you talking about the Boston Marathon," he told me. "I was wondering if I could run with you."

I made a joke out of it, turning to Evelyn and asking her permission. But my answer wasn't "yes"; it was "hell, yes."

"We'll run Boston," said the admiral. "I'll get two tickets."

My sudden status as a "celebrity" had no impact on my status at the 82nd, or my hopes to stay on there instead of being discharged. Which is not to say they didn't take notice.

At first, the reaction was uniformly positive. I suddenly got a lot of feedback from leadership—the upper brass and officers in charge of the division—indicating they approved of what I was doing. That was good; I'd been largely ignored before.

"He's showing resilience," they'd say, either to the media or to other soldiers. "It's inspiring. . . ."

I guess it's important to mention that my running in the marathon and even in the Army Ten-Miler were not part of my job; the Army didn't order me to take part in those races, and officially my being in those races didn't and shouldn't have made any difference on my standing in the unit. I was certainly a good example to others, and hopefully my actions reflected well on the army. I am honored to think that other soldiers saw me and realized that I was able to achieve what I did at least in part because of the standards the military taught me. I hope that I embodied not only the highest values of the army, but also reminded civilians that others in the service have those values as well.

Great things. But not reasons to keep me in the division, or even in the army.

Nor was the fact that I was now famous, or infamous, or at least a little better known than I had been before. Fame and notoriety are fickle things, not standards to be admired and upheld. And not excuses to keep me on active duty.

Fame or notoriety had nothing to do with my own desires either. I didn't want to stay in the army because people knew who I was, or even because people might look at me and realize how great an institution the U.S. Army is. I wanted to stay because I could contribute to the service. Even as a blind man.

Keeping a job in civilian life after a major injury can be very difficult. Keeping it when you're blind can be a hundred times more difficult.

A blind man in the army?

At the time, at least, it seemed to be an impossible mission.

The military is surprisingly open to many things . . . but blind soldiers is not one of them. As far as I knew at the time, there were no other blind men serving.

But I had always chosen to do difficult things. My entire career was based on that. This was just one more.

Be a Ranger. Be a Green Beret. Be a blind soldier.

I was realistic. My days as a combat soldier were over. I was not going to get a chance to lead a Special Forces ODA. That part of my life and that dream were now over.

But the army is a big place. There are a lot of jobs to be done, jobs that don't require the ability to see.

Like what?

Arranging support for units when they are deployed. A lot of that involves knowing what needs to be done, and who to talk to, who to e-mail, to get it done.

Recruitment. Mentoring soldiers. Handling the dozens of small details that need to be looked after to support a unit in the field.

I didn't want special treatment because I was blind. What I wanted was a chance to prove that I could contribute. If I couldn't hack it, then I would go home. Not necessarily happy, but at least satisfied that I had been treated fairly and had tried my hardest.

I put out feelers, but got nothing back in return.

There was also a selfish element in my desire to stay, I have to admit. I loved being a soldier, and I didn't want that part of my life to end. I wasn't ready to give up the institution I had been a member of for more than twenty years. There was a certain comfort level with the army. It was my home.

It was Evelyn's as well, as a spouse and a civilian. In January, she heard that Womack Army Medical Center at Bragg was opening a brain-trauma unit and needed civilian speech therapists. It was a perfect match for her—not only did she have the speech skills, but she knew quite a lot about the medical side of dealing with injuries and the military procedures related to treatment.

But the real question was me: Was *I* ready for her to go back to work?

Evelyn wasn't just my wife and lover by that point. She was a critical caregiver, and my eyes. I relied on her, and her mom, incredibly. Her going back to work would change that. With her not at my side, I'd have to be more independent, and maybe more creative.

We talked about it a lot. It was definitely time for her to go back to work, and not just because of family finances. She had always been an independent woman and a high achiever. Devoting 24/7 as my caregiver, as noble as that was, meant giving up an important part of herself—a part that I loved deeply. And without that part, she would never be whole.

So I told her to take the job. She was reluctant but excited at the same time; it was a good opportunity and it was also clear that I had reached a stage where I didn't need as much care from her.

The first real test for me was, ironically, blind school, which I returned to roughly around the time Evelyn went to work. I arrived a lot savvier than the year before. This time I made sure my orders allowed me to stay outside of the Augusta hospital ward. A friend of mine at the local army base arranged for transportation to make sure I could get around. And I think I moved through the program with a lot more confidence than I had during the first few weeks.

Every morning, I trained for Boston, not only with roadwork but also in the gym with various weight machines.

I was in rehab when the 82nd finally decided I had to leave my platoon and go to the WTU—the Warrior Transition Unit. It was a huge blow; it meant I was being kicked out of the army.

The title may sound impressive, but don't let that fool you. WTU was basically a dumping ground for soldiers who were to be medically discharged. The *concept* was good—if you got hurt, you would be assigned to WTU, recover, then be transferred back to your unit or, if very bad off, be given a medical discharge. It let your original unit replace you on the rolls, an important consideration for them, just as it would be in the civilian world.

But what ended up happening over time was that medical discharges became *the* overwhelming option. Actually, non-option. While recent official statistics claim that today 45 percent of soldiers in WTUs "return to force," my perception when I was faced with the transfer was that no one ever returned to regular army duty.

Maybe that perception was unfair, but that's the way I saw it. And let me assure you, I was far from alone in thinking it was a one-way ticket out of the service.

The process for leaving the military with an injury can be a little baffling to civilians, and certainly has its share of red tape. But basically, your case is reviewed by a medical board, which evaluates the severity of your injuries and then makes a recommendation about whether you should be discharged or kept on active duty. Technically, the board only recommends; army commanders make the final decision. But the board's recommendation is almost always followed. While it can be appealed, it is not easy to win an appeal, especially when you are trying to prove that you should stay in the army.

The medical review generally happens in the WTU. But while you're waiting for it to take place, you have no work assignment, and little incentive to do anything at all. Worse, there was no one there to go to bat for you if the review said you should leave when you want to stay. And the attitude among other units, where you might try to transfer after being put in WTU, was "Oh, you were in WTU, so you don't belong here." In civilian terms, it was a résumé killer.

Looking back, I can understand the 82nd's point of view—a little. I was on their roster as a platoon lieutenant but in no position to actually do that job. They needed to move me so they could fill that position. And since I wasn't really on command's radar, they didn't exert any effort finding me something to do elsewhere.

Desperate, I called the one command where I was on the radar: SOCOM. I told everyone who'd listen I wanted to stay.

"I don't care what I do, I just want to stay on active duty," I said. "Office work—I'm sure there's something for me to do. You can't tell me that because I'm blind, there's nothing I can do."

SOCOM has a special program called the Care Coalition, which is dedicated to helping SOF soldiers and families. They immediately started helping, reaching out to SOCOM command and Admiral Olson himself, trying to get support.

The admiral became my greatest champion. "Anything, anywhere," he wrote in an e-mail showing his approval.

Buoyed, I contacted Special Forces 7th Group and tried to get a spot on a B Team.

That was a bit too far. B Teams are considered combat units since they deploy in support of A Teams, and no one was eager to see a blind guy in combat.

But I got word back that there might be possibilities at group level, working in units that support the group as a whole.

"Anything," I told them. *"Anything."*

The Care Coalition began canvassing commanders who had or would have slots to fill. I was in a new race, one that I had no control over: a race to find a job before the army bureaucracy slapped me into the WTU.

This race, though, had to be run by someone else. I could fret all I wanted, I could make phone calls and cajole, even beg, but none of that would yield a position. It was really the Care Coalition that I had to count on—and even with a powerful ally like the admiral, there was no guarantee.

I did the only thing I could do—I kept running.

I had done well at the Marine Corps Marathon, but the Boston Marathon felt like a whole different level. It's the oldest marathon in the U.S. and by far the most prestigious. At least a half million people line the streets to watch the event, and the results are broadcast around the world. I wasn't intimidated by all that, nor by the fact that I'd be running with a four-star admiral, but I wanted to make sure I was in good shape for it. So I

decided that I would run another marathon beforehand, and settled on the Bataan Death March as a warm-up for Boston.

Warm-up, literally. The Bataan is held in the White Sands Desert of New Mexico. Besides the weather, there are a number of
other difficult features, including a stretch called "the sandpit,"
which has loose sand and is very difficult to run through.

The race honors the survivors of World War II's Bataan Death
March, a forced march across the Philippines from Bataan in the
spring of 1942. Having routed American and Filipino troops at
Bataan, the Japanese forced the prisoners of war to walk some
sixty miles to their internment and labor camp. It is estimated
that over ten thousand men, primarily Filipino but including
at least one hundred Americans, died during the march; many,
many others died in the days immediately following it. Conditions were so awful that the men responsible for ordering the
march were prosecuted as war criminals. Survivors of the
march are often present at the race to tell participants about
their ordeal.

I enlisted Chet Graylock, an army friend of mine, to run the
race with me. I'd known Chet since my days with LRS, and we
fell into an easy rhythm from our first practice session. I think
we ran the race in about five hours, an excellent time given the
conditions. The race has some strong uphill climbs, with the el-
evation topping out at some 1,650 meters. I must have had five
pounds of sand in my shoes within the first fifty meters. I learned
my lesson: If I ever run in that terrain again, I'll wear gaiters over
my shoes to keep the sand out.

On the other hand, the sand acted like sandpaper. My cal-
luses were gone by the time I finished; it was like getting a pedi-
cure.

I was still very much a novice at Bataan. I didn't have a
recovery routine beyond popping a few Motrin. And I was still
working out what sort of gear to wear. I know now that the right
shoes, socks, and body glides are all important—and personal
choices. Reducing chafing and blisters helps guarantee good
times and quick recoveries. Unfortunately, finding out what

was right for me was a long process of trial and error, and I had the sore muscles to prove it after that race.

■ ■ ■

My military achievements as well as time in service as an offi-cer qualified me for a promotion to captain, and in the spring of 2008 I was notified that I would be awarded the rank. (Techni-cally, this had nothing to do with my staying in the army, though having the support of the command to get the promotion in the first place would actually help, at least psychologically.) Typically, officers receive their captain's bars at a ceremony where the in-signia is "pinned on." By custom, the new captain can choose the person pinning on the bars; most officers select someone who has been supportive and has special meaning to them. Often that's a family member or a service mentor.

When the person in charge of arranging the promotion cere-mony asked, I thought of Admiral Olson. He'd been very support-ive and was going to run Boston with me. So I suggested him.

I have to confess, I thought we were talking about something very small and informal—in his office, maybe. I'd walk in, get the bars pinned on, and walk out. In my experience, that was how it was done: I really didn't have much experience with four-star officers.

"Admiral Olson would be happy to participate," came the reply. "He'll fly up to Bragg to pin on the bars."

The admiral also intended on visiting JSOC and the rest of his units there and doing a training run with me so we knew what to expect at the Boston Marathon.

OK.

Even so, I didn't realize what a to-do I had caused until I got a call from the U.S. Special Operations Command's protocol of-fice that went something like this:

PROTOCOL: The admiral will pin you at Special Forces 7th
    Group.
ME: Great.

PROTOCOL: Who's doing the catering?

ME: Catering?

PROTOCOL: Do you have the guest list?

ME: Guest list?

PROTOCOL: Who's in charge of the seating arrangements?

ME: Seating arrangements?

And on and on. The admiral's visit was a *big* deal. Everyone in command had to scramble. I guarantee that a half-dozen general officers and their staff must have been pissed with me. I had inadvertently created a ton of work for them.

And myself. I scrambled to get a caterer and make sure all the details were taken care of. Now I understand what wedding planners go through when contemplating a celebrity wedding.

Seventh Group graciously hosted the event, even though they were about to deploy oversees, which must have added a lot of logistical hassle. Evelyn, my mother-in-law, and I drove up that morning to their headquarters and found a massive traffic jam.

"Must have been an accident," I said.

No accident, just increased security—and traffic for my ceremony.

"What is the nature and purpose of your visit?" demanded the security people when we finally reached the entrance to 7th Group.

"Uh, are there some chairs out in front of the building there?" I asked.

"Yes, sir."

"That's for my promotion."

"Oh, I'm sorry, sir!" He quickly directed us to a reserved parking spot.

It was crazy. I felt like a "real" celebrity.

The 7th Group command sergeant major, George Bequer, ushered us inside. Admiral Olson met me, very graciously greeting my wife and mother-in-law. There were even flowers for the ladies.

It was a packed house. Colonel Sean Mulholland and a host

of other brass were there. I had to give a speech, something I was still a novice at. Besides thanking everyone, I assured them I wouldn't put them through this much trouble ever again.

Ceremony over, we had a light lunch—then the admiral and I ran 6.5 miles around the airfield, trailed by a security detail and some aides. In our entourage was Colonel Fred Dummar, the deputy commander at 7th Group; it was the first time he and I ran together but far from the last.

Six and a half miles is not a light workout, but the admiral was a practiced runner and had no trouble with the BRD or matching my pace. We ended the run right in front of his aircraft.

"Job well done, Ivan," he said, giving me a hug. "See you in Boston."

Off he went, still at work.

■■■

While it looked like I might be able to get a job at 7th Group, there were still complications and bureaucratic hurdles. Among them was the need to be classified as an SF officer.

That was not trivial. While I'd already been through the Q Course and had served for years in Special Forces, technically I was supposed to retake two parts of the course as an officer in order to qualify for a classification as an 18 Alpha, the official job title of an SF officer. Luckily, the general in charge of the Special Warfare Center and School, which oversees the course, already knew me—and in fact had presided over my commission ceremony when I became a second lieutenant. General James Parker had come up through the ranks himself, and in fact I had helped recruit him as the keynote speaker at our class's graduation. He had sworn myself and two other SF lieutenants in before the ceremony, and his goodwill now was like a magic wand waved over my orders—my MOS or military occupational specialty was changed from infantry officer to Special Forces officer.

With that important technicality out of the way, all I needed now was an actual job.

Before they could find one, a clerk from the 82nd called me up and told me they had cut orders for me to report to WTU.

Uh-oh.

I knew if I reported to the unit, I was done. Even looking at it optimistically, I would face a huge bureaucratic hurdle to go to USASOC. I called the Care Coalition and told them what was going on.

Hours passed, then days. Nothing. Finally, the day I had to report to WTU came.

Still nothing.

I went over to USASOC, the Special Forces Command, and sat in the G1's office, waiting and hoping that orders could be cut to get into 7th Group. Afternoon came, and time kept slipping away. I needed to either have new orders or report to WTU before the close of business, or I would be AWOL: absent without leave.

Sitting in the office, waiting, I kept calling people. Finally, literally minutes before the end of the day, the orders came through—I had a line item number and a piece of paper saying I was now a member of the Army 7th Special Forces Group headquarters staff, working for its commander, Sean Mulholland.

I don't know how much of an option Colonel Mulholland had in giving me a job—Admiral Olson, after all, had made it clear that he wanted to find me a place in the SOCOM family. But while the colonel found me a position, he also made it clear that I was not going to receive special treatment because I was blind.

Which was exactly right.

"I'm going to ride you hard," he told me straight out. "No free rides."

"Yes, sir."

He didn't just say that to me, either. *USA Today*, a Gannett newspaper, found out and did a story on me. "The only reason that anyone serves with 7th Special Forces Group is if they have real talents," the colonel told them in his usual blunt style. "We don't treat (Castro) as a public affairs or a recruiting tool."

And he didn't. Mulholland made me executive officer of the

headquarters company. It wasn't an easy job. One of the exec's most difficult if delicate duties is to deal with "problem kids"—guys who for one reason or another were going to be leaving the unit. You learn a lot about people, helping them solve problems ranging from being overweight and losing an ID to family strife and addictions. I also had to coordinate efforts for the families of anyone who was wounded or killed in action. That was a job very close to my heart.

Another job I loved, though it entailed more work than I expected, was coordinating a race for the group's "Jingle Bell Jog," a pair of 5k and 10k fund-raisers for the group.

But most of my day-to-day work was support, small things that most of us don't think of when we think about the army, yet are absolutely critical to the unit's well-being. The days were varied—I might be making sure some routine repair to one of our buildings was being performed in the morning, then counsel a soldier on how to get housing in the afternoon. Most of it was pretty mundane—necessary but trivial—though there were bright spots, like working with the language lab at the John F. Kennedy Special Warfare Center (an SF command) to prepare soldiers for the cultures they'd meet when they deployed. Not the sort of thing that wins you a medal, but it was important nonetheless.

18

Boston

Then came the Boston Marathon.

The marathon is always held on Patriots' Day, the third Monday of April, which that year happened to be April 21. Evelyn, my mother-in-law, and I flew up the day before, Sunday. Believe me, if you want to travel anywhere, do it with a four-star; his staff will take very good care of you. They had everything arranged—pickup at the house, air flight, ride to the hotel. They arranged for me to stay at the same hotel as the admiral and his wife, whom I met soon after I arrived.

There are downsides to being the boss of one of the country's military commands; among them, you never really get to take off. It was a weekend and after hours, but the admiral's aides were never far away, and he was in constant communication with various commands. Now maybe they were just talking about baseball scores, but I doubt it.

The size of the entourage around him, including security, would put a rap star to shame. And yet, there was one person in the room who could pierce the bubble immediately: his wife. No matter how high up you are, how important or famous, your spouse always has right-of-way through the crowd, straight into your heart. And Mrs. Olson didn't have to push. It was as if the seas parted for her with the slightest gesture. You could tell by the comfortable way they interacted that there was a deep connection there, no doubt forged over many years of trials and hard deployments, stretching back to Admiral Olson's first days as a SEAL back in the 1970s.

In the military, you form one image of a general or an admiral. Then you meet them outside of the uniform, in shorts and a T-shirt, going to get a bagel with a bit of cream cheese for breakfast. There's distance between those two images, even when you know it's the same person.

And so it was for me that weekend, and that race day especially, as we headed toward the starting line in Hopkinton, outside of Boston. It was impossible to forget Admiral Olson *was* an admiral—we were riding in a blacked-out Suburban with a state trooper escort, going lights and sirens opposite the traffic—but he was also "just" a runner as well, ramping up physically and mentally.

Two large buses filled with runners from SOCOM joined us near the starting line. After greeting everyone, the admiral and I plotted strategy for the race. Don't be fooled by Admiral Olson; he is classy but he is the epitome of a warrior. Not just because he was a SEAL, but because he is genuine, crafty, and humble. He had the course plotted in his head and was ready to compete.

We were in the third wave of starters, behind the first two groups of accomplished racers—you don't want to be in front of those guys and gals, because they'll mow you down. The crowd was raucous, cheering and shouting; I felt as if I were walking through a riot, albeit a pretty polite one.

As the clock ticked down, Admiral Olson stepped over to his radio operator (or RTO as we say in the military) so he could relinquish command to his deputy commander. Then he took the tether—and we were off.

We had a strong start, crammed in with the pack as it funneled down East Main Street in Hopkinton. The mass of runners began to slowly separate into large packs, cheered on by even larger crowds as we continued on Route 135. We hit a good pace during the Clocktower stretch, around Ashland, as the pack around us winnowed a bit more.

Every so often we ran past the admiral's RTO, who kept popping up along the route to assure him there were no emergencies. It was a bit like a *Where's Waldo* comic panel, though obviously with much higher stakes.

We were shadowed the whole way by one immense personal security officer, who was running with us. Not to brag, but we outran him.

There's a stretch on the course where you run near Lesley University. At one time strictly a women's college, the school has a tradition that involves the coeds lining up along the race route to encourage the participants. This encouragement takes the form of big wet kisses—wet more for the sweat of the racers than the young women's lips, I'm sure.

I paused there to get my encouragement.

The rest of the race is pretty much a blur. What I mainly remember is wanting to finish, and feeling slightly overwhelmed at the same time.

This was Boston, the marathon of all marathons to many people, including myself. To finish here, let alone to do it after coming through what I had in the past year and a half, was indescribable. But you don't really think about that when you're running. You can't. You think about how your legs are holding up, how you're breathing—and even that level of detail is often beyond you. You just push your body to get through it, push to finish strong.

Our time at the finish line was 4:25.06.

The RTO was waiting for us.

"I got command again," said Admiral Olson, grabbing the radio. He congratulated me and was off, back to work: that was his warm-down.

The very next day, I flew to Bethesda to get an angio-gram. My surgeon, Rocco Armonda, had run the Boston Mar-athon himself—somehow we both made it down for the early morning surgery. (He finished ahead of me, by the way, at 3:43.15.)

19

Green Beret Again

Going back to 7th Group was like going home. But that was good and bad: I liked the camaraderie and the dedication, but there were a lot of times that I felt inadequate—that the group had just brought me back because I was wounded or because I had run Boston with Admiral Olson. Even with all the assurances from everyone and the jobs I was given—there was still part of me that worried that I was essentially a charity case.

I didn't want pity. I wanted a fair chance. But it's difficult to quantify fairness. Any sort of concession to my handicap could be interpreted as pity. And yet my handicap was obvious, and I did need to make concessions to it.

I'm not sure what it's like on the other side of that equation. I'm guessing it's not easy. What concessions should a commander make to someone's disability? Certainly some, but where do you draw the line? I'm not sure I can say, even today. I worked, and worked hard, but I would be lying if I said that I was treated exactly as a sighted person would have been; it would have been impossible.

I don't know if they could have done anything differently.

The feeling of inadequacy came from me, not them. It was impossible not to compare what I could have done, what I would have done, had I not been blinded. I suppose there's no real way to know whether I would have become a team leader had I not been blind, but I was well on my way to that goal, and I believed then—and still believe—that I would have made it.

Would I have enjoyed it?

Hell, yes. Hell, yes.

Always in my mind—way in the back maybe, but there somewhere—was that perfect picture of what that A Team leader's life would have been like. The fact that it couldn't happen only made it more tantalizing. Reality is never as perfect as our fantasies. I knew that intellectually; knowing that in my bones was another story.

The hardest thing for me, personally, was watching the unit deploy into combat without me. When I'd joined the army, all I wanted to do was to jump into the fight, literally. I wanted a Ranger scroll and an Airborne tab, maybe even a mustard stain on the wings. (A "mustard stain" is a bronze star indicating a combat jump; a gold star indicates five combat jumps.)

Now I had to stand by as other guys went on to achieve what I couldn't.

■■■

Just a quick explanation for a few of you who aren't familiar with the way that assignments have been traditionally handled in Special Forces. Historically, the different groups have been associated with specific geographic areas across the globe. This makes for great continuity, both at the unit and personal levels. Dealing with the same army units over a period of years builds a kind of institutional memory that is extremely important in times of crisis. Everyone is on the same page, to use the old cliché; there is a lot less time wasted on trivial things like where is the administration building, what are the transportation procedures, or what sort of weapons are needed.

On the personal level, knowing who to talk to when there's

trouble, or potential trouble, not only saves time, but often means the difference between getting the straight story and getting BS. And you don't want the latter when bullets are flying.

These geographic associations remained in place during the Iraq and Afghanistan conflicts. But because of those wars, the different groups were put in rotation to go where they were needed. Which was why 7th Group was assigned to deploy to Afghanistan soon after I arrived.

■■■

My status as a semicelebrity—"Blind Guy Runner"—brought with it some honors as well as notoriety. Evelyn and I got to meet President Bush when he visited Fort Bragg to inspect the 82nd Airborne.

Ushered into the VIP tent, we waited in a reception line for what seemed like hours.

"Here he comes," whispered Evelyn finally.

I snapped to attention.

"Good to meet you," said the president, taking my hand.

Then he turned to Evelyn and started flirting with her.

"Who's this beautiful lady right here," he said, brushing me off.

I like this guy, I thought. He's just like me: flirting with the girls.

Maybe he wasn't flirting. He spoke with Evelyn and me for probably eight or ten minutes. He sounded genuinely sorry that I had been injured. He asked for details about my care. The president had an entire division waiting for him, but he still took the time to make sure I was being taken care of. I sensed some of the weight that command brings; I also sensed the humanity in the man.

■■■

One day not long after the unit returned from Afghanistan, Colonel Mulholland came into my office and asked how I was doing.

"Great," I told him. "I'm just wondering if I could make it to major."

That must have caught him by surprise. To make major, you have to serve as a company commander or hold an equivalent post, and you have to take classes that prepare you for the rank. (Collectively known as the Maneuver Captains Career Course, the course lasts about half a year and is held at Fort Benning, Georgia.) Just a few months before I had literally begged for a position. I'd managed with a lot of help to find one, and even if I was doing fairly well in it, I was still relatively new. And now I was going to ask for another one?

But the colonel didn't hesitate, or even act surprised.

"Good," he told me. "Make a phone call and tell them I'm going to release you to the captain's course."

"OK."

"Anything else you need, tell me."

Was I nuts? On the one hand, it was a logical career step. On the other, I felt that my time in the military was limited—any day, the bureaucracy would catch up with me and say: *Hey, you're blind. We don't need you. Get out.*

Granted, they'd use nicer words than that. But the end result would be the same. They would wake up and realize that blind guys were not supposed to wear the uniform, and I'd be gone. So maybe going for a promotion was my way of saying to myself— and maybe to that bureaucracy—hey, I'm normal, I'm part of the program.

Or maybe it was just another difficult goal I needed to strive for.

I made the call to ask about signing up for the class. Things went great until I said, "Oh, by the way, I should mention I'm blind."

"Legally blind?"

"No, totally. I can't see at all."

"What? No way. This course? No way."

I hung up, demoralized. Reality is hard. You don't realize how much of life is set up around the basic premise of seeing until you can't see at all. If you're blind, the writing on the blackboard is just chalk dust in the wind.

But give me a challenge, tell me I can't do something, and now you've given me purpose.

I called back a few days later, and spoke to the same intake counselor.

"Look, I know I'm blind, and I don't want to take someone else's slot," I said. "If you have limited positions, I don't want to take anyone's seat. But if you have plenty of seats, and you have an open mind, with your help and the help of my peers, I guarantee I'll learn something. And you'll learn something from me."

The counselor didn't answer. I continued.

"The only thing you have to worry about is giving me an opportunity," I told him. "Be open-minded."

He still hesitated.

"What are the course requirements?" I asked.

He gave them to me.

"I'll improvise. And I'll pass."

"OK," he said, probably worn down by that point. "OK."

I suspect that there may have been some pushing in the background from my group commander, who was one of my strongest advocates. But the officials at the school were fair and open-minded. I passed the prerequisites and was accepted.

I managed to get my place in the course rotation that started in the summer of 2009, the same time as a good friend of mine, "Lunchbox," was going through. (Lunchbox is his nickname, though its origins are obscure; he's still active, so we'll skip his real name.) A New Yorker, he'd been with me in Colombia and the Infantry Officer Basic Course. He did me a huge favor, agreeing to share an apartment when we took the course. That solved a whole range of logistical problems in one fell swoop—it was suddenly much easier to get to and from school; I also had a study partner, and someone I could call on if there were any problems.

Leaning on other people is the thing you never get one hundred percent used to when you're blinded. But it's somehow easier to lean on good friends, because you know they can lean on you.

Lunchbox sat next to me in class; he was the blind-guy interpreter from day one. More guys helped out as the course went on; I'm grateful to all of them.

It's hard to find a parallel to that experience to explain what taking the classes were like. I don't suggest going through an entire semester of a college-level class with your eyes closed, but even if you did that, it wouldn't quite duplicate the experience, since you'd still be able to see things in the visual world once you were outside of class. I'm not saying this to make it sound like I accomplished some great thing. I didn't—I did what was expected of me.

I used a recorder to keep track of the lectures. Many of the handouts were in digital form, which allowed me to have my computer read them to me. Study groups helped a lot. If I had questions about what a particular diagram, say, looked like, I could get a quick answer.

One of the most important things you learn in the course is how to write operational orders at the company and battalion levels. Having been in the army for so long, I already understood what shape the orders would have to take. But I had to learn how to formulate them at a much higher level, using different forces such as airborne and ground. I had to train my mind to see the forces without actually having visual cues.

Briefing the orders for class was a special problem. These days, most briefs are given using PowerPoint; visual diagrams are an effective and efficient means of presenting information. But how do you make a PowerPoint slide when you're blind? As sophisticated as voice command software is, it's not yet at the point where it can translate the spoken word into complete slides.

My solution was outside the box—way outside the box. Rather than telling someone how to make the slides for me, I got a little crafty. I did my research at Hobby Lobby and Toys R Us, then I took my purchases—toy soldiers, jeeps, tanks, yarn, glitter, etc.— and used them as props and set pieces while I briefed my orders. Lunchbox gave me a great idea about how to tell different elevations and positions by changing the texture of the cardboard with the help of glue and items like glitter, which I could feel beneath my fingertips. From the macro situation—the overall enemy force we were facing—to the individual action—the terrain model I mocked up with the help of some cotton and Legos—I demonstrated what I wanted my force to accomplish in battle.

You have to be creative in today's army, especially when you can't see.

The instructors would test me orally in class. Multiple choice was easy; fill in the blanks a little harder. But that's always been true, at least for me.

■ ■ ■

I kept running while I was taking the course, once more racing in the Army Ten-Miler and the Marine Corps Marathon. I also did the Air Force Marathon—I wasn't discriminating between the different service branches.

I started giving more speeches, following that pledge I'd made to myself to spread the message of self-reliance. The Naval Academy asked if I'd give a talk and I readily agreed. It was the largest audience I'd ever spoken to and maybe the largest I've ever done. There are somewhere in the area of forty-five hundred midshipmen at the academy; add in the instructors and staff and I had an audience of around five thousand.

A speech is a speech. For me, talking in front of five people is the same as talking in front of five thousand. After all, I can't see to count how many people are there. I try to keep it short, simple, and appropriate to the audience. In this case, given that all these young men and women were going to be leading others very shortly, I talked about some of the things I'd learned about leadership and focusing on the mission. But it was an unexpected question that I remember most:

What was your biggest moral decision you had to make as a leader?

I'm not sure what the midshipman who asked that expected. I'm not sure what I would have said if I'd had a lot of time to think about it. What came to mind was that "negligent discharge" incident back in Afghanistan, where my soldier fired his weapon at the wrong place and time. I told the midshipmen about my struggle to both observe regulations and yet be fair to the soldier involved.

It was a perfect example of leadership, even though I hadn't thought of it in that way ever before. I had just been trying to be fair to everyone concerned—but maybe that's one facet of leadership in itself.

I graduated from captain's school in December 2009. As far as I know, I was the first blind guy to make it through.

■ ■ ■

While I was in Georgia, Colonel Fred Dummar had moved over from 7th Group to command the Special Operations Recruiting Battalion. Fred and I had gotten to know each other since that first meeting, running with Admiral Olson. He was quite a runner himself, with several marathons and ultramarathons to his credit, and volunteered to train with me when I joined 7th Group. We ran in a few races together; he was a natural guide, able to adjust his pace to mine and seeming to have a blind-guy ESP when it came to running. We got along professionally as well, and when he commanded the recruiting battalion he decided I could help the mission by talking to other soldiers about SF. Since the job would mostly involve explaining the unit's special camaraderie and the dedication its soldiers showed, he didn't have to work too hard to persuade me.

The higher-ups were another story. I think to some of them, a blind guy was not exactly the best way to advertise the assets of the army. Instead, they thought I would scare new recruits away by reminding them of the hazards of the job.

Let's face it: "Join the army and lose your sight" is not exactly a recruiting slogan for the ages.

Fred's take was different. To him, I wasn't demonstrating the downside of the army. Nor was I showing off what Green Berets are made of. Instead, I was proof of the lengths the unit goes to take care of its members. Once you're SF, you are family. Say what you want about me; Special Forces is absolutely the best of the best when it comes to looking out for its people.

I'm not sure what arguments Fred made with the powers above him, or how much resistance he had to put up with—I'm guessing a lot—but he won the day. And he was right: We weren't dealing with new recruits. We were dealing with people already in the army, guys who already knew the dangers. We were able to show them that their motivation would not go unrewarded, or be forgotten when the last bullet flew.

Whatever the arguments, Fred won them. The recruiting battalion was based at Fort Bragg, which was another plus—it meant staying put.

I'd spent a lot of time away from home and Evelyn during those six months. While I was able to occasionally catch a ride with a friend who was also taking the class, it was a long, eight-hour haul each way, which made even occasional visits impractical. It was the same for Evelyn, who was fitting into her new job very comfortably. We splurged a few times on airplanes, but couldn't afford many visits.

The most important thing to me was the fact that we had decided that we would try to start a family. I'd checked with the doctors. Despite my injuries, my sperm count was good; Evelyn, too, was healthy. So we started aiming at fulfilling the personal plans we'd made before I got injured. We were back on track. Maybe it was a slightly different track than we had started on—I hadn't planned on being blinded, obviously—but the general direction was the same.

∎∎∎

Whether you can see or not, those sperm tests are always a bit on the delicate side. As usual, I had some fun with them. When the nurse presented me with the specimen container and told me to fill it up, I asked what I should do with the overflow.

A joke she'd probably heard a million times, but she laughed anyway.

■ ■ ■

Professionally, Evelyn and I had hit a comfortable place. Evelyn was doing well at her job. And I was beyond the most difficult part of my recovery. I had been blind and coped with it long enough now that I knew I could be a father again, and a good one—or at least one who would struggle the way all fathers struggle.

Based on that decision, we made another: Let's buy a house that's big enough to raise a family in.

By this point, we had two houses; I had purchased the house next to ours back when I was a sergeant and was renting it out to another soldier. While both houses were in good shape, we realized they would be a little small if we had a kid or two as well as my mother-in-law with us. I also knew that there were certain things I wanted in a house. Some of this was because I was blind—I needed to be able to move through the house smoothly, there had to be an adequate security system, we'd need tile floors to make cleaning easier if I had a guide dog, and other things. There were also things on the wish list, like a big enough garage to use as a workout area, that were just the result of seeing what other people had or thinking about what sort of amenities we would want as we grew older.

I spent endless hours thinking about what I wanted my house to be. Evelyn and I found a builder and started talking to him about what we wanted. He took me to a model and had me walk through, getting a feel for the size of the rooms and the route I'd take from one to the other. I made a number of suggestions— his-and-her closets, bathrooms in each of the bedrooms, tile on the first-floor rooms. Then he went back and made changes in the blueprints to give us most of the important things that we wanted—every house is a compromise between what you want and what you can afford.

There were no roads in the development when we picked the

property, walking past wooden stakes and spray-painted markers on the ground. It was all up to the imagination—something I was used to by now. I saw the front porch, with the two rockers; I saw the patio we'd build out back. I felt the fire burning in the study while I worked. This was going to be a great home for us.

People ask sometimes what was done to adapt it for a blind person. Aside from bump dots on the washing machine and stove so that I can tell what the controls are set to, nothing. You can't tell that a blind guy lives here, which is important not just for security, but for its eventual resale value, something even blind homeowners have to worry about.

But there are subtle adaptations. The tile floors on the first level: If I have a guide dog, it's easy to clean up, for example. A good alarm system is a must, even if I do have a shotgun in the closet. The adaptations are things that I think all buyers would like, but are especially helpful for me.

The house was built in 2009, but it wasn't until I got back from the course that I had time to relax in it.

For some reason, things weren't quite as relaxing as I thought they would be. Work was going great, but somewhere toward the end of winter and the beginning of spring 2010, things at home started feeling a little off. The long conversations I had with Evelyn suddenly got shorter. We weren't getting pregnant; suddenly there seemed to be less time together. We were sharing less and less. At the same time, she seemed to be a little testier.

I put it off to stress at work, both mine and hers, and just the normal things couples go through in their relationships. We'd spent an immense amount of time together right after I got injured. Now we were with each other less and less. On the one hand, I wanted to be independent; on the other hand, I missed that intense intimacy.

With our anniversary coming up in June, I decided I wanted to do something special on that day. We had done a lot of traveling together, visiting Europe, the Caribbean islands, Florida, Puerto Rico, all before I was wounded. It had been years, though.

It was time to do it again. I asked a friend of mine where we could find a fancy, all-inclusive resort. She suggested one in Bermuda.

Perfect.

"It's too much money," Evelyn said when I told her my idea. "I don't want to go."

The next day, she told me she had to go to a conference in New York the weekend of our anniversary.

"I'll go with you," I suggested.

"I have to go with a coworker," she said. "Sorry."

Pffffffff.

The Care Coalition had asked me to help mentor a very severely injured and blinded veteran recovering from wounds. He was in Texas receiving treatment at the time. Evelyn suggested that I use that weekend to visit him.

It didn't feel right, but it was practical.

"All right," I said. "You go to your conference. I'll go see him."

I left the day of our anniversary, catching an early morning flight. The whole flight, I could only think of her.

The whole flight, I kept thinking, this just isn't right.

I called her just after I landed.

"Hey," I said.

"Hey."

"You ready for your flight?"

"I'm already in New York," said Evelyn.

"You are? I thought you were leaving tomorrow."

"I caught an earlier flight."

"Well, happy anniversary."

"Happy anniversary."

"I have to get off the plane," I told her. "I'll call you from the hotel, I—"

"Don't call me."

"What do you mean, don't call you? It's our anniversary."

"I'm going to get my hair done and go out tonight."

"You're going out tonight?" I was dumbfounded.

"Yup."

"Evelyn, what is going on? This is our anniversary, and I'm in San Antonio and you're in New York."   ·

She was quiet.

"I've noticed a change in you," I said, unable to stop myself. "What is going on?"

"I'm done," she said. "I want out."

"What?"

"Yes. I want to end this."

"Are you telling me that you want a divorce?"

"Yes."

"I'm not quite sure you know what you're saying," I said. "I want you to think about what you said."

I hung up and got up with the rest of the passengers to leave the plane. My body was shivering and sweating, shaking. My soul had been ripped from my body. As horrible and shocking as the mortar round's explosion had been, this was ten times worse.

FIVE

LIVING IS THE ONLY REVENGE

We're a day from the Pole. I'm a day from doing something no other blind American has ever done.

And yet, the more I ski, the more I think about what I've done here and throughout my life, the more I realize that's not what's important; it's not why I'm here. I don't need to be first.

The one "first" people talk about belonged to Roald Amundsen. He climbed the Axel Heiberg Glacier to reach the Polar Plateau, sledding across to the bottom of the earth with four other men and sixteen dogs. He got there on December 14, 1911, the first to the Pole.

About a month later, Robert Falcon Scott reached the Pole from a different direction. Scott and the four men who went to the Pole with him died, stranded when the support team they were rendezvousing with failed to follow through on the plans.

Was Scott a loser? Were the other men losers who failed to reach the Pole?

*Winning and losing has little meaning when you're strug-
gling to breathe in minus-forty-degree weather, the wind freez-
ing your breath to your face, the ice tripping your feet with every
step. Surviving, that's what's necessary. That's what you do.*

*And that's what I've done. There is no winning or losing at
being blind. There's only surviving.*

And yet . . . and yet I need to race.

*I understand that now. It has nothing to do with finishing
first or well back in the pack. It's just an excuse to keep going.
A goal that tricks you into moving ahead.*

*I needed that when I despaired of ever seeing again. I needed
it as a kid in Puerto Rico. I needed it trying to become a Ranger,
trying to become a Green Beret. I needed it when I thought I
was worthless, and even when I thought I was mediocre.*

*So much has changed in the years since I climbed out of
that hospital bed. I've been part of that change. Society is more
willing to accept that battle wounds and disabilities aren't life-
enders. The races helped. I helped.*

*But the races weren't important in themselves. No one cared
what place I came in. I didn't care, not really. They made it easier for me to push myself. They were the easy excuse to do something hard.*

And I needed that. We all need that, from time to time.

*I'm blind. I could use that as an excuse to do nothing. But
doing nothing equals failure. Blind or not, I have to push myself.
I have to move forward.*

I have to ski, even in the cold.

*That's what my early career was all about: pushing on.
Becoming a Ranger, wearing the Green Beret, seeking out every
challenge. That's why Amundsen went to the Pole. Scott, the
others. They weren't failures; they were strivers, no matter what
place they finished. It was part of their nature.*

*It's why we climb, we explore, we accomplish. We need chal-
lenges to survive. It's what being human is all about.*

*The difference between my early life and my life now isn't
so much the fact that I'm blind, let alone the media attention*

that I sometimes get. The difference is that I have to work with others to succeed. I'm not really racing against them, I'm racing with them.

I learned how to work with others in the military. Now I've had to extend that lesson to achieve even more: seventeen kilometers today, over mostly smooth ice. Ten more to go.

20

Move On, Move On

I must have called Evelyn fifteen times that day, without an answer. Her mom, who was at our house in North Carolina, didn't answer the phone either. I walked back and forth in the hotel room, shaking. A friend—actually someone I hadn't seen since college, and who had never seen me blind—came and tried to calm me down. I ended up seeing the wounded serviceman I'd come to talk to, but I doubt I helped him very much.

His therapist was there, and she asked what was wrong when we were alone. I spilled my guts. After a while it must have been too much; she tried changing the subject, doing everything she could to get my mind off it, asking about running, asking about whether I'd consider a triathlon, asking about the weather.

My emotions were too raw to be salved. There was no escape from the hurt I was feeling, just as there was no escape from being blind.

Unsure whether Evelyn would meet me at the airport as we had originally planned, I called a friend and asked him to come. That made for some awkward moments when I landed—Evelyn was there, and I'm sure he sensed that he had walked into a black hole of bitterness and despair. We were civil, but just; he excused himself and left.

Evelyn and I drove home together. We were silent for a few miles.

"What's going on?" I asked finally.

"I want a divorce."

"What's going on?"

"I want a divorce."

"After all this? We've come this far, through all of this . . ."

There was no good answer to that, so she didn't give one. Instead, she told me she had a new bank account. And a new phone number. She had put down a deposit on an apartment, and had already picked out furniture. She was moving out in July.

My mother-in-law scurried to her bedroom as we came in. I heard her lock the door behind her. Not that I'd thought there was any real hope there. I walked in slowly, pulling my bag, handrailing around the walls to our bedroom. Things were out of place, drawers empty, the closet half full. Evelyn had taken everything from our bedroom and moved it to another room upstairs.

"Evelyn?" I said, but she wasn't there. She'd run upstairs to the room above the garage, a little minisuite with its own bath.

I sat on the bench at the edge of our bed, wondering what I was going to do next. For the first time since I'd been blinded, I cried.

■ ■ ■

Sadness and sorrow have a stealthy kind of weight, accumulating slowly and almost without notice. They can press down so gently at first that you hardly notice them at all. And yet, there they are in the end, pushing you against the floor, compressing your entire being into a narrow sliver that can't enjoy even the happiest events.

If I hadn't lost my eyes, would I have grieved so badly at the loss of my marriage?

It's a pointless question, because without having lost my eyes, I would never have lost Evelyn. And yet she had done so much for me after I was blinded; without her, I would not be alive.

In retrospect, Evelyn accumulated a lot of fatigue from caring for me over the year and change. She was my nurse, my confidante, my guide, 24/7 in the months immediately after the injury; even after that, she was a critical caregiver and caseworker—and worked full-time.

The stresses on both of us changed quite a bit in those years. There was the injury, then the recovery, then the media attention.

"Our lives were constantly in flux," Evelyn remembers. She was happy—thrilled—when I ran the Army Ten-Miler. I was getting some control back.

But at the same time, my racing convinced her that I didn't need her—or at least that's what she thought.

"He made it look easy," she told a friend.

Meanwhile, she felt burned out. To Evelyn, her whole world revolved around me, and she didn't have time for herself.

"I'm just going to be a caregiver?" she asked herself. "Do I have the energy?"

The answer was no. She didn't want to spend the rest of her life being a blind man's aide. And I think the fact that I was getting so much attention made it even worse; it only emphasized how diminished her role and our relationship had become.

In her mind.

She says she still loved me—that in fact she still *loves* me.

Whether that's true or not, all I know, and all I knew then, was that my heart had been pulled from my body that day.

■ ■ ■

Looking back, there were subtle signs of her estrangement that I missed. She put up a Facebook page without mentioning it. She started getting a lot of text messages, which she didn't share. She didn't come to church with me. She had been pulling away, separating herself mentally and emotionally.

The way it came down, she went out of her way to convince me she didn't love me anymore. We weren't intimate. She stopped hanging around with me. She even stopped saying she loved me, and several times told me flat out that she didn't.

My mother-in-law was caught in the middle. She had known me a long time, and I think genuinely loved me. But she couldn't go against her daughter. She continued to help, taking me to work in the morning, cooking at night. In an odd way, that helped Evelyn, making it easier for her to avoid me as much as possible.

I begged my wife to go to counseling. She finally agreed to see a chaplain we both knew, but it was clear as soon as we went in that she wasn't going to change her mind.

"I want out," she told the chaplain.

"Why?" I interrupted.

"I just want out."

We were in the room for about thirty minutes. Finally, she looked at her watch, declared the session over, and left.

"There's no budging in that," the chaplain told me. "I'm sorry."

No budging. A few days later I managed to start a conversation with Evelyn and asked if there was something I could do to change, as if it was my behavior that was the problem. She told me I couldn't.

"Is it because of my eyes?" I asked finally.

"Yes, you're not going to get your eyes back."

"What do you think I would have done if it had happened to you?"

"I don't know what you would have done," she answered. "But I've done my part. And I want my life back."

We talked some more. She opened up in a way she hadn't since before the injury. We had been so close emotionally then, so free with our thoughts and feelings; I missed that, and it felt almost good.

Except for what she was saying.

"You're a burden," she told me. It was the sharpest knife.

"I don't love you anymore," she added, twisting the blade.

As hard as they were, the words convinced me it was over. It wasn't so much the words or even the bitterness of her tone. It was her openness, the glimpse into the old Evelyn. She wasn't lying, she wasn't hiding, and there was no going back.

My anger turned into hate. It's sad, because I loved that woman so much. She had fought so hard for me; she was my pit bull. After so much pain, after so much loss, we had started to return to our life together.

Now that life was over.

Gone. Done.

I got a lawyer and we worked out a separation agreement within a few weeks. As with most couples, a lot of our friends felt they had to take sides. It was impossible to avoid bad feelings and a lot of awkwardness.

The day she came back to drop off the keys I sat in the kitchen at the end of the table. The door shut behind her as she left. Nothing had ever sounded quite so hollow and empty as the house that night.

21

Down and Back

I went a little crazy after that.

Which was worse? Being blind or losing my wife?

I couldn't tell you. The answer would change from moment to moment. I was back in the deep hole that I'd only recently climbed out of. And now the person who'd helped me out of it was gone.

Worse, it felt as if she'd pulled me out only to push me back in, then grabbed a shovel and piled on more dirt.

Depression is a physical sickness that affects the mind as well as the body. Sadness is a mental condition that strangles the body. I can't find the line between them—I know experts say there's one—but for me in this case they were one and the same.

I wished I was dead. I wished the mortar shell had finished me off.

I drank. I listened to sad music. I drank some more.

I truly wished I was dead.

And yet . . .

And yet something pushed me to keep going. Something pushed me to crawl. I couldn't climb out of the hole, but I could move around the bottom of it, slide and grapple and touch the edges until maybe I found a handhold.

When you are blind, you use your hands to walk around the edge of the room, to feel your way through the space. You come to know the corners and the cracks. Lights and switches have a new purpose, marking space rather than illuminating it. You feel your way around the edges of a room before you enter it.

And so it was for me, feeling my way through the depression and sadness that I was left in when my marriage ended. My faith and my dreams, my memories and my hopes—they were the edges I examined. Anger was a wall with sharp peaks and ridges. I was angry with God. I raged against God. How could He be so cruel? Take away my sight and then my soul?

Why? Why? Why? Why?

There is no God, I decided. Because nothing in the universe could be so cruel.

Blind, in my forties. Divorced twice. I'll never find happiness again. God, you are a bastard.

I relived every moment I had with Evelyn. There was not a place in my house, not a place in town, that didn't remind me of her. Each memory was a knife. The past closed against me, from above and the sides, squeezing the life out of me. My hands bled as I felt my way around that space, and nothing could stop the flow or ease the pain.

But not all the edges of the walls around me were sharp. My son was a place where my hand might rest in warmth for a moment, where my thoughts would turn bright and hopeful. He was a strong young man, someone with a lot of potential, a good man. Talking to him gave me some hope. He had a future, and I wanted to be part of it.

Work. That was a strong surface. Mentoring other people, helping them climb out of their own holes, became the most important part of my day. Maybe I couldn't help myself, but I could help others, push them a bit, tell them that they could get over any obstacle.

And running. Always running. Running was my salvation.

I ramped up my training. I ramped up my competitions. If exercise was a drug before, now it was my blood. Pushing myself gave me something physical to focus on. It wasn't punishment so much as an affirmation that I was alive, that something more remained. If my legs could be sore, then I wasn't completely spent. If I could be physically tired, then I hadn't been wiped out.

I didn't really get over the loss of Evelyn. Even now, thinking of this, I can't say at all I'm over it.

But, perhaps I've gotten past it. Maybe that's a more accurate statement.

There was no milepost I passed. For months I obsessed about why things had ended. I examined her Facebook page with my program that reads text on the computer and asked friends for clues. I refused to accept that my blindness was the reason. It was too simple. There must be more. I searched my memory. I questioned people for clues, had them surf social media for the vaguest hint.

None of this did anything to ease my pain. Somehow, some way, the questions stopped being so important. I spent less time asking them, less time obsessing on the past. I slowly trudged away from despair.

And then I started living wild and reckless.

■ ■ ■

I flirted with a lot of women, going on dates, trying to find intimacy that would fill my void. In reality, I was probably looking for Evelyn in every woman I met. It was very unjust to them. It would take awhile to realize I didn't want to cause them the same kind of pain I was going through. Which I'm certain I might have. I feel ashamed and embarrassed at what I did.

In retrospect, it may be that I wanted revenge. It's a crazy idea, because making love to someone is not revenge. And certainly I wasn't angry with any of the women that I met, let alone trying to hurt them; on the contrary. I loved them, if only briefly. Without exception they were wonderful to me, kind and gentle and loving.

But there was certainly some sort of motivation behind my

behavior that wasn't pretty, and that I'm certainly not proud of. It was a kind of getting back, and not only at Evelyn. I was getting back at my fate, avenging that damn mortar shell, sticking it to God.

You're going to take me down! You're going to bring me to my knees!

The hell you are!

Look! Look what I can do!

There was real anger there at my fate. Real anger.

I drank even more. I drank instead of eating. I would come home after work, put on music and sit on the couch drinking vodka, wine, beer, you name it. I had to fill the void with something. I was drunk every night, then spent the next day trying to conceal it.

People put me up on a pedestal. They think I can't do any wrong, but I'm human just like they are. No one's perfect, I'm no saint. We all make mistakes, and I made a bunch.

I met some amazing, good, caring women. I don't know why they were attracted to me. I hope I treated them well; I try to treat everyone the way I'd like to be treated myself. Some of the women were runners, some not. I met women who were therapists, who were nurses, who were salespeople. I was taking a lot more love than I could give.

■ ■ ■

I don't know how long that phase lasted, or how it really ended. It was another glide over a period of months, I guess. I kept running and competing, doing my job. The army, as it had for much of my life, gave me discipline and strength, and focusing on my duties probably kept me saner than I know.

In the summer of 2010 I found myself in San Antonio to do a triathlon. While I was there, someone mentioned that she was part of a group taking a bunch of amputees to London to do a bike ride across part of Europe.

"Well, hey," I said, joking around. "You're taking all these amputees. How many blind guys are you taking?"

"Uh . . ."

"Have you ever thought about taking a blind guy?"

"Well, uh, no but—"

I could tell she felt embarrassed. Another time I would have laughed it off as a joke, but all of a sudden I really wanted to go to London and Europe.

"Maybe you should take me," I said.

"Well, we might have one more spot."

And they did. The event, "A Bridge Too Far," was a charity ride sponsored by a British group named Help for Heroes. Established in 2007, the charity has a wide range of programs, and counts "sports recovery" as one of its most important areas. I can certainly relate to that—competing gave me a lot of purpose again, and helped me recover from my wounds. Just as important, it shows the "able-bodied" that an injury does not diminish a person's worth and potential, even if that potential is radically altered.

"A Bridge Too Far" featured about two hundred people riding some three hundred and fifty miles through Belgium and Holland. The name of the event may be familiar to World War II buffs; it's a reference to the Market Garden operation during that war. Launched in that same area and involving soldiers from the American 82nd and 101st Airborne divisions, Market Garden aimed to break German defenses and open a way into the German heartland. The campaign ended in defeat for the mostly British force; one reason historians give was the failure to promptly take the bridge at Arnhem, the "bridge too far." (That's the same title as a famous 1977 movie about the battle.)

Market Garden is seen by many historians as a critical point in the 1944 campaigns, as momentum was lost on the central and southern European fronts (maintained by the American army) to make the push in the north. But the war was just history to most of us who were participating; we'd been through our own.

Just so you don't think these events are always idyllic rides through fields of clover, let me mention that my sighted partner was a real pill. We had been hooked up with the help of a local racing club, and while hearts may have been in the right place, everything else was out of whack. He seemed to resent the fact that people liked to come up and talk to me about my being blind. Somehow he could never find a place to stop to hit the bathroom, yet he could always spot a group of girls to chat up.

The event wasn't a race per se; we rode quickly and a fairly long distance, but we weren't competing against each other, at least not formally. I was just having fun being in Europe—and being around all these wonderful female accents. There's something about the way an English girl says "cheers" that makes me smile.

We were a little more than halfway through the race when one morning I went to help retrieve our bike from the back of the support truck. While waiting for it, I heard a woman with an American accent talking to one of the staff.

"Hey, hello, who's that?" I asked.

"Amber," she answered.

"Where are you from?"

"America."

"Really? When did you start riding?"

"I've been riding all along."

I was surprised that I hadn't heard her accent before. "Well, Amber from America, where in America are you from?"

"Denver."

We kept talking and joking. Well, I kept joking. Probably she was rolling her eyes at my lame attempts.

We got on our bikes and started riding. Eventually we hit a traffic light and while stopped, I started talking about her with my partner. I said something to the effect that I thought she was a little stuck up and full of herself.

The light changed.

"The light is green!" said a voice right behind me. "Go!"

It was Amber, of course. I rode hard away from that light.

I started noticing her accent a lot. At times in the hotel she would come up to me and very pleasantly ask how I was doing.

Absolutely *not* stuck up. I was the jerk, not her.

The event finished off at a museum. Amber came up to me after we'd finished riding and said hello.

"Hey, take me around, would you?" I asked. "I'd like to see what's here."

Now there's a pickup line only a blind guy can use.

We took a nice tour and later on met in the hotel and we just talked and talked. We went to dinner and somehow I ended up holding her hand under the table.

That was in the fall of 2010.

We returned home and stayed in touch, talking about just about everything imaginable. A part of me that had been closed for a long time seemed to reopen.

And finally I realized that I was truly alive again emotionally.

"Maybe we should get married?" I asked.

Did I say that out loud?

At first, only to myself. But the more I said it, the more I was convinced it was not only a good idea, but something we had to do.

If she would.

With a race coming up in Hawaii, I put a plan into action. I asked her to come see me run—who turns down a trip to Hawaii? I ran the race, my pace way off. She found me at the finish line, and interpreted my nerves as exhaustion.

"Could you do me a favor?" I asked. "My number on my back is bothering me."

She undid it.

"There's something written here," she said.

"Really? Read it."

"*Would you marry . . . me?* Would I marry you?"

"Well?"

She said yes. We tied the knot in the spring of 2011. We chose "Landing in London" by Three Doors Down featuring Bob Seger as our theme music. Appropriate, no?

22

Faith

By then, my anger with God had dissipated. Maybe faith was too strong in me to ever go away. I didn't rediscover it; rather, I came to understand it better.

People say things happen for a reason. I don't know that I believe that, but I've come to realize that I can't hold God responsible for my lost sight. When I say I am a man of faith, I mean that I believe in God, absolutely. That's faith.

Religion, though, is something that man creates to understand God. I go to church when I can; I enjoy services. But I understand that the word of the Lord that I hear is man's version of that word.

I was born a Catholic; that's my heritage. I was baptized and made my First Communion; I took the other sacraments, including the Anointing of the Sick, the sacrament a Catholic receives when near death. I say the "Our Father" and the "Hail Mary," prayers I was taught as a child. On my back I have a tattoo of St. Michael, the archangel and personal protector; Michael led God's angels against Satan in the Book of Revelations, an important book in the New Testament. Roman Catholicism is the religion that I identify with.

But I am a rebel when it comes to the religion, as opposed to the faith. I value Christian services that are outside of the Catholic Church as well. I have been to Lutheran, Baptist, Presbyterian services. There is truth and comfort in those services as well.

Who on this earth is not a sinner? Show me one person who has not gone against some teaching, some precept of religion, even if they hold that religion as the greatest truth revealed to man?

I pause before I eat every meal to give thanks to God. It's not something I make a show of. For me, faith is a personal thing, a quiet acknowledgment. I pray for others—praying for yourself is a selfish act.

Next to my tattoo of St. Michael is a cross. Both are surrounded by footsteps, some doubled, some single. Beneath these are words in Latin from Isiah 6:8—*Here I am, send me.*

The footsteps? The times when God has walked beside me, and the times that He carried me. In a circle, because it is never-ending.

As my faith strengthened, and as my relationship with Amber strengthened, God gave me a chance at a kind of happiness I had only dreamed of, even when sighted:

Another child, this time a girl.

I have to confess that when Evelyn left, I more or less gave up hope that I would have another child. Even when my relationship with Amber deepened, I really didn't see kids in my future. And then suddenly, there she was, pregnant. What a blessing.

On the one hand, I felt extremely happy. On the other—I can't tell you how profoundly protective and worried about our baby I was.

Maybe even overprotective and paranoid. And to be honest, I can't say I'm much better in those departments now. I don't think dating will be allowed until she's thirty, and even then I'll remind her boyfriend that I have a shotgun, and am a pretty good shot for a blind guy.

Not that there has been any reason to worry about my little angel, especially during the pregnancy. Amber was very healthy, and things progressed without any problem. We were getting close to the due date when we went out one night to one of our favorite Italian restaurants with some friends. Back home that night, Amber felt like she had a bad case of heartburn.

Hmmmm. . . .

We finally realized that she was having contractions and getting ready to give birth. Now, in the normal course of things I would have jumped out of bed and grabbed the suitcase, ushered her to the car, and then driven like a madman to the hospital.

I did do some of that, but since blind guys and highways don't mix, it was Amber who got behind the wheel. At the hospital, my primary mission was cheerleader, and I think I did a damn good job . . . at least until we heard a bloodcurdling scream from a nearby room.

"You're not going to scream like that, are you?" I asked.

Amber didn't hit me. Maybe I was out of reach.

A nurse came into the room and took a look. We'd been there about four hours.

"Good," declared the nurse. "Let's give a little push and see how we're doing."

Amber gave a little push.

"You're ready!" said the nurse, a little surprised. "Doctor!"

Our daughter, Bebe (a nickname pronounced in Spanish like "bay-bay"), was out in three or four pushes. I cut the cord; then held her in a blanket for Amber as she recovered from the strain.

Being blind can't get you out of certain chores: I was changing diapers within a week or so. It's actually not as hard as I thought, and one or two dads have confessed that they close their eyes through the process anyway. But honestly, a lot of the parenting duties fell to Amber. She's adapted well and does an excellent job. And Bebe grows by leaps and bounds.

My daughter knows that I can't see, though it's hard to say how deep that understanding is at her young age. She'll run up to me and have me feel her new dress. She will take my hand and put it on the couch or the table, taking me somewhere like her mom does.

Since she'll only know me this way, will she ever have a sense of loss when she thinks of me and my blindness?

I hope not.

Having Bebe has made me realize how much of my son's childhood I missed, both physically because of the deployments and divorce, and emotionally. Even when we were all living together, work was my main concentration. It was a young man's mistake, and I've tried to make it up to him. Just as important, I'm trying not to make the same errors with Bebe. Even when I'm on the road, doing a race or a speech, I try to call and tell her a bedtime story, sometimes with Amber's help, and sometimes completely on my own—it's amazing how easily you can memorize a story when you've heard it a hundred times. I've even been known to sing a few verses, though I'm not sure my voice is appreciated by anyone other than my daughter.

It's shocking the number of tea parties I've attended. Fortunately, pretend tea doesn't have any effect on the kidneys.

One of my ambitions is to someday run a race with my daughter. I'm looking forward to that proud daddy moment. My grin will break all sorts of world records.

■■■

In my maneuvering to stay in the army, I had sidestepped the medical board review of my status. Technically, they should have done that no matter where I was sent. And technically, the board could have declared me unfit for duty and . . . out.

For some reason, I managed to slip through the cracks—they never scheduled the review, and I was smart enough not to bring that to their attention. By keeping my head down and, most important, doing my job, I managed to stay under the radar. And if no one was asking to review my status, I certainly wasn't volunteering.

Sooner or later, though, I knew someone would catch on. That happened in 2012, when I went for blood work and a nurse asked about my active-duty profile, which in the army is a little like a cross between an insurance card and your medical records in civilian life.

As far as I can remember, he was the first person who actually asked about it. I tried to brush it off, but he was pretty adamant. I sensed doom.

Without explaining all the regulations and red tape, the military has certain basic physical standards that a soldier must meet; he or she is rated on a scale accordingly. That becomes part of your permanent record. The scale determines in general how you can be assigned. Most combat soldiers will have the highest rating, which means they are healthy and can do whatever job is required. Disabilities take away from that rating. While you can serve with some disabilities, if you are too disabled the army will retire you.

Being blind—well, you can figure that one out.

The nurse started the procedure to have my profile updated. Once under way, it was obvious to me that the medical board would have to conclude that I was not fit under their definitions. While my other physical limitations might be arguable, you can't fake being able to see.

There is a provision in the regs that allow what are called temporary profiles to be issued. In layman's terms, those are waivers that say, "Hey, this soldier is disabled at the moment, but we're going to put all that on hold." Strictly speaking, those are generally meant for someone who is either being treated or has just been treated for an injury. They're basically temporary waivers.

I prepared for my med board the way I'd prepare for a firing squad. There was no way I was going to do anything but admit to all my injuries; my medical records spoke for themselves. And, you know, I am blind.

So I decided I would admit to the obvious and then ask for a waiver. I lined up support from Colonel Dummar and on up the command chain to General Mulholland and, finally, Lieutenant

General Charles Cleveland, the head of the Army Special Operations Command, and Admiral Olson himself.

They said some nice things.

Colonel Dummar:

As his former battalion commander at the Special Operations Recruiting Battalion (SORB), I know that Ivan is a force to be reckoned with in Special Operations recruiting. Losing Ivan would deal a significant blow to the SORB.

General Mulholland:

CPT Castro has made tremendous strides to physically recover from his combat injuries. Throughout his recovery, he has served as a stalwart example of tenacity and perseverance to others in our community and throughout the Army.

General Cleveland:

Captain Ivan Castro is the embodiment of a Special Operations Warrior, and his contributions to the SOF Community have been nothing less than stellar. Since his traumatic injuries on 2 September 2006, Ivan has continued to epitomize the resilience, strength, fortitude and leadership that most aspire to achieve.

Their kind words paid off. Not only did I get a waiver, but I got one with an open-ended time commitment, meaning that it didn't have to be reviewed every six months or so.

Let's be realistic here. The army was not saying that a blind guy should go into combat. I wasn't saying that either. But what the army was saying, and what I say, is that there are *some* jobs in the army that don't require sight.

Obviously, my case was special. I'm sure the fact that I had run in those marathons and was helping spread the word about how great the army is helped me tremendously. But I think—I *hope*—that in the future soldiers who have been wounded but still want to contribute will be accorded that privilege. Most will not do so in high-profile positions or luck into publicity like I did. Most will just quietly do their job, making important contributions as team players without fanfare or even notice.

■ ■ ■

Through all of this, I was still running. By now, Fred Dummar had become a steady running partner; I would guess that he's guided me through more than half of my marathons. We spent a lot of time working to get in under four hours, something that's difficult for anyone over thirty but especially hard when you're blind.

Pacing is difficult, both over short stretches and through the entire race. According to Fred, when we started running together I would come off the starting line too quickly, not pacing myself for later in the race. That's a problem sighted runners share; with fewer cues as a blind guy, I had to train myself to pay more attention to my body, and recognize the urge to accelerate and somehow ignore it—not easy.

But more difficult is learning to react to your guide. If he's tense, I tend to tense as well. A sharp tug on the shoestring—does that mean a car is coming and we have to veer out of the way? Or is it a turn my guide forgot to tell me about?

Fred had to learn how to run relaxed. I'm not even sure that he can explain how that's done. It's kind of a watchful glide, which is what it feels like when we're in synch.

One of the many things that makes Fred such a good pilot on a run is his never-ending patter about what's coming up. A two-hundred-meter warning for a turn gives me time to adjust my pace; same with knowing that we're at the start of a long climb or a short downhill. One of the most difficult things for a guide to do, believe it or not, is to remember I'm blind. A lot of my friends, especially those who have known me for quite a while, somehow forget that in the middle of a run. It's not that big a deal—until I trip over a cone or bang into something hard.

Hey, all's forgiven in time, but those bruises *hurt*. Fred

manages to keep himself focused both on the race and on our path, maybe because he's never known me as sighted.

There are some things, though, that are hard to prepare for no matter how good your guide is. We were running in the fifty-mile Boogie Marathon in North Carolina. It's an overnight run that takes you through varied terrain, including a piece of road that borders a swamp. We hadn't been running for all that long when a thunderstorm moved in. Drenched, we continued onward, nearing that piece by the swamp.

"If you step on something squishy," said Fred, "you're stepping on frogs."

Yeah. I got a few.

But probably my best story with Fred came during a march rather than a race.

We were invited to New York City during a commemoration of 9/11; an all-night march through the city boroughs was held as a fund-raiser and I was one of the "celebrity" participants. We were somewhere toward the middle of the Brooklyn Bridge when nature called.

"Fred," I said, "I gotta take a leak."

"We're in the middle of the bridge," he said. "You have to hold it."

"Can't do it," I warned.

"Human wall!" commanded Fred, showing true leadership skills as he herded a dozen or more of our fellow marchers around me to provide cover.

Of course, if one person pees off the Brooklyn Bridge . . .

I wouldn't be surprised if the water level in the East River rose a good three or four inches. The race organizers may never forgive me.

As of this writing, I've raced in more than fifty marathons, and a smaller number of half marathons. Most are known beyond the world of runners, like the New York Marathon, the London Marathon, Hawaii's North Shore Marathon, the Rock 'n' Roll Savannah, the Chevron Half Marathon in Houston, and the Gasparilla Distance Classic (another half marathon).

I took the Goofy Challenge, or as the Disney people call it, the Walt Disney World Goofy's Race and a Half Challenge. That's a half marathon in the Florida amusement park, followed by a full marathon the next day; I raised it up a notch personally by doing the 5k the day before.

There's something special about being greeted by a giant mouse at the start of a long run, then sailing through a magic kingdom, cheered on by tourists and characters you've grown up idolizing. I've had a lot of fun at the Disney races, even running the marathon at the Anaheim amusement park, Disneyland, the same year as a Goofy Challenge, something runners call the Disney Coast to Coast. Those races are unique because of the atmosphere of the parks, and all the kids who are around. Everyone racing seems to be having a good time, and it's infectious.

I've also run in two fifty-mile races. I find the longer distance a little easier than a marathon. With a fifty-miler, you focus just on lasting that entire distance, or at least I did. There was no question of strategy, when to sprint, when to take it easy; I kept a solid but slow pace throughout.

Is running blind different than running with sight? Certainly it is, and yet there are more things that are the same.

When I run, I feel the ground beneath my feet. That's the first sensation, the most important one. I think every runner feels that, whether they can see or not. I may be more sensitive to the slope and the smoothness of the pavement, since it's all I have to concentrate on, but I think that part of the running experience is the same for me as it is for any runner.

All runners go in with a certain strategy about how they're going to approach a race. I adjust to the distance, and to how I feel. A 5k is a lot different than a marathon; running when it's cool is different than when it's hot—whether you can see or you can't, you're still going to be aware of all these things and adjust to them.

But the cues that sighted runners get are lost to me. I pick up other clues about what's around me, sound especially. There are many: footsteps echoing against buildings if we're in a city can tell you how many people are around, and how hard they're running. You can hear hard, steady breaths and know that it's time to kick it up; the murmur of the crowd as you're getting toward the end can cue your final kick.

But the real difference for me is my logistics. I need someone to run with me, which always involves a favor. I also need a ride there, and a ride back—more favors. I try to show my appreciation in tangible ways, paying their registration fee, for instance.

Do you care about my gear? It's nothing special, really. I wear toe socks; they cut down on blisters. Mizuno shoes have always seemed to me the most comfortable for my feet. Shorts with pockets, smooth, wicking shirt, sunglasses—I'm not a fashion plate or an endorsement billboard, I'm a blind guy running.

When I first started racing, I was very competitive, not so much with other runners but with myself; I wanted to get faster. I wanted to cut time off my last race—all runners do this, to some extent at least.

I've mellowed. I accept that I'm not setting world records; I'm an old blind guy who's broke, not Dennis Kimetto or Geoffrey Mutai. Now I try to make it more about having fun, and not getting hurt. The objective is finishing the race. There are marathons now where I'll jog for a stretch, or even walk. I always kick at the end; finish hard, that's my motto. And maybe my competitive streak is coming out.

Everyone wants to compare times. Those numbers don't interest me at all. My best time is 4:04 in a marathon. That was in the Poconos—I thought I was going to break four hours but came up a bit short. Now, that's not a time that a world class, professional marathoner would respect, given that the world record is about half that. But a world-class, professional marathoner can see, hasn't had two knees blown out (figuratively; my ACLs or anterior cruciate ligaments were torn in those early jumping exercises) hasn't taken shrapnel, and on and on. The important thing, really, isn't how long it takes or what your splits are; the important thing is you do it.

That's my attitude, at least. I hate it when people try to motivate me. I don't need motivation. It comes from within. If you're not motivated to do something, it's not going to happen. So giving me a pep talk isn't going to get me going.

Try harder! You can do it.

Hey, the hell with you. I'm already trying as hard as I can. I don't need you yelling in my ear.

In 2013, I was running the Boston Marathon with Fred Dummar and another friend of ours, Mike Sullivan, when we began hearing sirens in the distance.

"Someone must have gone down really hard," said Fred.

Mike noticed that some runners nearby were on their cellphones. He took his out and called his dad to see if he knew what was up.

Mike's dad, by the way, lives in Washington State.

"There's some sort of explosion," said his father, who quickly turned on the news.

A few moments later, we turned down the street to get on the final stretch of the run.

"That's it," yelled a cop. "Get off the street! Get off the street! You're done!"

Mike glanced down the road and saw a large bag or rucksack on the sidewalk. Police officers were donning bomb disposal gear to check it out.

We ducked down a nearby street, plunging into chaos. Runners were everywhere, trying to figure out how to get out of downtown Boston. Meanwhile, police and other emergency vehicles flooded the area. Fred somehow found us a cab and managed to get us back to our hotel; by the time we got there, I had some two hundred text messages and voice mails asking if I was OK.

It was only when we turned on the TV that we got the full story. A bomb had gone off near the finish line, killing three people and injuring over 260 more. The attack was a stark reminder that the war on terrorism hadn't ended. Evil hadn't vacated the world when we began pulling troops out of Iraq or Afghanistan. The same threat I faced was present here, and for the foreseeable future will continue to be.

(Three days after the attack, two brothers, Dzhokhar and Tamerlan Tsarnaev were named publicly as the men who had set the bomb. Tamerlan was shot and killed during a chase a short time later; his brother was apprehended the next evening. Dzhokhar was tried, convicted, and sentenced to death while we were working on this book in 2015.)

23

Easy Rider

If running is my passion, then biking is my thrill. Biking is easier on the body, or at least on mine; my bones and joints don't take a pounding. There's none of the zigzagging you sometimes get with running a race; it's all a straight line. If you have a strong cyclist in front of you, you can get the speed way up. People think because I'm blind I can't crank it, but that's not true. I can stoke up a pretty good head of steam, sprinting up a hill. My recovery time after a sprint is relatively quick, and I can take advantage of the slope that inevitably follows a climb to regroup. While it's easier to run downhill than it is to run uphill, you don't get quite the same recovery when you're on your feet rather than pedaling.

I work out most mornings on a professional-level spin bike, which is a lot easier on my hips and knees than road running. Not to mention that I don't need the BRD and a guide to help me use the bike.

Since I loved bikes and my work in the Special Operations recruiting unit, it was probably inevitable that at some point I would want to get those two things together. In early 2012, I started putting the idea into words, constructing a plan that would have an army cycling team do a cross-country tour. The idea was not that much different than the Golden Knights, our top-notch parachute team, which inspires onlookers all across the country, or the navy's Blue Angels, an aerial acrobatics team whose jets perform at air shows. The demonstration teams raise consciousness about the military's mission, while at the same time bringing positive publicity to the service.

It happened that I met the secretary of the army during a racing event in 2012 and mentioned the idea to him. He didn't veto it—hey, that's something, right? If someone doesn't say "stop," then that must mean, "go."

I was still getting some of the facts together when I got an e-mail from a group called World T.E.A.M. Sports early in 2012 asking if I'd be interested in joining other injured service people in a cross-country ride, I answered right away.

Hell, yes!

My answer was a little more professional than that, but that was the gist. I realized this would be a great chance to see how a cross-country tour worked; I could shamelessly steal the positives and avoid the pitfalls, noting them all in my proposal for the army.

And I'd see parts of America I'd never seen before at the same time. I don't know how many times a blind guy has ridden a bike across America; I'm guessing it hasn't been done a lot, though there don't seem to be any organizations keeping track. But whether I was going to be the first or the millionth guy to do it, I was interested.

I contacted the organization. The guy I talked to was a little cagy, telling me to fill out their application and see if I made the cut.

"I can do that," I said, and I did, filling out details and e-mailing them back.

The next day the same guy called to tell me I was in.

Guess I aced that.

After maybe sixty seconds of jubilation, reality set in—could I *really* ride across America?

Then the next question, even more serious: Who was going to go with me?

I'd done a lot of biking with Bob Miarer, who'd helped introduce me to the sport back when I was rehabbing from my injuries, and eventually rode with me to Florida. Bob was a great mentor and pilot, or "captain" as serious tandem cyclists call the rider in front. (The cyclist at the back is a stoker.) But he would have had trouble taking time off for the race. So I looked around for someone else to ride with and hit on Bill Lahman.

I'd met Bill in Colorado in 2008 at a camp run by the U.S. Association of Blind Athletes; I'd ridden with him in the triathlon. Bill had worked with USA Cycling on Olympic events and done a good amount of piloting. He was older—in his late fifties—but in awesome shape. He also had a good combination of ability and an easygoing personality, two qualities that don't always go together.

Actually, my relationship with Bill was about the only good thing that came out of that triathlon, an experience as comic as it was humbling. I had gone out not knowing that I was expected to compete. While there, one of the organizers asked if I'd like to try.

Why not? I run, I bike. I hadn't swum in a while, but I'm sure I can figure that out. I'm from Puerto Rico; I spent my childhood in the water.

Well.

The athlete I was supposed to pair up with for the swimming portion didn't show; the rumor is he'd heard that there were parasites in the lake and didn't want to take a chance of getting sick by swallowing them. Whatever; he didn't call or tell anyone he wasn't coming. I waited and waited. Finally, the organizer who'd gotten me involved came over and volunteered to swim with me.

We didn't have a blind swimming device, so we fashioned something with a piece of rubber and some rope. Just as I was getting it around my chest the klaxon sounded for our heat.

I dove in. The two of us swam well—for about ten feet. It had been several years since I'd been in the water, and to be charitable, all that rust weighed me down. I persevered, pushing on, until suddenly I felt something grabbing at my legs.

An octopus? Giant parasites?

No, the rope had come off my guide and was wrapping itself around my flailing feet. Fortunately, I had tied my end with a quick release knot and was able to get it off.

I was roughly in the middle of the course at that point. There were so many contestants that they were broken into different heats or groups; the next group started in the water as I freed myself from the rope. They were on me in seconds. My guide came back, doing a backstroke and calling to me, directing me with his shouts.

"Where?" I yelled.

"Here."

"Where?"

"Here!!!!"

I swam in his direction, finally pulling close enough to use his prompts as a guide. The rescue boat came up and asked if we wanted help. I was tempted—sorely tempted—to climb in. Pride kept me going.

That and the will to live.

The third wave started, and they began gaining on us. A woman nearby sounded as if she was flailing.

Don't grab on to me, I thought. *'Cause I am not saving you. I don't know if I can save myself.*

Against all odds, I made it to shore. I'm not sure I've ever been happier ever to touch land in my life.

Someone asked if I'd drunk the water.

"A little," I lied. The truth is, I probably drank enough to lower the lake's water level a couple of inches. People were throwing up left and right—maybe the fear of parasites wasn't off the mark.

I found Bill and the bike and continued racing. I probably set a new world's record for the event—slowest time ever.

But with the exception of my bruised pride, I'd suffered no ill effects from the competition, and I remembered Bill fondly. So I got ahold of him and explained about the ride across America.

There would be no swimming, I emphasized.

"Are you interested?" I asked.

"I did that in my youth," he said, making·it sound like he was eighty years old.

He was experienced, enthusiastic, and most important, available, able to take several weeks off to complete the trip. Bill decided that we'd need a different bike—he's a tall dude, and he wanted one with just the right feel—so he reached into his own pocket and bought one.

We met in San Francisco at the airport in late May, a few days ahead of the Memorial Day weekend kickoff. All I could think of on the plane was how long the flight was.

If it's this long and far in a jet, imagine what it's going to be like riding back the other way.

There were sixteen of us, with about the same number of interns and staff members; all the cyclists were past or present military, and had seen service from Vietnam to Iraq. We had a truck and a bus, along with other vehicles riding in support.

The description of the event that I heard made it sound like it was going to be a lot more competitive than it was; in fact, it had been made out to be a real race. Even when I realized it was more a rally than a competition, I figured hey, these are all bad-ass cyclers, wounded or not. But in fact most of the riders had very little experience as cyclists; a few weren't even in particularly good shape. That quickly caused problems as the group split into different ability clusters, which in turn caused a good deal of resentment and not a little grumbling as the race proceeded. And though the organization had run a cross-country event before, there was a good deal of miscommunication and confusion among the staff during the ride, something that didn't help as the hot summer sun baked tempers along with helmets.

We rode thirty miles the first day; it took us eight hours. That is decidedly *not* a good pace, even if you're just trying to bring attention to the abilities of the disabled and wounded. We eventually sped things up, riding between sixty and a hundred miles a day. We also got a heck of a lot more organized. But order was always a bit precarious.

I was more serious than a lot of the others, maybe all of the others. That probably bothered a few of my companions, maybe even all of them. I wanted to get across the country, and I wanted to do it at a good pace. For some reason, the trip tickled my competitive nature. I had to do it, I was going to do it, and I was going to ride hard and as fast I could. My mission was to ride, and ride every single mile hard.

Personally, it was great to experience America by bike. We crossed the Sierra Nevada, hit Colorado, Kansas, Missouri—the temperatures were outrageous during the day, as high as 123 degrees, the hottest anyone could remember.

We took a day off at Lake Tahoe. I could not have imagined how cold that water would be, even in the middle of the summer. I sensed the natural beauty of the lake, extending for miles. I sensed—or at least thought I did—how vast it was. Leaving the lake area, we rode downhill and felt the heat build in a matter of moments. We seemed to fly down Highway 50 to Reno. From there, we hit a lonely stretch, empty, or almost empty, on both sides of the road. At the border of Nevada and Utah we paused at one of those all-in-one stops: restaurant, gas station, casino all rolled into one.

There was a line for the slot machines on one end of the restaurant—the Nevada side. You could hear the chimes and whistles in the distance, the artificial *click-click* of the machine.

No jackpots, though. At least not that I heard.

While I was riding, I was focused entirely on what I was doing, concentrating on how the bike was going, how Bill was pedaling. I had to stay focused on what he did, reacting to his pace and balance. At rest stops and at night, though, I thought a lot about my wife and our little girl. With Bill's help, every day I wrote my daughter a note on a postcard, and mailed it back to Amber.

Day 0:
Bebe: As I embark on this Journey Across America, there is one thing on my mind, and that is making it back home to be with you and my beautiful wife. You and your mother are everything to me. May God bless and protect our family. I miss you and love you.

Your Dad, Ivan

Day 1:
Bebe: I love you and I miss you so much. Today was our 1st ride, and what an experience! We started today by crossing the Golden Gate Bridge from San Francisco and continued north to Petaluma, California. Today is Memorial Day and although you and mommy are always on my mind, I've also been thinking of those who have given all.

Love, Daddy

Day 9: Fallon-Austin, Nevada
Bebe: Today was our longest and hardest ride yet, and to top it off, it was chilly, although we did get some sun. As we finished, it started snowing. As we rode we could hear Navy jets and fighters on their practice runs. After we finished lunch we went to a jewelry store that had handcrafted their own silver and turquoise jewelry. I bought mammy a nice pendant and matching studs.

Day 14: Baker-Delta, Utah
Bebe: We were happy to leave Baker because we didn't have any cell phone coverage and everyone was getting poopy-faced.

On our way to Delta we saw a badger right by the side of the road. As we got closer to Delta we could smell the brackish water of the receding Lake Sevier, and as we got even closer to Delta the farmers were mowing alfalfa and

it smelled great. Miss you and we are looking forward to
seeing you in Denver.

—Daddy

Amber and Bebe met me in Denver, where we took a break
two weeks into the trip. It felt impossibly short; we were quickly
back on the road, heading out through Colorado to Kansas and
then Missouri. Along the way, I took time out to perform another dad duty: attending my son's graduation. He was more
important to me than crossing the country, or any of the other
things I'd done since being injured.

Back with the group, we continued eastward, heading over
toward Pennsylvania. We picked up police escorts in several
towns, and the media was a little more excited. We had a great
German meal in Pittsburgh. The cooking was excellent, but
heavy food and biking don't mix. My legs and stomach paid for
it the next day.

Three days later, we reached Maryland and made a stop that
was particularly important to me—the Bethesda Medical Center.

It was an unscheduled stop on the weekend; because of the
vagaries of scheduling, I hadn't called ahead or made any special arrangements to say hello. But I felt strongly that I had to
be there.

I'd come so far from that hospital bed—literally across the
country. Part of me was still lost inside the hospital somewhere,
stuck in a ward praying for a miracle. My hope of ever seeing
again was there somewhere, comatose, collapsed against a sheet
stained by perspiration and tears.

I rode my bike here. I was pretty messed up when I was here.
Look at me now.

The next day we rode to Arlington National Cemetery, the
longest ride of the trip—not in miles, obviously, but in every
other way. While the others went to lay a wreath at one of the
memorials, I snuck away with Bill to say hello to some old friends
I hadn't seen in a long time. Standing at their graves, I ran my

hand over their stones, my fingers lingering in the indentations that remind the living how brief life truly is.

Our arrival in Virginia Beach was anticlimactic. After four thousand miles and nearly sixty days, I think everyone was ready to get home. I certainly was. I went to the beach with Bill, dipped our tire in the water, and then left before the beach party that was planned to honor the trip. I'd been away too long from my baby and my wife to delay my homecoming even a few more hours.

People talk about how homogenized the country has become, how every region, every town, is the same. But my impressions cycling across America are just the opposite—I felt diversity in practically every mile. From the smells to the weather, the accents to the prices, there was a tremendous variation. Every part of the country feels different, even when you're on bicycle, and even when you're blind.

24

Boss, Coach, and Man of Marble

I've been privileged to receive a lot of honors since my recovery. Often with those honors, I'm given mementos—certificates or plaques, commemorative medals.

But the wildest one I *almost* got was a statue.

Billionaire Ross Perot is a big supporter of Special Forces. Among other things, he's a board member of the Special Forces Charitable Trust, and sponsors an award each year for Green Berets who have done something special to benefit the community. In 2013, the trust decided to honor me as the only blind Green Beret in service.

Mr. Perot was told about the plans and decided that, instead of a plaque, the trust should erect a statue in my honor at Fort Bragg.

I wasn't privy to the discussions—I found out about all of this well after the fact—but I'm going to guess command didn't say "no."

It would have been more like "hell, no."

The army doesn't erect statues to living guys, for one. And

let me add, that as flattered as I was when I found out, I don't think I deserve a statue.

Mr. Perot settled on a rare sword, which hangs in my office, close enough for me to grab if any of my underlings get out of line.

Statues and plaques and medals aside, I received an important honor in 2015 that I'd never thought possible: The army notified me that I had made the promotion list for major.

But the news was bittersweet. Always in my career I've viewed promotions as stepping stones, not achievements in themselves. Get one, move on to the next. But this one represented an end point.

The next higher rank in the army is lieutenant colonel. That's an important position, a gateway to colonel. Among other things, it requires a year of school, and service as a battalion operations officer or executive officer. And to go on and become a full colonel, you almost always have to serve as a battalion commander, one of the most important posts in the army.

Could I command a battalion, in combat or not, as a blind man? Especially one with continuing health issues?

More important, would it be fair to my soldiers? Would they get the leadership and the attention they deserved? It's not enough to simply do a job; you have to do the best job for your men and women. The mission is about them, not yourself.

After a lot of soul-searching I decided I would end my career as a major. Being away from home, even just to go to school, let alone pulling up roots to move to another command as a lieutenant colonel, would have put a great deal of stress on my family as well as myself. And in my mind, if I wasn't going to go on to colonel, what would have been the point?

Maybe there would have been provisions to cut me some slack because of my condition. But asking for slack is not me. And the army shouldn't give me any, either. I don't want favors because I'm blind. And I don't want to take something away from someone else: There are only so many slots to go around.

Running has helped make me realize that limitations are

important. You have to recognize them. Counting my early years in ROTC, I'd been in the army for three decades. I'd achieved everything I had set out to achieve here, despite having been blinded.

Now it's time to do something outside of the service.

■ ■ ■

As I'm writing this, that decision is only a few weeks old. It hasn't been an easy one, even though I know it's the right one.

Would I have liked to stay in the army and become a general if things had been different?

Probably not, but maybe.

I wanted to lead a Special Forces A Team into combat. Being an A Team leader—a "SFODA," Special Forces Operational Detachment Alpha team leader—would have been the high point of my career, no matter what happened afterward. But eventually I would have had to move on from that achievement. I frankly don't think I could have made general's rank; there's a lot of brainpower as well as dedication involved.

And honestly, it would have been hard even giving up an A Team to become major. Once you're a major, you're doing a lot of important things, but jumping out of airplanes with guns to fight in combat is not one of them. So I might have retired at this rank even if I hadn't been hurt.

My new career: entrepreneur. With the help of some friends, both old and new, I've created Special Operators Challenge, a company that hosts and creates outdoor sporting events. Running events, primarily, but not just any running events—our events challenge people to run and think outside the box.

And sometimes *inside* the box. Literally.

Our events will combine traditional races, such as a 5k and 10k, with things like obstacle courses and other challenges. Ever eat a bratwurst while running a 5k? Ever have to run through a few hundred meters of mud during a 10k race? Slog through a row of tires? Climb logs, run through a stream? That's the sort of thing we plan and sponsor.

The events are for kids as well as adults. We have a huge trailer full of different obstacles and gear. Some of our events are inspired by the different obstacles I encountered during my Special Forces training, and bring those sorts of challenges to the civilian competitions. At the same time, I want to use the company to help support local charities. At our first event, held in 2014, we took canned food and other donations as part of the entry fee. We then handed out these donations to the local food banks, spreading the kindness of the community to those in need.

We're still in the getting-it-all-together stage. But I have taken some of the things I learned in the army, especially in command, and tried to put them into place here. First of all, it's "our" company, not "my" company. We're a small group, and I want everyone to feel as if they own part of the success. It's the team concept that I learned way back in Long Range Surveillance.

I also want complete transparency. Everyone on the team knows what our finances are, and everyone has complete access to our records. This way, everyone knows what's going on.

As a blind man, I understand how corrosive the lack of information can really be. Not knowing something—not *seeing* it—adds friction to the smooth path we need to take to success. It's like a pothole in the road when you're running. Hit it and you fall.

Trust is an important quality in a team member. In combat, if you don't trust the other guys on your team, you're probably going to end up dead. Things aren't quite that dire in business, maybe, but trusting the people who work alongside you is important to success as well.

Responsibility comes along with trust. Abuse trust, even once, and you're off the team. I have zero tolerance for anyone who steals or otherwise hurts the company or their fellow team members.

Another thing I learned from the army: Be the best.

In a business setting, that means offering the best product

you can, whether it's the best race, the best T-shirt, the best meal. Simple things make a big difference to your customers. To give one example from our company: It's customary to hand out tokens to people who participate in a race. Very often these are cheap T-shirts and thin medals. We're out to buy the highest quality T-shirts we can find, and hefty, high-quality medals fashioned to look like dog tags that people might actually want to keep.

Small things, certainly, but those little touches end up leaving a lasting impression.

The company isn't the only thing I'm working on. Recently I received nonprofit status for the Special Operators Foundation, an organization I hope to use to give back to the community in a more comprehensive way than I can on my own. We envision helping military special operations personnel and their families to continue their education through grants and programs. I don't see this as a simple scholarship program. Instead of just handing someone money to pay their tuition, I plan to hire mentors who can counsel and guide the recipients as they go to school, and hopefully help them get jobs or promotions when they graduate. (My role with the foundation is strictly as an advisor; I'm not paid.)

And then there's talking.

Ever since the first media reports of my entry into the Army Ten-Miler, I've been asked by various groups to talk about my experiences. I like to do this, not so much because I like to hear myself talk—although I'd guess I'm as guilty of that as anyone else. I like to hear other people's stories. The details of how they overcame challenges inspire me to keep going. That interaction, whether it's at a gala fund-raiser for a nonprofit or a small gathering of veterans struggling with PTSD, helps me in ways I can't adequately explain. Maybe it's just the notion that we're all together in these struggles, that my blindness doesn't make me an island, that's important.

I'm an example to others of what they can do. I cherish that. If I can get the hell out of bed and run a race when everyone around me said I was broken, when I can't see to get across a room without help, then you can, too. Nothing will hold you back, no matter how down you are, no matter how broken you are.

You may not be on the course you thought you were going to be on, but you can be on *some* course.

Don't *dream* of doing something. Do it.

▮▮▮

One question I'm often asked: Have you experienced post-traumatic stress?

I have not. I don't relive the war, or the moment I was hit—except of course in recounting it for others, and here. Why or why not isn't clear to me.

Doctors and counselors kept asking me about that as I recovered. I told them no. I'm not sure they believed me. In fact, I didn't realize until I got down to Augusta for blind school that I was on antidepressant medication.

"What the hell am I doing on antidepressants?" I asked.

I was referred to a psychiatrist, who seemed to want to diagnose me with PTSD, and pressed me to stay on the medication. I finally told him I wouldn't take the pills.

"If I start having symptoms, then I'll take them," I said. "But until then, give me an opportunity."

I quit them cold, and haven't gone back. I'm blind, not clinically depressed. There's a difference between being "depressed" in the sense of being sad or down, and being medically depressed. I'm not disparaging people who are the latter; I'm just saying I'm not.

Nor is post-traumatic stress the same thing as clinical depression. There's a lot we don't know about PTS; I'm certainly among the ignorant. The only thing I can say is that everyone is different, and we all deal with stress and trauma differently.

I'd never gone into a deployment or a mission with fear that I would see something horrible or have any doubt that things would go wrong. I can tell you that when I was a private in Desert Storm, the lack of information and experience was unsettling;

after that, I had a few nightmares, though they quickly ended. So maybe ignorance was, or is, part of the problem. Later on, with more experience and knowledge about myself, and more confidence in my abilities and mission, I didn't really feel afraid. I was mentally prepared. In my mind, there's a relationship between knowing what's going on and fear and its aftermath. But I'm no expert about any of that.

Another question I'm often asked:

Was the war worth it?

Honestly, I'm a soldier. I do what the army tells me. I hope that the politicians who send us to war make the right decisions, and I hope that they support us all the way through. I don't hold my injuries against any of the civilians who sent me to war. That was their job.

Politically, I'm on the conservative side, but I like to think of myself as an independent. I can see positives in both parties, and negatives.

■ ■ ■

Amber decided to do some running a little more than a year ago and got some information about a local road running club. Thinking she might like the company, she showed up for one of their practice sessions. I tagged along to cheer her on.

I have to confess I was disappointed. The club was very disorganized that day. No one greeted the runners, and things just seemed very ad hoc. There was no stretching beforehand, no cool down, very little camaraderie.

So I went over to the organizers.

"Hey, I have some ideas," I told them after introducing myself. "And I have a little experience running."

One thing led to another, and pretty soon I was coming every week, giving pointers and in general acting like a coach, even after Amber moved on to different activities because of her work schedule. I found I like being a coach.

The club has a wide range of ages and abilities, people who

are in great shape, and people who are greatly out of shape. What's important for each one of them is to want to get better. If they push themselves to achieve, and keep at it, they will improve.

They're a friendly group. They even laugh at some of my jokes.

We've formed some good bonds. There was a kid who was overweight and couldn't run. We worked with him for months. Not only did he get into shape, but he decided to serve our country by joining the air force.

Yes, wrong service, but what can you do?

We got him a set of running shoes as a going-away present. "Every time you lace these shoes up at basic," I told him. "Know that we're thinking of you. And run *fast!*"

He did. Last I heard, he's been promoted and is thinking of the service as a career.

Why is coaching so fulfilling? There are certainly frustrations, but I love standing near the starting gate and listening as the runners come around the turn.

"Arms up!" I yell. "Hey, you're not pushing. *I see you!*"

A few may snicker at that last remark, but they all kick butt a little harder. There's something about having a blind guy telling you that you can do better.

■ ■

Over time, Evelyn and I became friends again. Not great friends; we don't see each other all that much. Our relationship is way different than it was. There's still an undercurrent of pain, probably for both of us. But I don't hate her anymore. And I think she still cares about me, if not in the way she did when we were first married, at least to the point where she worries about me and doesn't want me harmed.

That may not sound like a lot, but it's a vast distance from when we broke up.

Why and how we got to this point, I don't know. Partly, I think, it's because we had such great years together, and no matter what happened with either of us, those years and that emotion and good feeling could not be completely obliterated. We were together for ten years. How can you love a person so much for that time and then only be left with hate?

You can't.

I also know exactly how much Evelyn did for me when I was injured. She took care of me. She got me out of that bed, out of the massive hole I'd fallen into. She's the reason I'm alive.

Evelyn has told friends that she feels guilty at times for leaving, but so much has happened there is no going back.

No matter what, she will always be in my heart. I owe her so much that I can only hope she finds the happiness she wants, the happiness that eluded her after I was injured. I think she deserves that.

We both lost quite a lot when I was blinded, things that will never come back. She's met a guy roughly my age she likes; maybe they'll find their own version of happiness.

■ ■ ■

Every day is a little different. I get up around five, hit the coffee machine, then work out for an hour or so in the garage. That's primarily cardio, spin, or rowing mostly these days. Depending on what else I have scheduled, I'm off to base to continue my workout at the gym. There I use a lot of the machines, working on strength training.

With my service time winding down, my day-to-day duties have declined. A lot of what I do now involves representing the army at various events and occasions. I don't mind it, certainly, but there are times when the combat soldier in me thirsts for something more exciting, some new challenge.

The only challenge they've got for me, though, is retirement.

I think about September 2, and the guys who died alongside me, every day. When the day comes around, I think about them a little harder. I don't mind saying that tears come with some of those thoughts.

I wonder where Ralph and Justin would be now if they hadn't been on that roof. I wonder where I would be.

The only consoling thought is this: If I hadn't been there, then one of my guys would have been there, and he would have been the one blinded or worse.

From that perspective, I'm glad it was me, not them. I can take it.

My life is not easy, but that's not because I'm blind. Everyone has some sort of obstacle, some sort of limitation. Mine is sight.

Life is difficult not because of that, but because every day I choose to get up out of bed and push myself to do something else, to make a difference for other people, or hit some sort of goal. It's hard, but I want it hard.

I need challenges other than being blind every day. Because being blind isn't what defines me; overcoming challenges is.

That's what the South Pole was all about. And I didn't even know it until I was out there and almost forced to give up.

Ironically, I've gotten to do a lot of things in my life because I am blind: marathons, biking across America. It's a bizarre calculus, but it's not compensation.

There's nothing in my life that I would love more than to somehow get my sight back. *Nothing.*

But that's never going to happen. I don't pray for it anymore. I don't dwell on it.

I have to move on. I have to keep going, until there are no more challenges to meet. Fail or succeed, win or lose, I have to push on.

SIX

GONE DARK

South Pole Diary:
December 13, 2013
The South Pole

Today I woke up, did a short video with some of the others, packed, and skied the last ten kilometers to the Pole.

Everyone got more and more excited as we made those last few kilometers. Days of hardship, bruises, frostbite, bad falls, altitude sickness, hemorrhoids, headaches—we forgot all of them as we sprinted to the Pole.

I thought of Amundsen and Scott as I closed in on the monument that has been my goal for more than a year. I thought of all the explorers who'd braved the elements to reach this spot.

I thought of Ralph, and I thought of Justin. I thought of Angel and I thought of Barbieri. The dead. The survivors. I thought of everyone who served with me, who pushed me to be more—and I thought of everyone who helped me reach that goal.

I couldn't have made it without them. I needed their help, even if sometimes it came in the form of competition. And I realized as I skied it's OK to admit that. It doesn't make me a loser to say that I need help to reach my goals. It doesn't make me any less of a man to admit that being blind is hard.

And I need it to be hard. Because that's how I have achieved. I've only gone as far as I've gone because I've had difficult goals. Those goals—whether they were becoming a Ranger or running in the Boston Marathon—helped me organize my days and my life. They gave me drive and purpose. Even if in the end, the real goal was something more than just a piece of rebar with a flag, an inhospitable piece of ice at the bottom of the world.

The real goal was to be myself. To be a man always moving forward.

That's what the South Pole was all about. That's what my life in the military before I was injured was all about. That's what the marathons, the ride across America, my new company all mean. Training, deployments, marriage, failures and successes: The things that come hard, those are the things I value.

Until this trip, I didn't want to admit that fighting and succeeding takes help. Now I see it. I couldn't have made it to the South Pole, to anywhere, without a lot of help. I had to allow people to help me, even as I struggled to help myself. It's a precarious balance, as disorienting as skiing through the sastrugi.

If you're a fighter, you find a way. Because that's who you are, and that's what it takes to win, no matter how winning is defined.

25

Postscript

Driving down the road with a friend, we're listening to the radio when Lynyrd Skynrd's song, "Simple Man," comes on.

I tell him to turn it up. I lean my head back and listen to the music. The words resonate. I'm a simple man. I have simple desires. Simple fears.

I think of my son, and my daughter. I think of my parents. I think of the guys who died alongside me.

There's some power in music to make us reflect. A few notes from a familiar song can conjure powerful images. There are three songs that sum me up:

"Simple Man," Lynyrd Skynrd

"One Last Breath," Creed.

"When I'm Gone," 3 Doors Down.

The first, a statement of where I begin and who I am; the second, a tale of my internal struggle to refind myself; the third, a song of my soul and moving on beyond this life. If my life had a soundtrack, this would be it.

■■■

When the music fades, we talk about war, what a man has to do to get through it. Courage is important, but more so is friendship—you fight for the guys on your left and right. No matter what brought you to the army, whether it was a thirst for adventure, or patriotism, or even the need to feed your family, when the shooting starts, it's your brothers you think about most, your soldiers, your joes. You fight to save them, or not to let them down.

When you tell me so-and-so has a certain medal from Iraq or Afghanistan, it doesn't really mean that much to me. When you look at the men who served in WWII, Korea, Vietnam—getting medals for valor back then was very difficult. It's easier, and probably less fair, today. In today's day and age, awards often are based on whether you're liked or not. Your position can make all the difference. A lot of guys who go above and beyond never get the recognition because no one takes the time or effort to write them up.

On the other hand, I know plenty of guys who have gotten medals for basically sitting in air-conditioned comfort for months. I've known units where *everyone* got a Bronze Star—except for the commander, exec, and sergeant major, who got *Silver Stars*, an even higher award.

I'll never call myself a hero. I wasn't one. A hero is someone who puts himself on the line to save someone else. When bullets are flying and you run out there to pull someone out of fire, then you're a hero. I was in the wrong place at the wrong time, and paid for it with my eyes and a good chunk of my body. I battled back, but that doesn't earn me anything, except a chance to breathe tomorrow.

The guys who pulled me off the roof while the mortar rounds were coming, those guys are heroes.

I dislike the word "warrior" as well, even if, in the dictionary sense of "one who fights," it fits. It's just so overused. Not every soldier is a warrior. I've heard a rumor that the army is going to start using the word "warrior" instead of "soldier."

Come on. When I think of the word "warrior," I think of

Conan the Barbarian and Mad Max. I think of someone ripping heads off and drinking the blood.

That's over the top, but truly, the word is way overused.

But it's not anywhere near as bad as "wounded warrior." I *hate* that term. It sounds so pompous and overbearing.

I'm a combat soldier. Just that. Yeah, I was injured. Yeah, I'm blind. But those things don't define me. "Soldier" does.

Less than one percent of the population volunteers for the military. I think people should be grateful, say thank you for keeping us all safe and preserving our freedoms. But you know what? Soldiers aren't unique. There are many people who serve us outside the military. Firefighters, policemen—they risk their lives. Doctors, nurses, teachers—we all depend on many people day to day. So soldiers aren't that special. We're part of the team.

Having said that, I think we should be aware of the sacrifices some are called to make. This last Memorial Day, I went to a ceremony at Fort Bragg honoring the men who'd been killed in action during our recent wars in Iraq and Afghanistan. I had four sets of boots with me, one pair for each of the men who'd died with my unit in Iraq around the time I was hurt:

-Ralph Porras
-Justin Dreese
-Angel Mercado
-Thomas Barbieri

Each man walks with me, not only on Memorial Day, but every day.

Some days I don't think too much about them; other days they are constantly on my mind.

I think, too, about the other guys who were with us. I think about the times we shared. I think about how short and tragic life can be. And I think about what can be achieved in that short time.

I want to make it very clear: I am just a service member, one of many. Every service member has a unique life and a different story to tell. I am blessed to be able to tell mine, and theirs.

▪▪▪

I've seen the colonel who put me on the roof where I got hit. We didn't talk about what happened. To this day I don't think he entirely understands what the situation was. Whether he ever thinks about his decision, I haven't a clue.

He was very complimentary, telling me he'd followed my career and was very proud of me and admired my ability to be a role model.

I had no answer to that. I said nothing.

Sometimes I feel guilty that I'm the one whose time on earth was extended. I feel sad, and obligated to do more. And I can never do enough. I go through phases of sadness. I still curse my blindness when I can't do something. But eventually I get to the point where I realize that even if I can't do one specific thing, I can do something else. I can't be selfish and grieve for myself. There's too much more to do, too much more life to live.

When I die, I want a big wake—a weeklong party. A week at Ivan's. I'll have sunglasses on in the coffin. Everybody that comes to see me better have their own pair.

Flip-flops and Hawaiian shirts. Classic rock, seventies music, dancing—you guys better be partying. I'll be in heaven.

Well, maybe not. But you guys better be having fun, that's all I have to say.

▪▪▪

We've traveled some distance as a country over the past several years. I don't know that there is more acceptance or understanding of people with handicaps, but there do seem to be more efforts to accommodate them. That includes sporting events. The Boston Marathon has separate categories—and qualification times—for people who are "mobility impaired" and "sight impaired." (The qualifying time for the latter is five hours, meaning that you have to have run a previous marathon in that time or less.)

Me, I've traveled an enormous distance as well. I've run over fifty marathons. I've skied, I've climbed. I've dived. I've cycled across America. Ridden horses. All blind.

Blind is the absence of sight, but that doesn't entirely define it. Blind is not blackness. Blind is not the end of light, but a different condition of living. For me.

Black is not the absence of other colors, but a color of its own. It has depth and subtly, and an infinite number of shades. Stare at a black painting for an hour and you see the permutations, undulations of texture that make up black.

White is a color, not the opposite of black, not the lack of color, but something of its own.

My world is not black, nor white. My world is blind, a meditation and collaboration between what is physical and what my mind constructs, from touch and memory, from sound, from the smooth glide of my fingers against the wall and the unexpected stubbing against my toe.

Blind is my reality. It's real. My world is your world, though we perceive it differently: you mostly through your eyes; me, through everything but my eyes.

Plato held that everything we see is a shadow on the wall of reality. If that is true, then all we have in the end are shadows anyway. My interpretation of reality remains different from yours, but not that much different. My eyes no longer see, but my feet walk the same earth, and my hands touch the same walls, and my ears hear the same songs.

In the end, we have the metaphors in common. We can choose whether to be bound by them, or to reach beyond them. To feel sorry for ourselves, or to be ashamed of those low moments and strive for something better.

As horrible as losing your eyes may be, it's not the worst thing that can happen to a man. It has taken me a lifetime to realize that, and many other things.

AFTERWORD

Ivan Castro's Commendations

Valorous Unit Award
Meritorious Unit Commendation
Army Superior Unit Award
Purple Heart (2)
Meritorious Service Medal (with Oak Leaf Cluster)
Army Commendation Medal (with Silver Oak Leaf
    Cluster)
Joint Service Achievement Medal
Army Achievement Medal (with two Oak Leaf Clusters)
Combat Infantry Badge (with one star)
Expert Infantry Badge
Drill Sergeant Identification Badge
Master Parachutist Badge
Air Assault Badge
Pathfinder Badge
Military Freefall Parachutist Badge
Colombian Jumpmaster Badge
Dutch Parachutist Badge
German Parachutist Badge
Ranger tab
Special Forces tab

Quotes I Live By

Over the years I've drawn inspiration from a number of sources. Here are some quotes that seem to sum up things for me.

You'll learn I've been where you're going.

—MIKE FIELDS

The trouble with not having a goal is that you can spend your life running up and down the field and never score.

—BILL COPELAND

Failure is the condiment that gives success its flavor.

—TRUMAN CAPOTE

It's not whether you get knocked down, it's whether you get up.

—VINCE LOMBARDI

As we express our gratitude, we must never forget that the highest appreciation is not to utter words, but to live by them.

—JOHN F. KENNEDY

Never leave that till tomorrow which you can do today.

—BENJAMIN FRANKLIN

No matter how bad it gets, it can always get worse.

—*FAMILY GUY*

When you can't make them see the light, make them feel the heat.

—RONALD REAGAN

Freedom is never more than one generation away from extinction. We didn't pass it to our children in the bloodstream. It must be fought for, protected, and handed on for them to do the same.

—RONALD REAGAN

Conformity is the jailer of freedom and the enemy of growth.

—JOHN F. KENNEDY

The only thing we have to fear is fear itself.

—FRANKLIN D. ROOSEVELT

This generation of Americans has a rendezvous with destiny.

—FRANKLIN D. ROOSEVELT

It is not fair to ask of others what you are not willing to do yourself.

—ELEANOR ROOSEVELT

Do one thing every day that scares you.

—ELEANOR ROOSEVELT

If you're going through hell, keep going.

—WINSTON CHURCHILL

You have enemies? Good. That means you've stood up for something, sometime in your life.

—WINSTON CHURCHILL

Success is not final, failure is not fatal: It is the courage to continue that counts.

—WINSTON CHURCHILL

That's the whole challenge of life—to act with honor and hope and generosity, no matter what you've drawn. You can't help when or what you were born, you may not be able to help how you die; but you can—and you should—try to pass the days between as a good man.

—ANTON MYRER, *ONCE AN EAGLE*

A good plan violently executed right now is far better than a perfect plan executed next week.

—GENERAL PATTON

It is foolish and wrong to mourn the men who died. Rather we should thank God that such men lived.

—GENERAL PATTON

Courage is fear holding on a minute longer.

—GENERAL PATTON

We herd sheep, we drive cattle, we lead people. Lead me, follow me, or get out of my way.

—GENERAL PATTON

The soldier above all others prays for peace, for it is the soldier who must suffer and bear the deepest wounds and scars of war.

—DOUGLAS MACARTHUR

Nearly all men can stand adversity, but if you want to test a man's character, give him power.

—ABRAHAM LINCOLN

I walk slowly, but I never walk backward.

—ABRAHAM LINCOLN

If the freedom of speech is taken away then dumb and silent we may be led, like sheep to the slaughter.

—GEORGE WASHINGTON

The weak can never forgive. Forgiveness is the attribute of the strong.

—GANDHI

Even though I walk through the valley of the shadow of death, I will fear no evil, for You are with me; Your rod and your staff, they comfort me.

—PSALM 23:4

God is our refuge and strength, an ever present help in trouble.

—PSALM 46:1

Be on your guard; stand firm in the faith; be men of courage; be strong.

—1 CORINTHIANS 16:13

Come to me, all you who are weary and burdened, and I will give you rest.

—MATTHEW 11:28

Then I heard the voice of the Lord saying, "Whom shall I send? And who will go for us?" And I said, "Here am I. Send me!"

—Isiah 6:8

I drink to make other people more interesting.

—Ernest Hemingway

Never mistake motion for action.

—Ernest Hemingway

Anyone who has never made a mistake has never tried anything new.

—Albert Einstein

We cannot solve our problems with the same thinking we used when we created them.

—Albert Einstein

There is no such thing as closure for soldiers who have survived a war. They have an obligation, a sacred duty, to remember those who fell in battle beside them all their days and to bear witness to the insanity that is war.

—Harold G. Moore

One day my grandson said to me, grandpa, were you a hero in the war? And I said to him, no, I'm not a hero, but I have served in a company full of them.

—Dick Winters

While I thought that I was learning how to live, I have been learning how to die.

—Leonardo da Vinci

A beautiful thing never gives so much pain as does failing to hear and see it.

—Michelangelo

Acknowledgments

This book is based largely on memory, and though we've made every effort to validate facts, there's always the possibility of human frailty where the past is involved.

The reconstruction of what happened when I was injured was the most problematic, since though I was there, I was obviously not in a position to remember it. Even the moments leading up to the actual attack have become hazy. At one point very soon after regaining consciousness, I told a nurse that I had been eating an MRE when I was hit. But based on conversations with others and our research, I think now that's wrong, as were several other early perceptions. As I detail in the text, I still have a lot of questions that will probably never be answered.

Jim and I talked extensively to the other guys who were with me on that mission. Everyone has a slightly different memory of what happened, and when. One remembers me using the M24 to watch a car approaching; another doesn't remember a car at all. (Neither do I, actually.) The exact time of the attack varies greatly from person to person—we're talking hours, not minutes.

But obviously there *was* an attack, and as best I can tell it happened the way I've written it.

Dialogue has been reconstructed from memory. It is not meant to be word for word, but rather to give a flavor of the conversation.

We have not used the full names of certain individuals who remain on active duty because of the nature of some of their jobs. We have not included any details on missions or procedures that are or were classified for fear of jeopardizing future operations or the safety of others.

■ ■ ■

Many people helped bring this book to fruition. We wish to especially thank Amber, Evelyn Fred Dummar, Chris Turner, Dennis Castellanos, Gerrard Torres, Brian Mundey, Chuck Labuda, Rafael Ortiz, Arthur Lyon, James Sevill, and everyone who served with me. Thanks also to Jackie and all my friends at the Fayetteville Running Club (FRC) and Cross Creek Cycling Club (C4). Thanks also to Tony, Victor, Willie, Angel, Lilo, Chaka, Mike Sullivan, Mike Fields, DJ and JP Roberts, Mike De Rosa, Joe Frank, and Ed Parker, everyone at Walking with the Wounded and the South Pole Allied Challenge, Prince Harry, Alexander Skarsgård, Dominic West, and Eva, better known as "Mommy." Thanks also to Irma.

I want to thank my good friend Miguel Torres, Cliff Burgoyne, Chet Grelock, Bob Miarer, the Special Forces Charitable Trust, Step Up for Soldiers, and Tom Russell.

I also want to say thank you to all of my family and friends who have been by my side and helped me, especially my sister, Olga, my brother, Joseph, and my nephew Gleyder.

I am so blessed to have my kids in my life. And so blessed to have had my mom and dad. They are the ones who taught me how to live my life, and gave me the foundation, strength, the education, and the will to work and survive that made me the man I am today. Thanks also to the rest of the Castro-Dones family.

Darlene Matos provided important material support in North

Carolina, as did her husband, Ruben. Debra Scacciaferro helped with editorial support and encouragement in New York.

Our thanks to our editor, Charles Spicer, associate editor April Osborn, production editor Jessica Katz, copy editor Catherine Reveland, and everyone else behind the scenes at St. Martin's Press. Many thanks also to our fantastic publicity team, the sales people, and Lisa Pompilio, who created the cover.

Our literary agent, Jake Elwell at Harold Ober Associates, stuck with the project through its various permutations. His suggestions on places to grab a good cup of coffee in Manhattan could use some work, but we like him anyway.

I would like to thank my coauthor Jim DeFelice, who took the time to meet me, and who took all the risk and the time to work with me on the book. He's been very easy to work with—I don't know if he's more a father figure, or just a good friend. I admire his talent and skill. Without him, this book would never have been written.

Finally, Margot was a spiritual presence and a great inspiration to both of us. See you at the beach, babe!

Collaborator's Note: Working with Ivan

I first met Ivan Castro in the fall of 2012. *American Sniper* had come out earlier that year, and a friend of a friend sent me an e-mail telling me how much she had liked it.

Then she added that she knew another person I should write about, a blind marathon runner, Ivan Castro. She told me a little bit about him, and I was intrigued. He and I arranged to meet in the New York area when he visited a few weeks later.

A couple of things interested me about his story. There was the fact that he ran marathons. As someone who was a some-time sprinter in my early high school days, the distance alone scares me. How do you do it blind?

Then there was his fight to stay in the army. We rarely think about the consequences of serious injury to a serviceman's career. It's not part of our consciousness about soldiers. When someone gets wounded, we just assume that they want to go home when they've recovered. They've done their duty; now's their time to rest.

But obviously that's not true in every case. A twenty-something has a lot more life ahead of him or her. Why leave the army just because you've gotten seriously injured? True, if the injury is severe enough, it's unlikely you can handle a combat infantry job, but there are a lot of jobs in the military far removed from combat.

One of the characters I'd invented in my fiction series, *Dreamland*, was a paraplegic who flew drones; he'd had to fight to stay in the air force. Now here was a real-life Green Beret whose attitude toward service was more or less the same.

The unit Ivan spent much of his career in remains something of a mystery to most Americans. For some reason, army Special Forces doesn't have the "sex appeal" that the navy's SEALs do, but that's the way most of the guys there like it. The Green Berets have worked pretty hard to stay under the radar. Some years back, I worked on a book detailing Special Forces operations during the First Gulf War. We were given tremendous access to SF soldiers. The only problem was, I was only allowed to write about things that had gone wrong. That wasn't going to polish their image.

They didn't care. They didn't want anyone knowing what worked.

So highlighting SF was a big reason I was interested in writing with Ivan. But the most important reason was Ivan himself. He came across as a humble, easygoing guy, a prankster and born comedian. The things he takes seriously—the army, workouts, his family, his friends—he takes *very* seriously. But his ego is not on that list. And woe be it to you if you take yourself too seriously.

We spent a couple of hours talking at that first meeting, feeling each other out. I have known blind people, but not very many; I would guess that if you took all of the conversations I've had with them and added them up, you'd still have less than half of the time Ivan and I spent on that first meeting.

And I'll say this for Ivan—he can talk.

When you're in the room with him, sitting down, you tend to forget that he's blind. If he doesn't know you, he's usually wearing sunglasses, which hide his injury. And he really doesn't make a point of his blindness as a general rule.

Don't get me wrong—it is certainly a limitation. If he's in an unfamiliar place, as we were that day, he needs guidance to get around. The location of the men's room takes on far greater significance in a building you've never explored before.

We talked a few times after that initial meeting before deciding to work together. We started talking regularly, while both of us continued to meet other commitments. The book project simmered along on a very low flame.

Ivan kept running. He was at the Boston Marathon in 2013 when the terrorists struck; fortunately, he was not near the finish line when the bomb went off. And a few months after that, as we've described here, he entered himself in the competition to go to the Pole.

You have to know Ivan to really appreciate how huge a leap that was. While he was born in the New York area—probably one of the reasons we bonded—he spent a great deal of his childhood in Puerto Rico. That's warm. And he likes it that way. What he knows about snow comes from those globes your crazy Aunt Louise brings back from a trip to Santa's Workshop at the county bazaar every December. He thinks winter at Fort Bragg, North Carolina, is fierce.

So when he told me he was training for the South Pole, I was surprised, to put it politely.

"What the hell are you going to do at the South Pole?" I asked.

"Race. Prince Harry's going, and we're going to beat the pants off his team."

"Have you ever skied before?"

"No. But I never ran a marathon before I did it, either."

"Yeah, but that was in warm weather. The South Pole is cold."

"How cold can it be?"

He went on to train in Norway and Iceland. He formed a friendship with Prince Harry and several other members of the expedition. He was always upbeat, but I could tell that he was having trouble dealing with the cold.

Then came November. Ivan left for England and the hoopla before the expedition.

I forget now if I talked to him right after he met the queen or before. The meeting was definitely a highlight for him. But all the media attention, the press conferences, and the interviews were clearly distractions. He wanted to get into the race.

More than a month went by before I heard from him again. There were a few updates on the Web and through his wife, but they were all pretty generic. It was only when I talked to him by phone from South Africa a few days before Christmas that I was sure he'd made it. His voice was hoarse and he was talking about food, something he almost never does.

It wasn't until a few months later, when I heard the tapes he had made of the trip that I realized how great an ordeal it had been. Ivan never had talked about quitting anything in the year and a half I'd known him. But though he didn't say a lot in the voice recordings he made every night, his despair at that point in the trip was obvious.

When I realized how important the trip had been for him, I started rearranging the outline for the book. I think it was then that we both started to realize how important teamwork has been to his life, both in and out of the army. And we started talking about how he has come to rely so heavily on others to get his newest goals accomplished.

For a guy who was on an A Team, relying on others is both strange and familiar. Strange, because to get to that stage of your military career you have to demonstrate incredible resourcefulness and achieve a great deal. Familiar, because what is an A Team but a group of people who depend very heavily on each other?

■ ■ ■

How do you write a book with a blind guy?

For me, it started pretty much like any other memoir I've collaborated on. We talked a lot, both over the phone and in person.

I think we talked every day for a few months when we were really cranking. Ivan made a few trips to the New York City area; I spent a week at Fort Bragg with him.

Visiting Ivan for more than a few hours means, inevitably, that you have to work out with him. I've never had a blind workout partner before. Suffice it to say, he kicked my ass. Constantly. Twice a day.

I'm not sure that those sessions gave me any insight into his character that I didn't have already, but I did sweat a lot.

One of the things being with Ivan made me aware of was exactly how much of most people's communications are nonverbal. We point at things all the time. We gesture with our hands to emphasize our points. An eye roll can add or change meaning to the most complicated remark.

You can't do any of that with Ivan.

He does have a lot of strategies and a few devices to help him sort out the world around him. His watch talks. An app on his computer reads everything on his screen—extremely fast, by the way; I can't understand the thing.

He's so good at getting around that a lot of times, certainly in his own house, you forget he's blind. And outside his house, he seems to know everybody in town. That's not just true at Fort Bragg, where he's lived for quite a while. Ivan is one of those people who's good at making friends wherever he goes. He's constantly talking up waitresses in restaurants—he's a hell of a flirt.

He does put it to good use, I must say; I always get a good table when I'm with him.

Ivan is loquacious in general, though that's not a term he would use. A question about an incident in the race to the South Pole is likely to net you a half-hour answer as he reconstructs the context of the event before getting to the question itself. I don't think that's a result of his blindness; he was always articulate, according to people who knew him beforehand. But I think his injuries have made him focus more on interior things. As we tried to capture in the book, Ivan has a reflective and

philosophical side, a result of introspection not normally associated with someone who likes to jump out of airplanes into
combat.

Admittedly, the idea that a paratrooper or any soldier for that
matter is not introspective is a mistaken cliché. Still, I can't help
but think that the isolation that is one of the side effects of blindness has driven him a little deeper into his own head than he
was before the mortar round hit.

■■■

If you talk to Ivan's family and friends long enough, you'll hear
them mention his humility. Ivan is a celebrity; people around
the world know who he is. According to Fred Dummar, the easi-
est way to get a free cab ride in London is mention you're with the
blind guy who went to the South Pole with Prince Harry. But
Ivan doesn't carry himself like a celebrity. In fact, you'd be
hard-pressed to meet an easier-going guy when you're kicking
back. If it's easy to forget he's blind, it's even easier to forget
that this is a guy whom presidents and a queen have fawned
over.

Olga, Ivan's older sister, and I were talking one night by
phone when she mentioned that she really didn't understand
what his blindness was like until roughly two years after he'd
been hit.

Ivan was visiting her, staying at a hotel not far from the house.
She brought him back to the room and stayed chatting a little while.

"Turn off the light on the way out," he said when she got up
to go.

She did, then watched him make his way back, into the
darkness.

That's his life, in the dark. That's what blindness is.

"I'm in awe of him now," she says. "He's like—wow! He's an
inspiration for so many people. He's been in marathons, he's been
at the South Pole. Nothing has stopped him. The things he has
done without eyesight are more than most people with it. . . ."

We're so proud of him. He's a superman. He's my hero. But he's still our little baby in the house."

Amen to that. I'd never call him a baby—he'd kick my butt, blind or not—but I'm proud to call him my brother. And he's definitely one of my heroes, whether he likes the label or not.

—JIM DeFELICE